WAKE UP
AND
SMELL
THE MONEY

WAKE UP
AND
SMELL
THE MONEY

Fresh Starts at

Any Age—and Any Season

of Your Life

Ginger Applegarth

CFP, CLU, ChFC

with Leslie Whitaker

VIKING

VIKING
Published by the Penguin Group
Penguin Putnam Inc., 375 Hudson Street,
New York, New York 10014, U.S.A.
Penguin Books Ltd, 27 Wrights Lane,
London W8 5TZ, England
Penguin Books Australia Ltd, Ringwood,
Victoria, Australia
Penguin Books Canada Ltd, 10 Alcorn Avenue,
Toronto, Ontario, Canada M4V 3B2
Penguin Books (N.Z.) Ltd, 182–190 Wairau Road,
Auckland 10, New Zealand

Penguin Books Ltd, Registered Offices:
Harmondsworth, Middlesex, England

First published in 1999 by Viking Penguin,
a member of Penguin Putnam, Inc.

1 2 3 4 5 6 7 8 9 10

Publisher's Note
This publication is designed to provide accurate and authoritative information in regard to the subject matter covered. It is sold with the understanding that the publisher is not engaged in rendering accounting or
other professional service. If financial advice or other expert assistance
is required, the service of a competent professional person should be
sought.

Applegarth, Ginger.
Wake up and smell the money : fresh starts at any age—and any
season of your life / Ginger Applegarth.
p. cm.
ISBN 0-670-87397-7
1. Finance, Personal.   2. Investments.   I. Title.
HG179.A663   1999
332.024—dc21   98-53707

This book is printed on acid-free paper. ∞

Printed in the United States of America
Set in Sabon

To my parents,
Bill and Alice Applegarth

Acknowledgments

Without the help, moral support, and encouragement of four very special people over the last two years, you would not be holding this book in your hands today. In early 1997, I was in an accident that seriously threatened my ability to write. However, rather than give up on the project (and on me), these four women conspired to make sure that *Wake Up and Smell the Money* still became a reality.

Leslie Whitaker, my collaborator, stepped in to help me put words and ideas to paper, patiently working around my physical limitations. An accomplished author in her own right, Leslie was not merely a scribe but worked with me, writer to writer, from developing the concept to editing the final draft. Colleen Mohyde, my literary agent, never allowed me to lose faith in the book's completion, although there must have been innumerable occasions when she privately wondered if it actually would be finished on time, if at all. Pamela Dorman, executive editor of Viking Penguin, was especially supportive. Finally, Karen Sitts, my assistant and financial paraplanner, basically ran my life and my office for me for two years during my recovery and writing phases. I owe a tremendous debt of gratitude to her for ignoring the usual employer-employee relationship and just doing whatever was needed to get us through to the next day.

I also had assistance from others at critical points in the writing process. Working on a very tight deadline, Emily McDowell assembled the final draft by editing chapters, coordinating charts with text, and researching missing data. Jesse Margolis built our Microsoft Access database and then cheerfully loaded in all the research I had accumulated over several years. Vivek Dhingra also provided important research at the beginning of the book-writing process.

In the true Applegarth tradition, my children, parents, and siblings provided unwavering and attentive support, for which I remain forever grateful. Finally, I would like to thank Craig McKeown, M.D., director of New England Eye Center, for his patience and skill in restoring my postaccident sight so that I could write the words you are reading today.

Contents

Introduction

When my parents were courting, they spent a lot of time gazing up at the moon and imagining their future together. They were not thinking about retirement and old age—after all, that was a long way off, and they expected that Social Security and their own hard work were going to carry them through that season of their lives. They focused instead on what lay ahead in the next few years: marrying and starting a family together.

Then, World War II postponed those dreams. My father was in military intelligence, so not only was he gone, but often my mother didn't even know which continent he was on. The one constant in their lives at that time was the moon. They knew they could both look up and see the same moon in the sky at night. It was the one daily bond they could share to ease their loneliness and the fear that their dream of living a long life together might never come true.

After they married, my parents continued to gaze at the moon and dream about their future. As the years passed and retirement neared, their faith in the Social Security system never wavered. In fact, the notion that the government would break its promise and not provide them with Social Security income during their final years seemed about as ludicrous as a man walking on the moon!

Today—a few decades and moon walks later—the moon still seems a distant and magical place. But when lovers gaze up at the moon and dream about their futures, they have more cause to worry. The financial safety nets that might have rescued their parents are disappearing fast. Social Security, for one, is in jeopardy; pensions and job security are a thing of the past. According to a recent survey, most Americans under the age of sixty-five believe that the chance of taking passenger trips to the moon during their lifetimes is about as likely as Social Security providing a significant portion of their retirement incomes. In other words, space travel still seems remote, but so does a secure retirement.

The moon and the stars continue to exert considerable power over our lives. From a distance of hundreds of thousands of miles, the moon controls the movement of the vast oceans of the earth. Just as the moon controls the tides, the sun controls the seasons. Mother Nature gives us four seasons. Each year, the cycle repeats itself, and we know what to expect from the outdoors. In winter, we ski; in summer, we swim. Spring and fall bring a burst of color, from blooming flowers to changing foliage. And as the temperature changes, our behavior—from what we wear to those extra five "winter pounds" we put on—changes as well.

But at the same time as Mother Nature imposes her cycles, so does human nature. Mother Nature gives us four seasons a year, but human nature gives us many more. Human nature arranges the seasons of our lives from early adulthood until when we die, and not always in the anticipated order. Some of our human seasons are controlled by events that seem as distant as that bright spot in the dark night sky, while we create other ones ourselves.

It would be great if that same sun that determines when spring appears would also let us know when we are going to get that big job promotion, start a successful business, or meet the partners of our dreams. But the seasons of our lives are different from the seasons of the year: They are irregular, and often unpredictable, and they may hit us two or even three at a time.

The good news is that while we can't control Mother Nature's seasons, we can create, or at least influence, our own seasons by making our own choices and decisions. Life isn't the way it used to be, with Americans moving in lockstep through the traditions of school, marriage and perhaps children in their twenties, career advancement and buying a house in their thirties, paying for their children's college in their forties, and then focusing on retirement. I am forty-six, and my children are twenty and twenty-two. But I have friends my age who have children who have barely reached the toddler stage. Our concerns are similar—we all have to worry about retirement and college; the difference is that we are facing them at different ages and at different stages of our lives.

As much as we may like to, we can't completely control our destinies, which is why I am paying for college while some of my friends are paying for diapers. It's not just our own human nature at play here; it's those of our families, friends, bosses we may or may not get along with, the inattentive driver in the car behind us, or the house seller eager to unload, or the one whose ego is too tied up in his newly remodeled kitchen to negotiate. So we control what we can today, plan as best as we can for tomorrow, and prepare ourselves for the best and worst of what the seasons will blow our way.

This book is all about how to manage your financial life as it unfolds. All too often we are so overwhelmed in the day-to-day minutia of just getting by in our lives that we can't see the big picture. And a wonderful, once-in-a-lifetime season may have just passed us by—as when you wake up on Labor Day and realize that the entire summer just went by without your spending an entire day outside enjoying it.

I promise you that I practice what I preach. My human seasons, in terms of age, don't fall into today's norms. I married at twenty, had my first child at twenty-three and my second at twenty-five, bought a house at twenty-two, got divorced at thirty-two, and opened my own firm at thirty-eight. Those are things that, for the most part, I chose to do; I created those seasons. But then other things happened to me along the way that I did not create, and my choice was either to sit back and give in to the forces of human nature, or to say, "I did not choose this, but it is not going to beat me." This is not to take all the credit for myself, because I believe that our viewpoints toward life and our attitudes are shaped a great deal by our parents.

My parents, who spent so much time looking at the moon together to imagine their future, and then gazing at the sky for four years during World War II, knowing that it was the one thing that they could share every day, also dreamed about how they could raise their children. And they raised their children to be fighters, and to be awake and aware of money at an early age. They also learned, thanks to the Great Depression, how nothing in life—except, of course, for Social Security, because it was a government promise!—is guaranteed and, as a result, they planned accordingly. That's the reason this book is dedicated to my parents.

It's a good thing they raised us to face challenges rather than run from them, because I have had my share of adversity during several different seasons of my life. When I was twenty-five, a misdiagnosed ligament problem from my pregnancies resulted in my being bedridden for five years, followed by surgery and a body cast for a year. Five years ago, my foot was accidentally run over by a car and I was not expected to walk again. In fact, I did my entire book tour for my first book, *The Money Diet*, from a wheelchair! I am now walking several miles a day and feel terrific. But in each of these situations, I really only had two choices: Let the event—whether due to human nature, Mother Nature, or some combination of the two—control me, or try to take as much control of the results of the event as possible. That's why this book is about controlling what you can and planning for what you can't—what human nature or Mother Nature might send your way. If I could do it, you can too.

In *Wake Up and Smell the Money* you will learn all about the six seasons of your financial life. Don't be surprised if you find that your current situation has you going through two or more seasons at a time; mine did, and frequently still does. Frankly, experiencing events in more than one season is what keeps life interesting. Very few women today want to marry as young as I did and have children right away. And very few men still want to be on that corporate treadmill of working their way up slowly through the same company for thirty years and getting a gold watch and a small pension when they retire. The wonderful thing about life these days is that it is so diverse and offers so many opportunities to achieve our dreams. But along with these opportunities that human nature offers and the reality of today's world, there are risks to consider and traps to avoid in every season. *Wake Up and Smell the Money* will show you how to learn about, plan for, and enjoy the financial seasons of your life so that you can maximize your potential for gain and protect against loss in each event, making the happiest life for yourself that you can in the meantime.

In my twenty-five years as a financial planner, I have seen emotional pain caused by financial issues on a daily basis, and the joy of making wise, thoughtful decisions that paid off. The last financial season in this book is called Happy Endings, but for me, happy endings don't have to wait until retirement. They should happen every day of your life, because that's what will bring true joy and peace of mind. You'll be in control of your financial life, and you won't have to worry about causing additional financial pain to yourself or others (due to fear, lack of knowledge, or inattentiveness), or spending your retirement years blaming yourself every day for what you should have done.

Rather than worry about your future when you gaze at the moon, you'll feel reassured. When the moon rises each evening, waxing and waning just as our lives do, you can enjoy dreaming your dreams—as my parents did fifty-five years ago.

WAKE UP
AND
SMELL
THE MONEY

I

Beginnings

Generations of our ancestors had to cope as temperatures rose and fell, plants bloomed and wilted, all before central air-conditioning and heat insulated us from the full effects of changing weather. Whatever food sources they lived on—crops, animals, or both—before climate control and genetic engineering, they didn't have much control over when those crops were ready to be harvested or when the animals were ready to reproduce. Even if they did not live in areas with snowy winters, they knew when it was spring, summer, fall, and winter because there were still changes in nature—because summers were hotter and winters cooler—even in the desert.

You may or may not be living in an area where you feel the full effects of the changing seasons every year because of changes in nature around you—fall leaves, winter snow, spring blossoms, summer heat. But even if you aren't, the media has probably conditioned you to seasonal changes with its holiday ads and snow-filled store displays, and all those beach scenes in the summer. The net result is that if you are like most people, when the seasons start to change you know it—there is some kind of stirring inside that lets you know that your body is attuned to all those changes in nature.

If you think about your own life in a similar fashion, you have a pretty good idea of what will happen to your body: You know that it will age and mature. This actually results in certain personal, emotional, and financial patterns that we tend to follow as we go through that process—and we are not alone, because everybody else must progress through it as well. And there is no way to separate the personal from the emotional from the financial, because they are all irrevocably intertwined. Just think of the milestones of getting your first apartment, getting married, changing jobs, buying a house, having a child, deciding to reduce your take-home pay so you can invest in your company retirement plan, getting divorced, or starting a business.

On the surface, these milestones may seem personal, emotional, or financial in nature—but if you think about it, you will see that they have profound implications for all three areas of your life. And the great thing about these milestones is that wherever you are in life, and whatever mistakes you may have made in the past, you can make a fresh start and truly turn your life around and prosper with the proper guidance. Our culture tends to focus on personal and emotional gratification, so sometimes the financial implications of our decisions don't even enter our heads at all (that's why more than one therapist has sent me clients over the years). Proper financial guidance actually includes a large dose of personal and emotional support as well—just ask any good financial planner.

"WAKING UP" TO THE SEASONS OF OUR LIVES

After more than twenty years of experience as a financial planner, I tend to see my clients in terms of what financial "seasons" of life they are in—and their financial seasons depend on what is happening in their personal lives. I experienced this reality firsthand just a year ago when I said goodbye to my youngest child as she entered her freshman year in college. I made the long drive back home by myself with no one in the front passenger seat and the back of the Jeep completely empty instead of being stuffed to the gills with boxes, CDs, bedding, lamps, etc. I realized that I was going home to an empty house and an entirely new phase of my life after spending over two decades feeling like the "parent in residence." All of a sudden, I was freed of the enormous day-to-day responsibilities that parenting requires, and I only had to think about myself when I was planning my social life or deciding whether to stay late at work. I cried as I drove home, thinking that this was the end of an era, but part of me was excited as well because I knew that enormous changes were going to take place for me. Financially, of course, things had changed as well. I was at the point that every parent plans for and dreads—paying those high college costs—and some of it was going to have to come out of my monthly expense money. (My twenty-one-year-old son has postponed college in favor of world travel on his own shoe-string budget, so college sticker shock has been delayed.)

If you think of your own life in terms of seasons, it may help make sense out of the experiences you have had to date and those you expect to face in the future. This book divides our financial lives into six phases or seasons—Beginnings, Taking Root, Settling Down, Building Up, Fresh Starts, and Happy Endings. You will be able to identify yourself in some or all of them at different parts of your life. You may be entering adulthood and moving away from home for the first time (Taking Root), or starting a new business (Fresh Starts), or quitting work to stay home with your children (Settling Down). Because human lives are so complicated these days, you may be straddling several seasons at once—retiring from your job at the same time you are entering into a new marriage (Happy Endings and Settling Down), or switching jobs at the same time you are buying a house (Fresh Starts and Settling Down). All of us should try to focus on saving and investing (Building Up) all throughout life so that we can meet our financial and nonfinancial goals.

Most of us fear the future because we fear the unknown—and this is especially true if we are worried about money—so we deep-six those money worries and stay asleep at the financial wheel. By planning for the things you expect to happen, for those you want to happen, and for those that may throw you off track along the way, you will have done all you can to make sure that your next season is more prosperous than the current one, no matter what the current one looks like. And "planning" simply means "waking up" and understanding the reality of your own financial situation.

Every once in a while (and sometimes more frequently than that!) Mother Nature shocks us with an unexpected event, such as a tornado, which reminds us that many things are beyond our control. But in general, we can forcast her seasonal cycles. We also can anticipate the cycles of our own lives, and we try to stave off the aging process by getting on the treadmill, quitting smoking (or at least trying to), or following the latest "healthy" diet. (Sometimes we go a little overboard: A potential client came to meet with me with no money and with the only goal of saving for liposuction; I turned the assignment down.) Taking the same conscious approach to our economic health by looking ahead to what is likely to happen at each new stage of life—rather than denying that change will ever occur, or avoiding thinking about it altogether—will make it possible for you to have a secure financial future.

WHAT SPURS "WAKING UP"?

New clients often come to me for financial planning at the start of new seasons in their personal lives, usually marked by significant life events—someone just had a new baby, or started a new job, or bought a new house, or celebrated a significant birthday (usually forty or fifty). Or perhaps someone just emerged from a personal crisis, such as the loss of a job or the death of a spouse or parent. Sometimes new clients are reacting to events; other times they are anticipating them. And sometimes a new client has suddenly begun to wake up and pay attention to his money because he bounced a check or realized he had $15,000 sitting in a money-market account during a three-year period in which the stock market almost doubled. But they are all thinking, "I had better get my financial act together."

Whatever the impetus, their lives have been forever altered: they are ready to look at their finances for the first time. Although they may be fearful, they are ready to discard past habits that have not served them well, and to learn new strategies for achieving their financial goals, even if they aren't quite sure what those goals might be. Because you have picked up this book, I am guessing that you probably are in a similar position.

I know that I love my job because I still get excited before my first meetings with potential clients. What will they be like? What are their issues? Which financial seasons are they in? Where are they in the process of "waking up"? Often, we don't even talk numbers in the first sessions—I want to get to know them as people first. Potential clients usually fall into one of three categories:

1. They have been jolted awake by external events.
2. They are experiencing a slow dawning of awareness of their financial situations.
3. They are already wide awake and need expert advice to help them stay on the right path to financial success.

Which category or categories best describe you? Many people feel that more than one of these descriptions apply to their situation.

Whether you are twenty-three years old and have just put yourself through college, forty-five years old and have never balanced a checkbook, or sixty-two with retirement only a few years away, you must step back and rekindle the curiosity you had as a child. Remember how it felt when you were ready to learn a necessary skill? (Even seasoned investment professionals have to do this if they have neglected their own financial planning and all they know is the stock market.) You must start here—at the beginning. If you are ready to see your financial situation with new eyes, you will no longer be plagued by the same feeling of anxiety that comes from being out of financial control, or from being uneducated about your financial situation. These concerns may have kept you up at night for years, or you may have been pushing that uneasiness off to the side and pretending that it doesn't exist. I can guarantee that you will feel better if you face your financial demons head-on. But you have to start with where you stand today, and that's what this chapter is about.

EVEN SMALL "AWAKENINGS" CAN BREED LARGE RESULTS

It is true that the older you are, the less impact your choices will have because there are fewer years for their effect on your finances to compound. Still, even small changes in the amount of savings you put away every week, or your investment strategy, or the fact that you acted fast to get a greater rate on refinancing your mortgage, might make or break your chance of reaching an important financial goal.

So start now! Don't wait for your credit card balance to creep higher, or your job to change (making you suddenly responsible for rolling over a big chunk of your retirement savings to an IRA in which you pick the investments). Don't hold off until the start of a new year, or until a personal crisis hits, or there are so many candles on your birthday cake that they singe your eyebrows. In fact, it's always easier to focus clearly on your finances during a relatively uneventful period in your life, when you are not forced to make decisions on a deadline, or when your thinking is not clouded by your emotions and outside stress.

No matter what season you are in, my goal is to motivate you to change the way you think about the continuum of your financial life and to take control of it—simply by being aware of it. My clients have taught me over the years that nothing is more motivating than seeing the dollars and cents results of their decisions five, ten, twenty, and thirty years down the line. When I started to see clients with Starbucks as line items in their budgets, for instance, I began to run the numbers to show them the consequence of spending that little extra money on their coffee break. Let's say you spend $3 a day on cappuccino. Now, let's assume you decide to give up this small indulgence and invest that money in a retirement plan with a 10 percent yearly return instead. How much would you save over time (in addition to freedom from coffee nerves and all that excess weight)? Here's what reducing your spending by *$3 a day on anything* will net you long-term:

In ten years: $17,500
In twenty years: $63,000
In thirty years: $180,000
In forty years: $484,600

Another one of my favorite motivators is to tell clients about the survey of a Harvard Business School class of the early 1950s. At the time they graduated, only 3 percent had specific financial goals for their future. Twenty-five years later, that 3 percent owned 97 percent of the class's wealth.

A recent survey predicted that sixty-five million American families will fail to achieve their financial goals because they don't have a plan. The same survey found that households with annual incomes below $100,000 that have a financial plan save *twice as much* as those without one.

While you cannot control many things that happen in your life, you do have the power to make numerous decisions that will help to secure your financial future. For example, you can pick a better investment strategy that will get you a 12 percent return instead of 7 percent, or learn how to negotiate a better pay raise and/or better benefits before your annual review. You can make your car last longer so you don't have to shell out $22,000 (the current average price of a new car) plus interest over the next five years; or you can negotiate a less expensive divorce (or better prenuptial agreement). You have the option of selecting a less expensive home, and a cheaper auto insurance package that is just as good as the one you have now, and you can make the best tax choice about when to start taking retirement plan distributions after you retire. You can start your own business, make sure your child qualifies for all the college financial aid possible, choose the right mortgage with the best interest rate and point package, save the most on income tax year after year, and on and on—all by making conscious and well-informed decisions.

So why wouldn't you?

FINANCIAL "NAPS" IN THE PAST: HARDER TO WAKE UP IN THE FUTURE?

Some people let worries about where they are now, or what they may regret having done in the past, prevent them from looking too closely at their financial situation for the future. But much of what determined your current status may have been due to changing circumstances beyond your control, or ones in which you gave up control. Many clients blame themselves, for instance, when they are laid off (even though fifty others were laid off at the same time), and go into a spiral of depression. Because their emotions have taken over, they may go wild and spend more than usual to make themselves feel better, or spend all day in front of the TV because it's just too hard to go out, hit the pavement, cut their budget, and look for a new job right away. I see clients all the time who, now that they're waking up, start obsessing about the past. They bemoan what they should have done differently, and what they could have done differently, and the sad thing is that all they did was *nothing* while their lives—and their financial seasons—were changing around them.

There are also those who have *selective* vision about their pasts (rather than the 20/20 hindsight that we are more prone to praise), especially when it comes to money matters. They blame themselves for decisions that actually were quite defensible at the time. For example, I had one couple as clients who, when they realized they needed to borrow money to repair their roof, began to feel guilty about $3,000 they had spent on a trip to a lush island three years earlier. "We know we shouldn't have taken that trip." Then I found out in a later session that it was that trip, their first time alone in eight years and four kids, that saved their marriage. But they didn't remember that part.

Others take all the credit for happy accidents that have made them wealthy beyond their wildest dreams. My best example is the client who happened to luck out, and ended up making millions even though he was a lackluster business school student. No big firm would hire him, so he had to accept a job with a small start-up software firm that couldn't pay him much but gave him stock options instead. You guessed it—the company went public and he made a fortune on those stock options. But to hear it now, he was the *only one* in his class perceptive enough to realize the potential of this software company and that's why he is so wealthy today.

YOUR CHANCES FOR WEALTH HAVE NEVER BEEN GREATER

In fact, the possibility of dramatic and rapid change in your economic status is more likely today than ever before in history. Technology has increased the rate of change, especially in the area of personal finance. It wasn't so long ago that things did not change much in a person's life. The rich stayed rich, and the poor stayed poor.

That doesn't always hold true anymore. Today most of America's billionaires are not recipients of "old money" at all, but decidedly "new money" earned through new opportunities that arose through changes in our culture—including entertainment, sports, computers, and other forms of technology. Eighty-five people listed on the Forbes 1982 ranking of the four hundred richest people in America got their money from inherited wealth, and four got theirs from the software or computer industry. In 1996, the number who had inherited their wealth dropped over 50 percent to thirty-nine, while those whose money came from the software or computer industry jumped 525 percent to twenty-six. In fact, in 1996, three of the ten richest people in the United States made their money from one company alone—bet you can't guess this one—Microsoft.

While I can't predict whether you will stumble into a huge pot of new money, it is certain that your financial opportunities will change as you age and live your life—you just have to be awake and ready to seize them. As each season passes and a new one begins, you will no doubt experience sadness at the end of the old one and excitement about the new one. Just as I did when I became an "empty nester," you will also probably experience a good deal of trepidation that may increase as you get farther into the season if you don't have a plan in place. You may enjoy the first few days of June but find the 100-degree afternoons in the middle of summer oppressive if you don't have an air conditioner. In December the first snowfall may delight you, but in midwinter two feet of dirty gray snow piled up against your doorstep will seem like nothing but a hassle and an eyesore.

Whether you are starting out or starting over, building up or scaling back, each financial stage will present its own opportunities for "waking up" and taking charge. My goal is to help you prepare for each of these financial seasons by being by your side throughout this book, helping you design and therefore control your economic future. The idea behind *Wake Up and Smell the Money* is that it will act as a lifetime guide—one where you can fill in the worksheets, make notes in the margins, write down and change your goals, assets, income, etc. so you can keep track of your progress.

There are plenty of people who let outside events determine the course of their financial lives. Others may call these people passive, but in fact they *have* taken action—by deciding *not* to act.

This is especially true of couples in which one person refuses to work on financial issues with his or her partner. In those cases, the active partner becomes resentful about all the responsibility that the abdicator has shrugged off. After fighting about it for a long time, if they stay together, they usually wind up avoiding the subject of money altogether. This is unproductive and dangerous, because the lack of communication will exacerbate whatever money problems they have, and money problems are the number one cause of divorce. I will only consent to meet with couples when both partners agree to attend, because only then can I get a full picture of their financial situation. There are two sides to every story, *especially* when money is involved!

If you are married or involved in a long-term relationship, I warn you that you can't begin to get a handle on your finances without your partner's involvement. I had one friend whose husband was so uninterested in their finances that it wasn't until she was literally on her deathbed that he allowed her to teach him how to balance the checkbook. Don't—either of you—wait that long to share the responsibilities.

(If you are really stuck for a way to get cooperation from your partner, skip ahead to my No-Argument Plan [see page 137].)

My view—and I hope you come to share it—is that it is far better to wake up and know the reality of your situation than to always wonder about where you stand. Then you can make the best possible choices, secure in the knowledge that you have done the best that you could for yourself and your loved ones. Once you begin to make conscious and thoughtful decisions about how you manage your money, you won't go back to being asleep at the financial wheel.

STRONG STARTS MAKE FOR HAPPY ENDINGS

Before you can turn any season of your life into a growing season, you need to take six preliminary steps to lay the groundwork for a prosperous and secure future. Strong starts make for fabulous finishes, so don't skip ahead to the sections of the book that most concern you based on your current financial season—be it retirement, college funding, buying a vacation home, getting out of debt, or designing the best possible investment strategy—until you take these initial steps to get you on your way. Here they are:

1. Examine Your Own Beginnings
2. Pay Attention to Your Spending
3. Get Wired: Use Technology to Your Advantage
4. Forget About Money: Dream a Little (or a Big) Dream
5. Take Stock of Your Present Situation
6. Choose Wealth

STEP 1: EXAMINE YOUR OWN BEGINNINGS

What's your first memory of money? What's the first thing that you ever bought? Did you have a piggy bank or some special place where you kept your money? Did you get an allowance and what chores, if any, did you have to do in order to get it? What were the financial lessons you learned in your childhood? Do you remember saving up for something? Did you have a lemonade stand or a paper route? Or did you get no lessons from childhood at all except how to cajole money out of your parents?

Answering these questions will help you uncover where your financial habits originated. You may not realize it, but you've been molded by every single money experience that you've had, and those experiences have an enormous effect on how you handle money now.

Frequently, when I ask clients these questions, they, especially married couples, will realize that they are acting *exactly* the way their parents did and the way they said they never would. The wife, for instance, will have married someone who handles money the same way her father did, and will realize that she behaves exactly as her mother did around money. Others realize they were taught bad habits, or nothing at all.

Among the methods for handling money that are passed down from generation to generation are:

- New England thrift—there are lots of things you could spend money on to make your life happier and easier (such as hiring a cleaning lady), but you don't because it would feel as if you were betraying your family and your personal values.
- Never Spend Principal—if you are over sixty-five and still following this credo, or if you are younger and buying another investment, it's time to review your strategy. It's OK to spend some of your capital gains as well.
- Buy for Others—but never for yourself.
- Count on Your Inheritance.
- Use Money as an Excuse—to avoid a social life or emotional connections with loved ones. For example, "I never go out because I don't have the money," or buying your children gifts to compensate for not spending enough time with them.
- Shop 'Til You Drop—did your mother or father shop for recreation? Is that what you do now?
- Obsession with Investing—you look at the financial pages every day to find out how much you gained or lost, and adjust your daily spending accordingly.

Sometimes instead of copying your parents, you may be reacting against them. Many people who were raised in the Great Depression, for instance, reacted by spoiling their kids with an oversupply of toys and clothing. At the other extreme, of course, were those who behaved as though another depression was just around the corner. Because of my accidents and divorce, my own children worry that everything could be wiped out overnight. They are both frugal (a good thing), and I know they will always be able to live within a budget. I expect they will be affected by these childhood experiences for the rest of their lives. On the other hand, they are both able to spend money and enjoy doing so in a healthy way, without feeling guilty about it.

Often, what you uncover isn't good or bad—it just *is*. You gain a great deal of personal insight and peace of mind simply by identifying your habits and figuring out where they came from. With that knowledge in hand, you can often achieve some kind of balance—keeping the good and helpful stuff you learned and discarding the rest—by cutting through the financial fog that may have surrounded you for years.

If you weren't taught much about how to manage money growing up—and most of us weren't—it's very difficult to know what to do when you are first on your own, even if you've been on your own for twenty years and this is the first time you are really thinking about it. Making the most of any financial season requires the development of good money habits. The most important one is gathering knowledge about your options in any given situation. Others are: brainstorming about your goals, taking stock of what you own and owe, and tracking your spending—all critical steps that we'll guide you through in this chapter.

Money permeates everything, as the following exercise will allow you to demonstrate to yourself. Try taking a piece of paper, maybe even a page out of your appointment calendar, and drawing a line down the middle. Carry this piece of paper with you for a week (better yet, a month). On one side of the line, put a check mark every time you *do* anything that has to do with money. On the other side, put a check mark every time you *think* about anything that has to do with money (plus a one- or two-word description of each thought). If you are like most people, you will be astonished at how often you think about money. You may be sitting in your office thinking, "Boy, I'd love to change jobs." Or "I can't afford to go out to lunch." Or "I'm going out to lunch," but then you feel guilty about it. Or "I wonder how my mutual fund did yesterday." Or you see a car wrecked on the side of the road and before you even wonder about injuries, you may think to yourself, "I know I should get more insurance."

Usually the thoughts are negative. People rarely spend time congratulating themselves about their money. That's why I've included a scorecard on the next page that should help you keep track of some of the good decisions that you are ready to begin making—from here on out. Keeping track of your ATM withdrawals, checking the interest rate on your credit cards, and so on, are all very important steps that you can begin to take. (Don't be intimidated when you look at the list of twenty items. I'll guide you through every one of these as we go through the book.) Check off the ones you've already done, then three months from now, take out the list again and use it to track your progress.

Personal change takes work, and most important, it takes time. But it's also possible, no matter how old you are. A rule of thumb I used in my first book, *The Money Diet*, which still holds true is that it takes one week for every year of your life to change your financial habits. So if you are twenty-five, it might take six months. At fifty, it might take

Pat-Yourself-on-the-Back Chart

I wrote down my financial goals.	
I wrote down my nonfinancial goals.	
I figured out my net worth.	
I filled out my Current Cash Flow chart.	
I developed a budget.	
I figured out where I spent my money last week.	
I cut my spending by 10 percent this week.	
I balanced my checkbook.	
I looked into/started using personal finance software like Microsoft Money or Quicken.	
I checked the interest rates and late fees on my credit cards.	
If I have credit card balances, I shopped for lower interest rates.	
I checked current mortgage rates against my own mortgage(s) to see if refinancing makes sense.	
I talked to my kids about how they will help save some money for college or post-high school training.	
I gave up the temptation to spend _____ and saved _____.	
I explained to my child where the money in an ATM machine comes from.	
I figured out what my current investments are and what investment categories they fall into (in other words, my asset allocation).	
I reviewed the investments in my 401(k) plan.	
I wrote a will, or checked to make sure my current one is up-to-date.	
I checked my life insurance policy to see if I have enough.	
I checked my benefits at work to make sure I have enough disability insurance.	
I checked my car insurance policy to make sure I have enough coverage, and I asked for the cost savings on raising my deductible.	

you a year before you are completely comfortable doing something a new way. If people are really dedicated, they may change before that. But give yourself some leeway. If you backslide, give yourself a short break, and then start again. It's only natural to make mistakes, and if you are too hard on yourself, you'll lose your motivation entirely.

Mistakes are okay. *Forget about them!* You'll see as you read on that I've made just about every one in the book—and so have most planners I know. I've also been witness to scores of people who have transformed their lives, which has been tremendously gratifying. And I can't take the credit for it. They were smart enough to come to a planner and do what it takes. I gave them guidance, but they made the changes.

If you are making changes, you are making choices. Not making changes is making a choice, too, because you're making a subconscious one to not "wake up." Becoming conscious of the control that you can have over your financial destiny is a great beginning—the best—and the only one that will succeed.

STEP 2: WAKE UP TO WHERE YOUR MONEY GOES

Disconnection from our money is a distinctly modern development. Thousands of years ago, when value was invested in tangible objects as diverse as animal teeth, stones, gold, shells, ivory, rock crystals, coral, and sheep, you could look at your money, touch it, and smell it (especially the sheep). Much later, when coins and then paper bills were created, money was still closely guarded by its owners. Before banks earned people's trust, people hid their money, which made them feel safer because they could take it out and count it.

Today, largely because of technological advances, we have very little direct contact with our money. We may carry a little cash around, but that is our *only* personal connection with our money. (The rare exception: some older people, remembering the Depression, still keep cash stashed away. Just recently, at a Vermont yard sale, a couple spent less than $5 on a box of baking items—and included with it was an old cigar box containing over $10,000 in cash!)

When we look at our financial resources, what do we see?

Pieces of paper—bank statements, ATM receipts, checks, loan papers, pay stubs, credit card statements;

Pieces of plastic—credit cards, ATM cards, debit cards; and

Computer screens—if we go into the bank and the service representative pulls our accounts up on the screen, or if we use personal finance programs to try and maintain financial order on our own.

None of these forms carries the emotional weight of a dollar bill. And our separation—both emotional and physical—from our money is only going to increase. Experts predict that at some point all your bank accounts will be managed by one card containing your unique holographic fingerprint, which you will use for every financial transaction. You will put your finger on a pad and get scanned, just like an item at the grocery store. At that point, you will be *completely disconnected* from your money.

The problem with being disconnected from your money is that it becomes very easy to lose control of it. With Automatic Teller Machines (ATMs) and overdraft protection, you can overdraw your account (something you may be too humiliated to do at the bank, where the teller knows how much you have in your account). In addition, with banks that don't print balances on their ATM receipts, you may not even know when you have gone in the red because your line of credit kicks in to cover the overdraft. And since almost 30 percent of Americans don't know how much is in their checking account, lots of people are in for big surprises every month.

In a recent year, Americans used their ATM cards over seven billion times, averaging more than six hundred million times a month, in some cases racking up transaction charges of as much as $2 or $3 a shot. (Now, to encourage ATM usage, some banks are charging a fee to walk inside and use a live teller as well!) Few people are able to recall where all their money went, because we have to make such an effort to keep track of that money. How often have you opened up your wallet and had absolutely no idea where your money had gone?

We also have debit cards that can take money out of your account while you are in stores and restaurants, not just at bank machines. Those are much better than credit cards, because you cannot spend more than what you have in your checking account (plus its overdraft limit), and most statements tell you how and where you used the card. However, people frequently forget to record their debit purchases in their checkbook because it feels as if they are using a credit card. Consequently, there has been a huge increase in overdrafts and bounced checks for accounts with debit cards. I have also seen an increase in the number of debit-card users who consider their checking account balance to be the amount in their account, plus the amount of their overdraft protection (the line of credit attached to the account so they don't bounce checks).

WEAR YOUR MONEY FOR A WEEK

If you work, Social Security and (probably) income taxes are withheld from your paychecks, but have you ever had the opportunity to see or feel that money? All you know is that numbers show up on your paycheck indicating that the money was taken out, and at the end of the year you get a W-2 form showing that the money went to the government. Perhaps thousands of dollars a year—often more than one-third of your income—never even passed through your hands! With renewed debate about privatization, which may give you some say over how your Social Security contributions are invested, you may gain more control over a portion of these contributions, but direct access still won't come until you retire.

Exacerbating our overspending problem is the fact that nowadays it's easier than ever before to spend money, and lots of it. All kinds of things that we didn't have to pay for before now come with tempting, costly options—cable television, having someone fill your gas tank and wash your car windows, and getting long distance directory assistance, to name a few. And a host of nonessential items have been added to the list of standard home equipment: things such as computers, software, video games, VCRs, microwave ovens, and camcorders. In fact, according to some surveys, home computers are now considered a "back-to-school expense"!

Added to these are new ways to buy—via catalogues, home shopping networks, the Internet—all of which make it easy to part with your money with the press of a few computer keystrokes or pushes on the telephone pad. Because you don't have to hand cash over, these transactions seem painless and inconsequential—until you get your bill.

It's also harder to keep a lid on spending if you are a parent. Kids easily fall prey to the marketing experts and now want expensive brand-name clothes and electronic gadgets and games. My forty-year-old friend was proud of her transistor radio when she was ten; her ten-year-old son started out with a boom box, complete with a compact disc player.

I'm all in favor of progress, but when it comes to money matters, I sometimes wish that we had retained some of the ways of the past. When my parents were developing their spending and saving habits, for instance, they didn't have credit cards. If they wanted to buy a washing machine, they either had to wait and save the money, or they had to go and make a deal directly with the owner of the appliance store. (And if they were late on the payments, they knew they might run into him at the general store or pass him on the street downtown!) They couldn't charge their vacations. They couldn't charge their dinners out. They had less leeway than we do and couldn't develop the less-than-perfect habits we can in just a few years as adults. We, on the other hand, can stretch out our payments for last week's groceries for ten years if we want to. Improperly used, credit can hang us with a string of debts.

Credit card companies, one of the prime beneficiaries of all these trends, are stalking a whole new generation of spenders by setting up sign-up tables on college campuses and along the Florida beaches during spring break. You can be dead drunk and sign up for a credit card—in a state that allows a 23 percent interest rate and a $30 late fee. No wonder it takes less than a year for the average college student to reach his spending limit! And if they go overboard, the companies know they can count on the majority of moms and dads to bail out their children in an effort to protect their youngsters' credit ratings. Decide *now* what you would do in that situation, and teach your kids how to handle credit *before* they get that first card.

My advice? To get a handle on your financial life, you've got to reconnect with your money. The best way to do that is to cash your next paycheck and hold the money in your hands. When you get tired of that, try to "wear your money for a week." I know it sounds strange, but I promise it works. Cash your next paycheck, or Social Security, or other income check, and keep it on your body for the next seven days— either in your wallet or in a fanny pack strapped around your waist. (Obviously, don't tell anyone you are doing this!) One of my clients wrapped the money in plastic wrap and taped it to herself! (If you have your paycheck direct-deposited, go to the bank and cash a check for that amount.) You will be acutely aware of your money, and as you pay for everything in cash, you will be acutely aware of how quickly it can disappear.

When we don't pay for things in cash, we tend to forget how hard we had to work for the money we are giving away when we buy something. The difference between doling out cash and writing a check or handing over a debit or credit card is palpable. It will feel like you are spending far more than if you had simply deducted that debit card or check amount in your check ledger, or added it to your credit card bill.

Some people ask me, "That doesn't sound very safe. What if you get mugged?" My response: "When you don't have the money ten years from now, wouldn't you rather blame the mugger than blame yourself for spending it on things you don't need?"

Another tried-and-true strategy that has worked time and again with my clients is to put only one week's worth of your cash needs in your wallet. Include the expenses you can't control, such as gas or the daily lunch money for the kids, but keep them in a separate place in your wallet. You probably have an idea of where you spend too much money. Let's use eating lunches out at work as an example. Give yourself a budget of, say, $25 and paper clip that amount of money together with a Post-It note that says "lunch." Pay for your lunches from the clipped cash and when you run out, it's brown-bag time for the rest of the week. If you have several spending categories, you can even keep your money in an envelope inside your purse or your inside jacket pocket. Forget about keeping track of coins. Just use any leftover change as you need it, or you will drive yourself crazy and give up on keeping track of your spending altogether.

Another technique is to write down where all your money goes on the backs of your ATM and debit card slips. Just do it for two weeks, and you will have a much better idea of how you are spending your money. People don't care if you take another thirty seconds at the checkout counter or restaurant to write down the amount of money you've just spent. In fact, I've gotten compliments when I've explained what I'm doing. "Since I've been tracking what I spend more carefully, I've been able to cut my spending," I say. Many people respond by saying they might try it, too.

It's especially helpful when you have children because you can refer to the slips and say, "I already gave you $12 this weekly to go to the movies." When I first started keeping track of my cash, I realized I was spending more money on my kids' clothes than on my own wardrobe, which didn't make sense because I had to show up in a suit at a Boston office every day. And I couldn't blame the kids: I was buying some stuff that they said they didn't need or even want.

Furthermore, everything you do instructs your children. So if you are disconnected from your money, and you aren't paying attention to where it's going, they are not learning how to measure its value either. Ask your children the next time they accompany you to the ATM machine where that money comes from. If they don't know, and they probably don't if they are young, explain it to them. Many kids think the ATM is just a "magic machine" that spits out bills. It's not a bad idea to ask yourself the same question from time to time: "What did I have to do to get that money?" It's a consciousness raiser that will help you hold onto your hard-earned cash.

By keeping close tabs on your spending, you will gain a much better sense of where your money goes. Study after study has shown that most people can cut roughly 20 percent out of their discretionary spending before they really feel it; chances are good that you will fall in that camp. Somehow it works, at least if you are a person who generally lives within his or her means.

Two tips: (1) Only track discretionary expenses (the ones you can do without) because there's nothing you can do about the necessities. To give you an idea of the difference between the two, I offer the following:

Necessities	Discretionary Expenses
Mortgage	Impulse buying
Basic food	Dining out
Basic clothing	Lavish gifts for others
Utility bills	Cable TV, caller ID, etc.
Gas	Car wash (vs. washing it yourself)

☞ **Wake-up Call:** If you track your checkbook spending by hand (not with software), always round your numbers to the nearest dollar—it's close enough. Pennies can cause big errors, and reconciling them can take hours.

Do whatever it takes to record your spending, but make it easy. I had one client who decided only to spend cash, so she divided her cash up into fifteen envelopes, each earmarked for a specific type of expense. After one week of that she'd had enough and gave up. She had created an impossible goal for herself. Start small, and keep it manageable.

Talking about the steps you are taking and sharing the saving techniques that work best for you within your own family or among your friends can boost the support you need in order to take control of your financial life. If you have a significant other, remember that he or she should also be involved. Form a pact with a close, *nonjudgmental* friend or family member that each week you will show each other where you spent your money. Pick a time, make it a weekly appointment and keep it! Showing someone else how you've spent your money is a real Spending Stopper—that way, it's harder to delude yourself about the fact that you spent $50 on a pair of shoes you'll probably never wear.

If you are part of a group of friends who regularly go out to lunch or clubs, or wherever, tell them you are trying to cut back and ask them to be supportive. Chances are some of them also know they are spending too much money, but are too embarrassed to admit it to the group.

STEP 3: GET WIRED: USE TECHNOLOGY TO YOUR ADVANTAGE

As much as I miss the personal contact that people used to have with their money, the flip side is that technological advances have made it much easier to save and invest. Automatic deductions from your paycheck for 401(k) contributions make it virtually impossible for you to skip a month. You don't miss the money because you never have access to it. Studies show that people who authorize automatic deductions of up to 10 percent automatically seem to decrease their spending by the same amount, rather than spending at the same rate and running up their credit card bills.

Think about automatic deductions into retirement plans this way: Every dollar you keep yourself from spending is a *$1 tax-free pay raise,* because you won't be taxed on that money (until you withdraw it) and if you don't spend it, you will save it for a time when you will really need it—during your retirement. It's as if your boss said, "I'm giving you a raise, but you don't have to pay taxes on it and you can't touch it now, because it's being invested." Here's an example: Make a dollar. Pay taxes on it. Spend the rest of it on nonnecessities. There's nothing left! It's as if you never earned that dollar at all—so why did you bother to work for it?

You can also give yourself a "pay raise" by using an automatic deduction to increase your savings. Have $50 a month, or whatever amount, deducted from your paycheck and deposited into a mutual fund or savings account. Any money that you save, that you otherwise would have spent, is equivalent to a pay raise. You can even write "$1 tax-free pay raise" on the back of your business card and put it in your wallet close to your cash. This can be a very powerful motivator when you are tempted to spend money unnecessarily.

Automatic bill paying is an excellent way to help yourself if this is one of your problem areas. One of my young colleagues had developed the bad habit of paying her bills late during college when she had no money (a very common problem). As a result, she now had a terrible credit report, but by signing up for the automatic bill-paying service at her bank, she began to restore her credit rating. She knew the money was coming out of her checking account, so she spent less.

Another option to consider is electronic banking through one of the more popular software programs such as Microsoft Money or Quicken. Ironically, by using an electronic program like this you gain more control over your money because you have greater access to your own numbers. This may sound contradictory to what I told you about the importance of a tangible connection with your money, but it's not. The purpose of reconnecting with your income is to wake up to your spending habits: this takes that process a step further and enables you to record your spending in the software program. Twenty-four hours a day, you can have access to your account and see which checks have cleared and what your balances are, rather than having to wait until you get your monthly statement in the mail. You can use these programs to enter all of the bills that need to be paid for the next several months or more, and then determine the exact date you want them to be paid—or you can enter them and choose the date of payment later. You can set up a personalized budget and see how your monthly and annual spending compare and where your problem areas lie. If you want, this information can actually be displayed automatically every time you open the program, and you can print out detailed reports.

These aren't just checkbook-tracking and bill-paying programs, but are powerful financial planning tools as well. These programs contain built-in advice from financial experts so you can get suggestions for improving your financial situation and help with juggling your long-term savings goals and your short-term spending needs. And if you list all your investments, the software will track your investment accounts, and update and display their values each time you open the program. No more flipping through the *Wall Street Journal* to figure out how much you "gained" or "lost" yesterday!

If you do your own taxes, programs such as Intuit and Kiplinger's Tax Cut can copy your year's tax data from both Microsoft Money and Quicken, and will also take care of most of your tax prep work. Believe it or not, entering all your financial data and setting up a budget usually doesn't take more than a couple of hours. In addition, these programs are designed to walk you through the process of filing your taxes on line, which can speed up your tax refund, if you are owed one. If you're in need of more financial information, get yourself hooked up to the Internet, which offers all kinds of business news articles and data, including analysts' reports on stocks and mutual funds, so you can research to your heart's content.

These programs can also be used as lists of all your important financial data, which is useful for getting a quick handle on your current situation. It's also helpful in the event of an emergency, such as the unexpected death of a spouse or business partner, because you won't have to search to dig out all the financial information you'll need, such as the names and amounts of life insurance policies, when you're under considerable duress.

STEP 4: FORGET ABOUT MONEY: DREAM A LITTLE (OR BIG) DREAM

Some of the most productive conversations I have with clients are the ones in which the word 'money' is never mentioned; the discussion focuses instead on concerns or dreams. A couple comes to me because a friend of theirs who is a parent was just diagnosed with cancer. They say they now realize they had better buy more life insurance. "The kids would really struggle if something happened to one of us." Only then do we begin to run the numbers. Another client told me that he was an aggressive investor, but then one day realized he couldn't handle as much risk as he had thought. "It's keeping me up at night," he confessed. Then it was time to review his investment strategy. After fifteen years of living as single adults, a man and woman meet and decide to marry. "We want this to be the wedding of our dreams, and we know it's not going to be cheap." Or a welcome pregnancy spurs college dreams (and financial fears), or a job change means moving and buying a new house. It's the recognition of need, or a decision made, or a dream put on the table. It's waking up.

The traditional way of setting goals in financial planning is to write a list of major life events, such as retirement, buying a house, and educating the kids, and then to try and figure out how much they will cost. That's the way I operated as a financial planner for over twenty years, and it took me that long to figure out that method didn't work for most people. You need to make a list, but you also need to attach a set of images to that list that will motivate you to implement your plan. Words on a piece of paper alone just won't do it. As usual, I learned this from a client, because every client teaches me at least one thing I can then use to help someone else.

I was in a meeting with a long-time client for her annual review and she was not making much progress toward her financial goals. Rita was spending too much and not saving enough, her insurance policies were overpriced and a mess (she never contacted the agent I had referred her to), and she had not consolidated all her IRAs to make life easier. Basically, she had not done *one thing* on the list that I gave her the year before.

Rita confessed to me, "I felt so guilty in the car driving here today that I was embarrassed even to meet with you. Then I realized what the problem is. You gave me that to-do list as well as those cash flow statements for the next twenty years and, believe me, I have studied them. But then I don't *do* anything about it. I guess I just don't have the motivation to make these financial changes. If I could just *see* the future, I *know* I could do what it takes." There was more conviction in her voice than I had ever heard from her. I had tried to make her "wake up" with numbers, but instead, I had terrified her.

All too often, we planners focus on the numbers, and when we show them to our clients they are so overwhelmed that they give up and don't do anything at all. Who failed? The planners, because we missed a crucial step—helping each client develop a vision. Without brainstorming you don't have one—and it is that vision of the future that will make it easier to make all those difficult decisions along the way. By brainstorming your goals, you will see the big picture and will know where you are headed.

The overwhelming majority of Americans have never written down their financial goals. In a preliminary questionnaire that I give to new clients, we have a section in which we ask them to list their goals in order of priority. Often they come back with eight or nine goals and numbers next to them that look like they have been erased and changed too often to count. These new clients don't have a clue about what's most important to them, because they have never really thought about their future in concrete terms.

It doesn't matter how smart you are or what field you are in; the issues that financial planning brings up can sometimes be hard to face. Some of my clients who know the least about their own financial situations are investment bankers. Lawyers seem to fall down in estate planning. I know one attorney whose wife had been bugging him to get a will, because for years she had been hearing his tales of horror about his own clients who had died without wills and proper insurance policies. But he was afraid to face his own mortality. So he wrote his last testament on a napkin at a restaurant, naming her as the executor and beneficiary of all his money. Then, he found the cashier, who happened to be a notary and could notarize his signature, and made the waiters give him their names and addresses and sign it as witnesses, and finally presented it to his wife, saying, "Are you satisfied now?"

Reminder card

Buying a House

Turning key in lock and walking over the threshold

Touring empty rooms, smelling fresh paint

Planning where your furniture will go

Having a housewarming party

Retirement

Moving to a retirement community with more social and intellectual activities than you ever imagined

Hitting the golf course every day with friends, driving the golf cart like kids

Meeting friends every day for breakfast

Waking up to beautiful weather every day

Feeling your grandchildren's hugs when they get off the plane for a visit

College

Hearing the applause as your child walks across the stage to collect her diploma

Taking photos of him in his cap and gown

Planning the family celebration

Hearing her say, "Thanks, Mom and Dad, for making this possible"

Credit Card Debt

Opening that final statement and seeing a $0 balance

Using scissors to cut up all your cards except one

Financial planning is about much more than facing your fears, it's also about reaching your goals, and brainstorming is the first step. But first, brainstorming requires you to dream. Forget what you think is doable and what is not. Focus only on what you *want* to do, regardless of how ridiculous or impossible it seems. Brainstorming about your financial future has little to do with dollars and cents. Instead, you should envision the goals you want to achieve in your lifetime. Think of the most pleasurable image you can. It should be as fun as vacation planning. Nobody starts out saying "Let's spend two thousand dollars in August." They envision where they want to go and what they want to see and do. Then they figure out how much it will cost. Financial planning should be approached the same way. You don't say, "I want my kid to go to a college that costs thirty thousand dollars a year." Or "I want to live in a five-hundred-thousand-dollar house when I retire." Or "I want twenty-five thousand dollars a year to put into my checking account for expenses." A great vacation leaves you relaxed and exhilarated. The right college is the one at which your child can blossom. Being able to meet expenses means making enough money so you can live comfortably and realistically. These days, a happy retirement is living in a manner in which you can *enjoy*—whether it is on the golf course, a cruise ship, Elderhostel learning adventures, holding your first grandchild, attending family reunions, or doing volunteer work. Or just sitting on the porch!

Achieving the goal of providing for your child's education does not amount simply to writing a five-figure check each year for four years (I know this from personal experience!). It means agonizing through the application process, enjoying the day the college acceptance letter arrives in the mail, then attending parents' weekends, hearing about all of the college experiences your child has (or at least the ones he will share with you!), and watching the graduation ceremony as your child walks across the stage to receive his degree.

And the pleasure you take from the education you have provided does not stop there. You have the satisfaction that knowing, year by year, how that college degree is helping your child advance along his chosen career path as well as in his personal development.

And what if your child decides to postpone college indefinitely, go into the military, work, or try to use his time in ways that *he* thinks are most educational? Society (school, parents, friends, family) can force him to go, but if he doesn't want to be there, it's a waste of money. Each child learns his own way, and sometimes, college is not crucial. When I was appearing on CNBC, the Internet chat room monitor was barely out of high school. My son has lived and traveled on four continents, and knowing him, I would rather have him do that than graduate from Harvard this year with his peers.

Successful financial plans, just as successful businesses, start with a vision. Each successful business started with a person or group of people with a shared vision who then brought in experts to help them make their vision a reality. They knew what they wanted to do in order to sell a particular product or service, but they needed to find someone who could help them turn their idea into a reality. They had experts tell them how to write a business plan, set financial goals, and obtain capital. You can start approaching your finances the way successful businesses do. If it worked for them, it can work for you, because after all, you *are* running a business. You have revenues (your income), expenses, and taxes, and your "products" are living well today and saving for the future.

Money alone is not motivating. It is what you can *do* with the money that motivates you to take action and change your life. A couple of years ago, I saw a potential client who had inherited $3 million and who had previously been living frugally on a modest salary. He was absolutely miserable, because he was afraid his values would change! The problem was also that Charles had never thought about the future, so when he got the money, he did not have a clue about what to do with it. Everyone under the sun—life insurance agents, stock brokers, real estate agents—tried to sell him stuff. As he said, "My friends keep telling me that I have it made. They expect me to be jumping for joy. But I am not any happier now than before; in fact, I am miserable, because I'm afraid I might turn into a different person, and I feel like I should be using this money for something useful, but I don't know what. It is disheartening because my friends are treating me differently, and a couple have even asked to borrow money from me. That really hurt. But if only I had thought about what I wanted in life beforehand, I could be enjoying it now, because I would have set a goal and then achieved it. *Life is so much more rewarding when dreams come true,* and my dreams have never been for more than just paying the rent and having time to hike and bike with friends. Instead, I just have a lot of money that everyone wants."

After spending a lot of time brainstorming about what he really cared about in life, and the legacy he wanted to leave, Charles, who was very interested in philanthropy, settled on a plan that was personally very satisfying and also economically sound. He gave part of his inheritance away to a charitable organization whose work he wanted to support, and in return, the organization gave him a tax deduction and an income for life through a special trust. The other portion he invested for long-term growth and a secure return, and plans to hand down the remainder to his nieces and nephews.

Brainstorming is the first step to making your dreams come true. It works *for* you in two ways. First, it helps you to see what you want more clearly, so it motivates you to do what you can to accumulate the wealth you need to achieve your goals. Second, when you succeed, it is all the more satisfying because you have worked for it. Think back to when you were a child, and you had a plan to save your money for something special, which included sacrificing something in the meantime. Wasn't it all the more wonderful because you had to wait for it?

So, let's get started with the brainstorming process. Forget about price tags and about how much things cost. Forget about the word "impossible." Forget about what you are *supposed* to want—what your siblings or your parents or your friends or colleagues say are important. This is all about *your* choices. I have a friend who drives a thirteen-year-old Volvo with 135,000 miles on it. He could afford a Ferrari, but he honestly sees no reason to buy one. He is constantly kidded in the office about his car, but his clients love his frugality. And he lets people think that he paid $200 for his shirts at Burberry's without ever revealing the *real* truth—that he wears perfect knock-offs at 20 percent of the cost.

I always thought it would be cool to retire and take a year to drive around the country in a rented mobile home, cooking my own meals, and keeping a journal for posterity and my kids. Some of my friends who consider it déclassé say to me, "How could you stand doing that?" But I think it would be fun, and it sure would be cheap! You, too, may have dreams that are less expensive than you imagine.

Start by looking at the chart called "Brainstorming Your Goals." You will see that I have divided your goals into two categories—financial (such as retirement security) and nonfinancial (such as spending more time with your family). You may find this hard to believe coming from a financial book, but I believe that both categories are equally important. On this chart I have listed a number of goals in each category, but there are spaces for you to add your own special ones.

Do not rush through the completion of this chart. The brainstorming process is actually one of the most important factors in achieving your goals (remember the study with the Harvard graduates?). Think carefully about what you write down, and make sure it is something *you* really want—something you are willing to perhaps sacrifice a little for now so that you can have it later.

Next, for each goal, close your eyes and pretend you are looking at a home movie of yourself enjoying that goal. Make sure that the image is very pleasurable. For example, for retirement security, if you are a golfer or tennis player, imagine seeing a film clip of yourself teeing off straight to the green or hitting a perfect backhand. Imagine the sound as the golf club or tennis racket hits the ball in just the right way. And imagine the warmth of the sun on your face, and the feel of the newly cut grass or groomed court. Use as many senses as possible. Bring a number of scenarios to mind for each goal—such as receiving your credit card statement in the mail and the outstanding balance is finally "zero," or being able to cut up all your credit cards except one because they are all paid off—and select the one or two that you think will most motivate you to work to achieve that goal. This is a crucial part of planning your financial future, because if you have no internal vision of what you are trying to achieve, you have no motivation to give up anything today in order to do so. When dinner and a movie are tempting you, it's hard to say no when "retirement," "college," or another goal is just empty words that are years and years away.

SETTING GOALS

You will notice a column on the right of the chart with the heading P*. Filling in this section is the harder part. Unfortunately, very few of us can meet every one of our financial goals. We have to set priorities. Look at each line of your list carefully, then rank each goal as follows: M = Must Have; C = Can Compromise (have part of, or less of, the goal); G = Give Up (willing to give up in order to achieve other goals.) Remember my clients with the questionnaires messy from changing their goal priorities? It's perfectly normal to do the same yourself: it's all part of the process of "waking up." This can be a difficult process, so reward yourself when you are done—with lunch or dinner out, flowers, or whatever is meaningful to you. You have just chosen what you want your financial future to hold for you, and it's worth spending a few bucks to reinforce and celebrate your choices.

Now take a look at both your financial and nonfinancial goals. Nonfinancial goals are really lifestyle goals because they have to do with your quality of life. Unfortunately, virtually every nonfinancial goal you've written down has financial ramifications and connections. The most obvious is the nonfinancial goal of "marriage" that accompanies the financial goal "pay for the wedding." (At least it *should* accompany it; I've actually seen couples still paying off wedding debts ten years after the event itself and it is keeping them from buying a house or having children.) Spending more time with your family might mean working only part-time or passing up a promotion with a pay increase. Developing a particular hobby probably means paying for equipment, lessons, and trade magazines. That's why our lifestyle goals and our financial goals are irrevocably intertwined.

Brainstorming Your Goals

Financial Goals	Visual Images	P*
Retirement		
Education		
New car		
Starting business		
Wedding		
New/redo house		
Protection against catastrophe		
Other _____		
Other _____		
Other _____		
Nonfinancial Goals	**Visual Images**	**P***
Work less		
More time with family		
Marriage		
Have children		
Less stress		
Travel		
Improve health/exercise		
Other _____		
Other _____		
Other _____		

*P = priority

Now do you see why it is so important to *consciously* make choices about your financial future? Otherwise, as I have seen over and over again in my years of working with clients, your lifestyle goals will keep you from reaching your financial goals, or your financial goals will make your life miserable until you reach them. There is a delicate balance between the two, which is why brainstorming is so important before you and I start constructing your financial plan together. Just like the client with a $3 million inheritance who was miserable, you can end up with *too much money and too little life.* Or you can have *too much life and not enough money.* If you don't want to be in either predicament, continue on to the next steps, and you won't be.

☞ **Wake-up Call:** It's not just your *financial* plan—it's also your *life* plan.

STEP 5: TAKE STOCK OF YOUR PRESENT SITUATION

Before you start focusing on your future, you need to know where you stand today. You have to start at the beginning with a realistic sense of where you are before you can plot your route to your financial goals.

The best way to measure your current financial status is to look at what you own and what you owe.

When I start to work with new clients, I always wait for the same two questions. It it so difficult to reveal your financial situation to someone else, even if that person is a financial professional, because in our culture our status is determined by our net worth. As I look at the form on which my client has revealed his assets and debts, I always get asked two questions: "Am I normal?" and "Will I have enough?"

Very often, people do not know how much they are worth. If you don't, you are not alone. In all my years as a financial planner, I can count on the fingers of one hand how many times prospective clients have told me their net worth and then, after completing a net worth worksheet, were correct to within $5,000. The record for being off is $1.2 million.

But I am giving you a fair warning: Being "normal" is not enough today. Both individually and as a country, we are saving at a far lower rate than we should. Over half of the nation's wealth is owned by baby boomers, but the average baby boomer has only $1,300 in his lifetime savings account. If you have managed to save more than that, that statistic alone should make you more confident about your own financial progress thus far.

Fill out the net worth chart on the next page. Remember to round your own numbers up to the nearest dollar, or $10, $50, or even $100—*whatever works for you.* Precise figures to the penny won't give you any more insight and rounding will save you loads of time. Also, don't worry about revising it each time you get updated figures. You simply want to take a snapshot regularly. Make changes just often enough to help you see the progress you are making.

I give my seminar participants net worth charts and make them fill them out on the spot, even though they have no bank statements, retirement plan booklets, or loan statements to refer to. Then I give them blank copies, and tell them to go home and pull out all that documentation and complete the forms again, because the real insight comes when you compare your real figures with the estimates you made when you were "flying blind." It is a good exercise that tells you how much you know about your money, and how in touch you are with your own financial situation.

With checks, credit cards, debit cards, and ATM withdrawal slips, sometimes our finances seem no more real to us than a Monopoly game. As a result, we have no clear picture of our present financial situation. Twenty-eight percent of us do not know how much money we have in the bank. I'm always stunned when prospective clients fill out our firm's Preliminary Questionnaire and discover that they thought they had $700,000 but instead have $400,000, or they actually have $70,000 instead of $40,000. These are differences of almost 50 percent of their net worth!

When you are mentally ready to face the truth, and you have an hour or so to do it, pull out all the most recent statements for every asset you own and debt you owe, including your mortgage, car loan statement, and credit card bills. This exercise may be nothing new for you; if you have ever applied for a loan, you have probably already had to do it. On the other hand, most people are surprised at the results, because they rarely focus on their financial situation as a whole.

If you are pleased and have more than you expected, congratulations—but you still have a lot of financial work to do to protect and grow your assets. Are you disappointed? Relax and try not to worry! That net worth figure is based on *past* events and choices. Armed with knowledge and a willingness to learn, you can seek the guidance you need to move forward financially.

In *The Money Diet* I told readers to forget the past, because if you constantly think of your past financial mistakes and failures, you will never make the changes you need to make in order to meet your goals. But many *Money Diet* readers wrote or called to tell me that it was only in recognizing the events in their past that they could change their future. Once again, I learned a valuable lesson I can now pass on to you.

Now that you have gotten your numbers on paper by completing your net worth statement, let's see how your financial situation stacks up against other Americans of similar ages with similar incomes. Look at the charts on the following pages to find the results.

Are you surprised? The most common reaction is disbelief, because we always think that everybody else has a lot more money than we do! Of course this makes perfect sense: we live in a culture where appearance means everything, and we are great at wearing the mask of affluence even after we have maxed out our credit cards and can't make the minimum monthly payments. If your assets are above these amounts, and your debts are below, wonderful—but that still does not mean you can slack off.

The next thing to take a look at is how you are spending your money. This is always the part of the financial planning process that clients hate the most! So if taking a look at your cash flow makes you cringe, you are in good company. That's why I'm going to alter the process here: Before I ask you how you are spending your own money, I'm going to show you how other Americans are spending theirs. It will probably make you feel much better.

Somehow, we always think that everyone else is doing a better job managing his money than we are. But before you make this judgment about yourself, take a look at the following two charts. They tell you how Americans in general spend and save, based on their household income. The first gives you the totals by category, and the second breaks it down in more detail.

Are you surprised again? Most clients are when I show them this, and it makes them feel so much better. Now it's time for you to do the exercise for yourself. Look at the chart titled "Current Cash Flow," and estimate what your expenses are for each category. If you don't have a clue, don't worry—many people don't. It just means that you need to "wake up" and pay attention. By the time you finish this book, you may actually know where every dollar goes!

Compare your current estimated cash flow to that of other households in your income group. But remember that these are averages, and some households are single-person households, while others have two parents and five children. Also, costs vary according to where you live—there is a big difference between rents in Manhattan and rents in Minneapolis. What is important is how *you* spend your money, so that you can save for the future, and meet your personal and emotional goals as well.

Now it's time to look at your current cash flow, to think about the goals you have written down, and then resolve to set a budget. Don't panic—what follows is just a generic budget, and I am going to give you *very specific* budget worksheets tailored to each season of your financial life. They are included in every chapter, and they cover just about any

Your Net Worth Today

When listing your assets, list all your retirement accounts together including the investments (such as stocks and mutual funds) in them. Do not list the investments in their individual categories.

ASSETS

Checking, Savings, Money Market Accounts	
Certificates of Deposit	
Mutual Funds	
Stocks	
Bonds	
Retirement Accounts	
Savings Bonds	
Trusts, Annuities, and Managed Investment Accounts	
Autos/Boats	
Primary House	
Investment Real Estate (second home, etc.)	
Business	
Personal/Household Items	
TOTAL	

continued on next page

Your Net Worth Today (cont.)

DEBTS

Mortgage/Home
Equity Loans

Installment/
Auto Loans

Credit Cards

Lines of Credit
(including checking overdrafts)

Investment
Real Estate

Life Insurance Policy

Loans (against
retirement plans, etc.)

TOTAL

YOUR NET WORTH

TOTAL ASSETS

Minus (-)

TOTAL DEBTS

Equals (=)

YOUR NET WORTH

What Americans Own According to Income

Household Income	Checking/ Savings/ Money Market	Certificates of Deposit	Mutual Funds	Stocks	Bonds	Retirement Accounts	Savings Bonds	Trusts/ Managed Accounts	Vehicles	Primary Residence	Investment Real Estate	Business	Other Non-financial
Less Than $10,000	700	7000	15,000	10,000	15,700	9,000	500	12,000	2,400	40,000	33,000	29,000	1,500
$10,000 to $24,999	1,100	16,000	7,000	4,000	11,000	5,100	500	20,000	4,300	50,000	21,000	20,000	5,000
$25,000 to $49,999	2,300	13,000	15,000	5,000	25,000	10,000	500	20,000	8,100	75,000	45,000	55,000	5,000
$50,000 to $99,999	5,600	12,000	22,000	8,000	20,000	25,000	1,000	32,000	11,000	115,000	65,000	25,000	12,000
$100,000 and over	25,500	28,000	30,000	40,000	51,000	66,000	1,200	95,000	14,900	225,000	160,000	260,000	20,000

SOURCE: Statistical Abstract of the United States

What Americans Owe According to Income

Household Income	Mortgage and Home Equity	Installment	Credit Cards	Other Lines of Credit	Investment Real Estate	Life Insurance/ Pension Loan
Less than $10,000	16,000	1,600	6,000	B*	6,500	700
$10,000 to $24,999	17,400	2,700	800	3,000	6,100	1,000
$25,000 to $49,999	40,000	5,600	1,300	1,500	18,000	2,000
$50,000 to $99,999	58,000	7,800	1,500	2,000	41,000	3,000
$100,000 and over	103,000	10,800	3,900	18,000	75,000	6,000

*B=Base figure too small

SOURCE: Statistical Abstract of the United States.

What Americans Own According to Age

Age of Head of Household	Checking/ Savings/ Money Market	Certificates of Deposit	Mutual Funds	Stocks	Bonds	Retirement Accounts	Savings Bonds	Trusts/ Managed Accounts	Vehicles	Primary Residence	Investment Real Estate	Business	Other Non-financial
Under 35 years old	1,400	5,000	3,800	2,000	10,000	4,700	400	20,000	5,900	69,000	40,000	19,300	3,500
35 to 44 years old	2,200	5,000	18,000	5,000	19,300	9,800	600	20,000	7,600	90,000	38,500	45,000	8,500
45 to 54 years old	3,400	10,000	20,000	12,000	25,200	30,000	1,000	25,000	8,600	95,000	70,000	100,300	11,300
55 to 64 years old	4,000	20,000	20,400	20,000	40,000	35,700	1,000	30,000	8,300	85,000	55,000	92,000	10,400
65 to 74 years old	4,000	25,000	30,000	24,000	25,300	23,000	900	40,000	5,600	70,000	60,000	80,000	11,000
75 years old and over	4,000	24,000	22,300	28,000	52,000	28,000	1,100	55,000	4,500	70,000	52,000	80,000	5,000

SOURCE: Statistical Abstract of the United States.

What Americans Owe According to Age

Household Income	Mortgage and Home Equity	Installment	Credit Cards	Other Lines of Credit	Investment Real Estate	Life Insurance/ Pension Loan
Under 35 years old	52,000	4,600	900	1,600	18,000	1,200
35 to 44 years old	54,000	5,000	1,300	1,800	28,000	3,000
45 to 54 years old	42,000	5,000	1,700	5,000	49,500	3,000
55 to 64 years old	28,000	3,900	1,000	4,000	34,700	3,000
65 to 74 years old	17,000	4,200	700	4,000	17,000	2,000
75 years old and over	15,000	3,100	600	B*	104,000	1,100

*B = Base figure too small

Source: Statistical Abstract of the United States.

How Americans Spend and Save (Totals)

Average national costs for various expenditures at various levels of household income.

Expenditures	Pretax Income											
	$20,000	$25,000	$30,000	$40,000	$50,000	$75,000	$100,000	$125,000	$150,000	$175,000	$200,000	$225,000	$250,000
Alcoholic Beverages	210	220	230	240	290	500	690	870	1,040	1,210	1,390	1,560	1,730
Apparel & Services	1,310	1,430	1,550	1,830	2,130	2,950	3,820	4,770	5,730	6,680	7,640	8,590	9,550
Cash Contributions	710	700	760	1,100	1,380	1,910	2,470	3,090	3,710	4,330	4,950	5,570	6,190
Education	210	250	290	400	540	940	1,310	1,640	1,970	2,300	2,630	2,950	3,280
Entertainment	1,080	1,280	1,470	1,830	2,160	2,950	3,820	4,770	5,720	6,680	7,630	8,590	9,540
Food	3,880	4,120	4,390	5,110	5,700	6,870	8,440	10,570	12,670	14,780	16,890	19,000	21,110
Furnishings	890	1,090	1,290	1,720	2,060	2,660	3,370	4,220	5,060	5,900	6,750	7,590	8,430
Health Care	1,630	1,670	1,710	1,850	1,970	2,260	2,710	3,390	4,070	4,750	5,430	6,110	6,790
Household Operations	330	360	400	500	630	960	1,300	1,620	1,940	2,270	2,590	2,920	3,240
Housekeeping Supplies	740	840	920	1,010	1,110	1,430	1,810	2,260	2,720	3,170	3,620	4,070	4,530
Miscellaneous Expenditures	660	720	790	950	1,040	1,170	1,390	1,740	2,080	2,430	2,780	3,130	3,470
Personal Care Products & Services	330	360	400	500	570	660	800	1,000	1,200	1,400	1,600	1,800	2,000
Personal Insurance & Pensions*	1,460	2,030	2,620	3,870	5,050	7,820	10,530	13,160	15,790	18,420	21,050	23,680	26,310

continued on next page

How Americans Spend and Save (Totals) (cont.)

Expenditures	Pretax Income												
	$20,000	$25,000	$30,000	$40,000	$50,000	$75,000	$100,000	$125,000	$150,000	$175,000	$200,000	$225,000	$250,000
Reading	120	140	160	190	210	280	360	450	540	630	720	810	900
Shelter	4,390	4,820	5,240	6,030	6,930	9,430	12,170	15,210	18,250	21,290	24,330	27,280	30,420
Taxes	980	1,500	2,010	3,970	4,110	7,430	10,430	13,040	15,650	18,260	20,870	23,470	26,080
Tobacco Products & Smoking Supplies	200	280	330	310	300	290	310	390	470	550	620	700	780
Transportation	4,580	5,300	5,990	7,320	8,330	10,130	12,510	15,640	18,760	21,890	25,020	28,140	31,270
Utilities, Fuels, & Public Services	1,950	2,050	2,150	2,320	2,480	2,840	3,420	4,280	5,130	5,990	6,840	7,700	8,550
Total	25,660	29,160	32,700	40,050	46,990	63,480	81,660	102,110	122,500	142,930	163,350	183,660	204,170

Source: Bureau of Labor Statistics.

*Include life insurance premiums, some of which are used to pay for term insurance (no savings buildup) and for permanent insurance that includes a savings element.

How Americans Spend and Save (Detailed)

Average national costs for various expenditures, at various levels of household income.

Expenditures	Pretax Income												
	$20,000	$25,000	$30,000	$40,000	$50,000	$75,000	$100,000	$125,000	$150,000	$175,000	$200,000	$225,000	$250,000
Alcoholic Beverages	210	220	230	240	290	500	690	870	1,040	1,210	1,390	1,560	1,730
Apparel & Services	1,310	1,430	1,550	1,830	2,130	2,950	3,820	4,770	5,730	6,680	7,640	8,590	9,550
Cash Contributions	710	700	760	1,100	1,380	1,910	2,470	3,090	3,710	4,330	4,950	5,570	6,190
Education	210	250	290	400	540	940	1,310	1,640	1,970	2,300	2,630	2,950	3,280
Entertainment	1,070	1,280	1,470	1,830	2,150	2,960	3,820	4,770	5,730	6,690	7,630	8,580	9,540
Fees & admissions	220	260	310	430	560	910	1,240	1,550	1,860	2,170	2,480	2,780	3,090
Supplies, equipment, & services	190	260	310	370	430	610	790	990	1,190	1,390	1,580	1,780	1,980
Pets, toys, playground equipment	230	290	330	390	440	600	770	960	1,160	1,350	1,540	1,740	1,930
TV, radio, sound equipment	430	470	520	640	720	840	1,020	1,270	1,520	1,780	2,030	2,280	2,540
Food	3,890	4,120	4,390	5,110	5,700	6,860	8,450	10,550	12,660	14,780	16,890	19,000	21,110
At home	2,640	2,680	2,760	3,120	3,370	3,770	4,490	5,610	6,730	7,860	8,980	10,100	11,220
Away from home	1,250	1,440	1,630	1,990	2,330	3,090	3,960	4,940	5,930	6,920	7,910	8,900	9,890
Furnishings	890	1,090	1,290	1,730	2,060	2,670	3,380	4,220	5,060	5,910	6,750	7,590	8,440
Floor coverings	80	100	160	390	470	340	290	370	440	510	590	660	730
Furniture	220	260	290	320	380	570	760	940	1,130	1,320	1,510	1,700	1,890

continued on next page

How Americans Spend and Save (Detailed) (cont.)

Expenditures	$20,000	$25,000	$30,000	$40,000	$50,000	$75,000	Pretax Income $100,000	$125,000	$150,000	$175,000	$200,000	$225,000	$250,000
Household textiles	60	70	80	110	140	200	260	330	390	460	530	590	660
Major appliances	140	160	170	170	170	210	270	330	400	470	530	600	670
Misc. household equipment	330	420	510	640	790	1,200	1,610	2,010	2,410	2,810	3,210	3,610	4,010
Small appliances, misc. housewares	60	80	90	100	110	150	190	240	290	340	380	430	480
Health Care	1,630	1,670	1,710	1,850	1,980	2,250	2,720	3,400	4,070	4,750	5,430	6,110	6,780
Drugs: prescription & nonprescription	320	310	300	280	280	310	370	460	550	640	730	820	920
Health insurance	860	870	880	940	980	1,030	1,190	1,490	1,790	2,090	2,390	2,690	2,980
Medical services	380	420	450	530	610	780	990	1,240	1,480	1,730	1,980	2,230	2,470
Medical supplies	70	70	80	100	110	130	170	210	250	290	330	370	410
Household Operations	330	360	400	510	620	960	1,290	1,620	1,940	2,270	2,590	2,920	3,240
Other household expenses	170	180	180	190	240	490	710	890	1,070	1,250	1,430	1,610	1,790
Personal services	160	190	220	320	380	470	580	730	870	1,020	1,160	1,310	1,450
Housekeeping Supplies	740	840	920	1,000	1,110	1,440	1,820	2,260	2,720	3,160	3,620	4,080	4,520

continued on next page

How Americans Spend and Save (Detailed) (cont.)

Expenditures	\$20,000	\$25,000	\$30,000	\$40,000	\$50,000	\$75,000	\$100,000	\$125,000	\$150,000	\$175,000	\$200,000	\$225,000	\$250,000
Housekeeping supplies	370	420	460	500	560	720	910	1,130	1,360	1,580	1,810	2,040	2,260
Laundry & cleaning supplies	110	110	120	120	130	160	200	250	300	350	400	450	500
Other household products	160	180	200	210	240	340	440	550	660	770	880	990	1,100
Postage & stationery	100	130	140	170	180	220	270	330	400	460	530	600	660
Miscellaneous Expenditures	660	720	790	950	1,040	1,170	1,390	1,740	2,080	2,430	2,780	3,130	3,470
Personal Care Products & Services	330	360	400	500	570	660	800	1,000	1,200	1,400	1,600	1,800	2,000
Personal Insurance & Pensions	1,460	2,030	2,630	3,870	5,050	7,820	10,520	13,160	15,790	18,420	21,050	23,680	26,310
Life & other personal insurance	230	260	300	390	490	740	980	1,230	1,480	1,720	1,970	2,210	2,460
Pensions & Social Security	1,230	1,770	2,330	3,480	4,560	7,080	9,540	11,930	14,310	16,700	19,080	21,470	23,850
Reading	120	140	160	190	210	280	360	450	540	630	720	810	900

Pretax Income

continued on next page

How Americans Spend and Save (Detailed) (cont.)

Expenditures	Pretax Income												
	$20,000	$25,000	$30,000	$40,000	$50,000	$75,000	$100,000	$125,000	$150,000	$175,000	$200,000	$225,000	$250,000
Shelter	4,390	4,820	5,240	6,040	6,930	9,430	12,160	15,210	18,260	21,300	24,330	27,380	30,420
Maintenance	590	600	630	750	860	1,120	1,420	1,780	2,140	2,490	2,850	3,200	3,500
Mortgage interest & charges	900	1,220	1,540	2,210	2,890	4,650	6,330	7,910	9,500	11,080	12,660	14,250	15,380
Other lodging	210	230	260	340	440	770	1,070	1,340	1,610	1,880	2,140	2,410	2,680
Property taxes	610	650	700	890	1,090	1,620	2,150	2,690	3,230	3,770	4,300	4,840	5,380
Rented dwellings	2,080	2,120	2,110	1,850	1,650	1,270	1,190	1,490	1,780	2,080	2,380	2,680	2,970
Taxes	980	1,500	2,010	2,970	4,110	7,440	10,430	13,040	15,650	18,270	20,870	23,470	26,090
Federal	640	1,020	1,400	2,130	3,010	5,590	7,900	9,870	11,840	13,820	15,790	17,760	19,738
Other	120	140	160	190	220	320	410	520	620	750	830	930	1,040
State & local	220	340	450	650	880	1,530	2,120	2,650	3,190	3,720	4,250	4,780	5,310
Tobacco Products & Smoking Supplies	200	280	330	310	300	290	310	390	470	550	620	700	780
Transportation	4,580	5,300	6,010	7,320	8,330	10,120	12,520	15,640	18,760	21,880	25,030	28,160	31,280
Gas & motor oil	800	920	1,020	1,190	1,320	1,510	1,820	2,270	2,730	3,180	3,640	4,090	4,550
Public transportation	220	230	280	550	700	810	990	1,230	1,480	1,720	1,970	2,220	2,460

continued on next page

How Americans Spend and Save (Detailed) (cont.)

Expenditures	Pretax Income												
	$20,000	$25,000	$30,000	$40,000	$50,000	$75,000	$100,000	$125,000	$150,000	$175,000	$200,000	$225,000	$250,000
Vehicle finance charges	170	230	290	360	400	450	540	680	810	950	1,090	1,220	1,360
Vehicle insurance	570	640	700	830	940	1,150	1,420	1,780	2,130	2,490	2,850	3,200	3,560
Vehicle maintenance & repair	520	580	650	780	880	1,040	1,270	1,590	1,900	2,220	2,540	2,860	3,170
Vehicle purchases (net outlay)	2,080	2,460	2,790	3,200	3,570	4,380	5,430	6,780	8,140	9,490	10,850	12,210	13,560
Vehicle rent, lease, license, etc.	220	240	280	410	520	780	1,050	1,310	1,570	1,830	2,090	2,360	2,620
Utilities, Fuels, & Public Services	1,940	2,060	2,150	2,320	2,480	2,840	3,420	4,280	5,130	5,980	6,850	7,700	8,550
Gas, electric, water, etc.	1,310	1,380	1,440	1,560	1,670	1,930	2,330	2,920	3,500	4,080	4,670	5,250	5,830
Telephone	630	680	710	760	810	910	1,090	1,360	1,630	1,900	2,180	2,450	2,720
Total Expenditures	25,640	29,147	32,706	40,046	46,992	63,466	81,664	102,079	122,500	142,914	163,329	183,744	204,165

Source: Bureau of Labor Statistics.

financial season and situation you are in right now and face in the future. The following budget is just to get you started.

☞ **Wake-up Call:** Are you one of the many people I know who have a phobia about really taking a nitty-gritty look at their finances? If so, ask a trusted friend or relative to help you fill out these worksheets—someone who will keep your financial secrets and who can act as a cheerleader as you begin to make changes in your financial life. A "Money Mentor" like this can spell the difference between success and failure for you. Of course, a financial planner can help you as well, and she is really the best place to begin, but if you have a real phobia you may not be ready to bare your financial soul to a stranger. (On the other hand, it may be easier.)

My Current Cash Flow

Category	Current Cash Flow
Alcohol	
Clothing	
Charitable Contributions	
Credit Card Payments	
Education	
Entertainment	
Food	
Furnishings	
Health Care	
Health Insurance	
Household Operations	
Miscellaneous	
Mortgage/Rent	
Other Insurance	
Retirement Plan Contributions	
Taxes	
Transportation	
Utilities/Public Services	
Total:	

My Budget

Category	My Budget
Alcohol	
Clothing	
Charitable Contributions	
Credit Card Payments	
Education	
Entertainment	
Food	
Furnishings	
Health Care	
Health Insurance	
Household Operations	
Miscellaneous	
Mortgage/Rent	
Other Insurance	
Retirement Plan Contributions	
Taxes	
Transportation	
Utilities/Public Services	
Total:	

STEP 6: CHOOSE WEALTH

As a final first step, I'd like to introduce you to a two-word phrase that I liken to a mantra: "Choose wealth." This phrase is the handiest way I know to help people realize that with every economic decision they make, or refuse to make, they are making a choice that will impact them both in the present and the future. Whether you surprise your wife with those $500 earrings or add that amount to a mutual fund, whether you stick to your budget for the kids' clothes, whether you purchase adequate insurance to protect you in the event of a medical emergency, can make a major difference in your life.

Wouldn't you choose wealth if you only had the chance? If you, like most people, are struggling day-to-day to pay today's bills, make debt payments, and to perhaps sock a little away for the future, it may sound too good to be true. But for most of us, "choosing" wealth is the only way to get it.

Let me illustrate how this plays out in the lives of three clients, the first two of which are *unconsciously* choosing wealth, one in the past, the other in the present:

Steve and Marilyn came to see me because, in Steve's words, "We want to be rich, but we don't make enough to save for the future." When we met, I saw on their Preliminary Questionnaire that they made $180,000 a year. For most people that would be enough income to live on handsomely, and save a bundle for the future at the same time. Then I saw a first and second mortgage that appeared to be the absolute maximum they could have borrowed. They had always been told they should buy the largest house they could afford and then grow into it, so they did. They were following outdated advice that doesn't hold up in today's economic climate.

They were each making retirement plan contributions at work, but less than half of what they could have. Most of their retirement money was sitting in low-interest money market accounts because they didn't "have the time to research the best investments." With two demanding careers, that alone meant that coming to a financial planner made good financial sense.

I told them there was a lot that could be done that they wouldn't even feel—changing their insurance, getting a better investment return, and cutting back a bit on spending. They looked at each other and their enthusiasm immediately faded, and I thought at that moment they would never be back. My suspicions were confirmed when I didn't hear from them for months, but then they reappeared. By refinancing their mortgages, they saved $450 a month. By raising the deductibles on their auto and house insurance, they saved $800 a year. By cutting back on spending on things they didn't really care about and services they could do *themselves (example: they began mowing their own lawn and loving it), they reduced the clutter in their house and saved over $5,000 a year.*

They didn't realize it, but Steve and Marilyn had been choosing wealth in the present. They had been choosing to have it *now*—just by failing to take the time to pay attention to their spending, but they were going to pay later. Until they decided to go to a planner, they had invested a minimal amount of time in planning their future, because they were so caught up in their work. But when and if they run out of money at age seventy-five because they didn't plan ahead, the fact that they worked late at the office every night isn't going to do them a bit of good.

Philip was referred to me by his insurance agent because he had a $40,000 income and $11,000 in credit card debt with an interest rate of 19%. He was struggling just to make the minimum payments. To his credit, he knew exactly what had happened. During a very stressful year after his divorce, he spent too much on his children out of guilt over their emotional reaction to the situation. He bought them anything they asked for—ice skates, dancing lessons, televisions for their rooms.

I did as much as I could for him and then sent him to a consumer counseling credit service. Counselors there advised him to transfer his $11,000 debt to a credit card with a 5.9% interest rate, which meant he would pay off the principal at a faster rate. He also got a part-time job that required him to work a half day on the weekends, which helped him fill the painful hours when he couldn't see his children.

Philip wasn't conscious of it, but he chose to have his wealth in the past—three years ago. He is paying now, and will be for years to come. The sadder part is that all the money he spent didn't ease his children's pain.

Frank and Bonnie have a $50,000 income, two grown children, and no mortgage. In forty years of marriage they have amassed a $500,000 retirement portfolio, plus a nice pension plan at Frank's job. How did they do this while raising two kids? Didn't they ever take vacations? Sure, but camping trips, not Disneyland. Eating out? Yes, but McDonald's or a family restaurant once a week. The *fancy restaurant was reserved for anniversary dinners and other special occasions.*

They still live in the same house they bought when they were first married, adding rooms as they added children. They always bought a "great looking" used car so it would feel new, and drove it until it died. Birthday presents had a family maximum (in 1998 it was $100). They invested their retirement plan money for the long term, mostly in the stock market, and that money has almost doubled in the last few years.

Each of their children has graduated from first-rate colleges. Frank and Bonnie will have more than they will need for retirement. In fact, because they are so much better off than they ever dreamed they could be, they are thinking about buying a beach cottage.

This couple consciously chose to have their wealth in the future. Some of the future has already happened—the kids got through college—and they still have plenty of money at retirement. I asked them if they felt like they sacrificed a lot in the process. Their answer was, "We never really felt we sacrificed; we just paid attention to things"—not just their spending, but also their investments, insurance, employee benefits, loans, college funding options, and so on. Frank and Bonnie planned ahead and chose to have wealth at the time in their lives when they needed it most. Steve, Marilyn, and Phillip have made important changes that will help them preserve their wealth until they, too, need it most.

You will know you are well on your way to achieving your financial goals when saving becomes more pleasurable than spending. You won't enjoy spending money that you know is going to increase your credit card debt, or that is going to put you into overdraft, or that you don't have in your budget.

I've never known anyone who was happy living beyond his means or living in denial of his economic reality. Never. Somewhere deep inside, you know you are digging yourself deeper into a financial sinkhole. When you overspend, you get a momentary thrill and then reality sinks in. This happens, for example, after every Christmas. People go into a frenzy. Then in January, when the credit card bills come in, they see for the first time how much they spent, and it's incredibly depressing. It makes some people sick. What good is a new house if you are not happy in it? Or what good is a new house if you both work so hard to save money for it that it has threatened your marriage?

☞ **Wake-up Call:** Learning how to secure your own future is even more important than putting in long hours at work. Today's business and personal lives are so hectic that it is easy to put this whole process off. Your employer won't bail you out if you run out of money at age seventy-five.

Everything, including your financial decisions, should proceed from your values. Remember when I said that your personal, emotional, and financial lives are irrevocably intertwined? Values are critical too. When there is discord between your values and the way you are living, you will be unhappy. When there is a gap between your expenditures and your income, you probably won't be able to sleep at night. People at peace with themselves have managed to align their values and dreams, their emotions, their personal lives, and their finances. Those are the folks who have happy endings at the end of every day of their lives.

2

Taking Root

At a college graduation a few years ago, I witnessed a family event that made me laugh, but also made me stop and think twice about what had taken place. After about twenty minutes of impatiently posing for family photos in the hot sun, a twelve-year-old began teasing her older brother (dressed in cap and gown) about how "stupid" and "geeky" he looked. The irritated graduate looked at his younger sister and said, "Listen, squirt, be thankful for how easy you've got it while you still can. You have a roof over your head, dinner made for you, a fridge stocked with food, a VCR, and an allowance. Mom or Dad will usually take you wherever you want to go, and," he then shot a glance at his parents to make sure they weren't listening, "you can even pretend you are deathly ill so you can stay home from school and play video games all day. Now that I've graduated, I have to get a job and save for an apartment and a car and anything else I want. And I don't think I would keep my job very long if I pretended to be sick so I could hang out at home."

Not long after that I was at a dinner with some longtime friends, and I noticed that Samantha, their twenty-two-year-old daughter, looked more and more uncomfortable as her parents talked about all the options for her future and how strange it was to have a daughter who was now "grown up." Finally, Samantha said wistfully, "The whole time I was growing up, I had this image in my mind that I would wake up one day and suddenly be an adult. But I guess it doesn't work that way. Some days I feel like a ten-year-old who just wants to hang out with my friends and then come home for dinner, and other days I can't wait to be on my own so I can come home whenever I want to and do whatever I want to. But I guess it's not suddenly 'poof—you're an adult': it comes in stages, just like growing up did."

Both of these conversations made me think about all the rites of passage that mark the changing seasons of our lives, and how they usually don't happen all at once. There are usually lots of little steps along the way—before and after each big decision—that make the difference between success and failure. Even one of the most dramatic rites of passage, marriage, is usually preceded by all kinds of decisions that come up during the dating process: planning the wedding and the honeymoon, and thinking about life as newlyweds.

Samantha is right. Taking on adult responsibilities is thankfully something that most of us don't usually have to do all at once. Even so, the shift toward financial independence can be daunting, especially if you haven't had a job before, or you have never had to think about money, or you are suddenly saddled with rent or student loans or car payments. But if you have a positive attitude, want to be financially smart, and have the right financial information on hand, you will be prepared to make decisions as they come up—rather than feeling so overwhelmed that you just want to pull the covers over your head. You will be making decisions by choice rather than by default. In fact, if you can identify with either of the two young adults I've mentioned, that's a good sign that you are ready to "wake up and smell the money."

Perhaps you are still in school or have recently finished up—be it high school, vocational school, college, or graduate work—and you are looking ahead to your first "real" job, one that marks the beginning of your career. Or perhaps you have been out of school for a while, working at dead-end jobs because you haven't really thought much about your future, and now you are ready to get serious about life. You may have lots of financial worries, or, although it's on your mind constantly, money may be the very least of your concerns. What should I do with the rest of my life? Should I move out or stay with my parents? Can I afford a car? How in the world will I ever pay back my college loans? Do I need more education—training or degrees—to do what I want to do? And what do I want to do anyway? If these are some of the questions bouncing around in your head, welcome to the real world. And if you are between the age of twenty and twenty-nine, take comfort in the fact that you share that world with 36 million other Americans your age.

Of course you are nervous about the future—you would not be normal if you weren't!—but consider this the first phase of a financial journey that will continue throughout your lifetime. And don't think you will ever have all the answers! I have clients in their fifties who are still asking themselves, "What do I want to be when I grow up?" or "Why didn't I bother to learn how to handle my money thirty years ago so I would have more of it now?"

Even when you come up with answers that help you achieve your current goals, you will find yourself revising them as time goes on. As the theme of this book, and the title of Chapter 5, "Fresh Starts," should tell you, the strategies you use to meet today's financial issues may not be the right ones for you as the seasons of your own life change.

This is absolutely the best time to start out on the right foot when it comes to financial matters. As you no doubt already know, and as I can testify from the trail of clients who "woke up" too late to meet their dreams, the longer you keep the same habits, the harder they are to break. That goes double time for money habits.

Fortunately, studies indicate that your generation is much more realistic about the future than your baby boomer parents continue to be, especially when it comes to the availability of Social Security and the need to rely on yourselves instead of your employers for financial protection. In 1997, in a nationwide poll of college freshmen, 75 percent chose "to be very well off financially" as a crucial goal of their education, and 41 percent chose "to develop a meaningful philosophy of life" as a crucial goal.

The irony is that in 1968, when your parents were your age, the numbers were *almost exactly reversed,* with philosophy of life being more important than financial wealth. (See what I mean when I said that you are more realistic than your parents? Here's where it started.) I am part of that generation, and I would be the last to say that having a meaningful philosophy of life is not critical, but what many of my peers failed to figure out is that you need a financial philosophy and game plan as well. That's why so many baby boomers will fail to meet their financial goals. In my own practice I see the sad results of those who abdicated their personal responsibility for their finances: baby boomers spending to keep up a standard of living they really couldn't afford, while neglecting to save for the future. We teach our children by our example. If we are stressed out by trying to live beyond our means, our kids know it. Later, they may find themselves repeating our mistakes because that's the way they were raised, or reacting against our spending habits and becoming much more careful with their money.

I spoke with one young woman at the request of her boomer parents who were worried about her because they felt she spent too little and was obsessed about money. It turned out that they were wrong. Felicia actually had a very healthy attitude toward money and wasn't obsessed or frugal. She was just being smart and living well within her means. Her parents, though they can't take credit, were the cause. As she explained to me, "I don't ever want to have the financial stress and frustrations that my parents do. Do you know what it was like, year after year, to watch them go through cycles of overspending and then vowing to cut back—and to argue about it, or try to hide it from the kids?" She is not the first adult child of a baby boomer who has had essentially the same reaction. I figure that in fifteen or twenty years, I will see more and more clients in my office who, like Felicia, have learned from their parents' mistakes.

The sophistication level of the average twenty-five-year-old new client who comes to see me now is light years ahead of clients that age who came to see me even ten years ago. And, as a young adult, you have time on your side. If you begin saving and investing now, you will maximize your ability to take advantage of the magic of compound interest. That means the longer you save, the faster your money grows: Each year, you will have a larger sum to earn interest or grow in value in the stock market.

Consider the case of a forty-five-year-old man who "wakes up" and decides to start putting aside $2,000 a year for retirement. By the time he reaches age sixty-five, if he invested well and managed to get a 10 percent return every year, he would have invested $40,000 in a retirement plan that had grown to $128,000. If his twenty-five-year-old son invests exactly the same amount and earns the same return over the same period of time as his father, and then stops at age forty-five, he also would have $128,000 after twenty years. But here is where the magic of compound interest really shows itself: If the son leaves his money untouched in his retirement plan for another twenty years, without investing another penny, his account will grow to $860,000, or more than seven times as much as his father's. Thanks to compound interest, the son would reap much more from the same investment because he has twenty more years for that money to grow.

Even five years can make a significant difference. If you put $2,000 a year in an investment that earns a 10 percent after-tax annual return for twenty-five years, you will earn almost $197,000. If you invest for another ten years and earn the same return, your investment will grow to almost $550,000. The chart below will show you how much your investment will grow over a longer period of time—a real incentive to wake up early and start saving now.

In a recent survey, 91 percent of Generation Xers (born between 1965 and 1977) agreed with the phrase, "If I work hard enough, I will eventually achieve what I want." This is not an unrealistic statement, provided that you start making smart financial decisions *now* that will affect your financial future. Think about it: if you are now in your twenties, when you reach age sixty-two, you may have another twenty or thirty years not just to live, but to live it up—if you've saved enough money so you *can* live it up.

YOUR WORK LIFE

■ Your First Investments: Job-Finding Tools ■

On my book tour for my first book, *The Money Diet*, I was truly stunned at the number of college students and young twenty-somethings who attended the financial seminars I gave at bookstores around the country. Often, they had the most nerve to come up and ask questions afterward, which I thought was a great sign. But the number one question I got was, "How can I save and invest if I don't have any money?" The answer is that you can't—so your first order of business is finding a

How $2,000 a Year Grows over Time

	5 years		$12,210
	10 years		$31,875
If you invest	15 years	at a 10% return,	$63,545
$2,000 a year	20 years	in the end	$114,550
for the next	25 years	you'll have	$196,694
	30 years		$328,988
	35 years		$542,049
	40 years		$885,185

job. The good news is that thirty million new jobs come on the market each year, and young adults' comfort level with technology (as opposed to that of their older job competitors) already makes them great candidates for many of those positions. An estimated one million new computer programming jobs alone will open in the years 1999–2007. A common example is that of the "downsized" executive who refused to learn computer skills because "my secretary always handled that for me." Times have changed, and even top executives are expected to know how to use the Internet, E-mail, word processing, and various databases.

Let's face it, college education helps. The high demand for well-educated job candidates gave these new, unproved graduates the "upper hand" over their potential employers when negotiating salary and benefits. The average number of job offers for college graduates in 1998 was about 2.5. And as you get older, you will find it will be increasingly important to have a college degree if you want higher income and more advancement.

The first order of business for most recent graduates and others new to the job market is finding your first "real" job. A growing proportion of young people nowadays, in fact, 70 percent of those ages twenty-one to thirty-two—especially in the computer industry—would prefer starting their own businesses to working for someone else. If this describes you, turn to Chapter 5, "Fresh Starts," for more information on putting out your own shingle. But even if you are starting your own business, you should read the following sections on résumés, clothing, and adjusting to the working world.

☞ **Wake-up Call:** As you start your job search, remember that just as you have been living in a "college culture," there is a very definite "corporate culture." This varies by industry and organization, but be prepared and keep your eyes open to *all* the changes around you—from as obvious as the mode of dress to as subtle as how an employe addresses a superior. Always call your job interviewer Mr. or Ms., unless or until you are told not to.

■ Résumés ■

If you are headed into the traditional job market, you'll need to be armed with a résumé—your calling card to the working world. It should be a flawless, brief, and descriptive list of your work and educational histories. Flawless means *absolutely no* grammatical, spelling, or punctuation errors allowed. I thought everybody knew that, until I tried to hire someone to transcribe tapes and work as an editorial assistant on *The Money Diet*. I received twenty-five responses, over half of which contained one or more substantial grammatical errors. I eliminated all of those candidates immediately, and I have to tell you that most employers will do the same, even if the ability to write well is not a requirement for the position you want. Even one misspelled word, or a sentence without a verb, can land your résumé in the trash can.

Write a draft using the most powerful words you can to legitimately describe your accomplishments. Highlight your skills, awards, and experience using verbs—"managed," "established," "coordinated," and other words that demonstrate your on-the-job initiative and special talents. If you have access to a college placement office, high school guidance counselor, or social services career counselor, he or she can help you polish your résumé. They can also be invaluable—and free—sources of information about who is hiring in the area and what they are paying. If you don't have access to free help, invest in a job-hunting guide, such as *Job Smarts for 20-Somethings* by Bradley Richardson, which covers the conventions of résumé-writing in detail, or Martin Yate's *Knock 'Em Dead!* books on résumés and cover letters. Another perennial favorite is *What Color Is Your Parachute?* by Richard Bolles, which is great for liberal arts graduates trying to figure out what fields they want to go into or who need help with phrasing their experiences into powerful job-getting words.

☞ **Wake-up Call:** Your résumé is your foot in the door. Ask your friends and parents to proof your résumé for errors and to suggest more striking descriptions of your accomplishments. Sometimes you forget awards and things that you have done (parents are great at remembering these!). Also, watch your phrasing: Powerful is one thing, but don't go over the top. Whenever I see a résumé with phrases such as "interfaced with" or "engaged in dialogue with," the first thought that comes to my mind is "This is too much BS!" Keep it simple.

An absolutely crucial investment is a package of high-quality paper with matching envelopes. Your résumé should be printed on heavy, 16–25 lb. paper stock, usually in white or cream, unless you are trying for a job in the design industry and have been advised to use attention-getting colors. The extra money you spend for high-quality paper shows that you care about how you present yourself.

I will never forget my astonishment when an Ivy League-educated child of some clients came to see me after six months of job searching had proved fruitless. One look at his typing-paper résumé, nonmatching envelope, and self-inflating language told me why. He thought his education was all it took to land a good job; he did not realize he actually had to *work* to get work! He did not seem to realize that there were lots of other job seekers who were smarter and hungrier about landing a top job, so he had not done his homework. A great presentation can beat an Ivy Leaguer with an attitude any day!

■ The Clothes Make the Man (or the Woman!) ■

You'll also have a much better chance of landing the job you want if you arrive at the interview looking your best. Investing in the best outfit you can afford, including accessories such as polished leather shoes (*never* sandals or extremely high heels for women) and a briefcase (leather or canvas, *never* vinyl) "is the only good reason I can think of to run up your charge card," says a twenty-something woman, one of the most financially conservative people I know. Like most recent grads, her wardrobe mainly consisted of jeans, sweaters, and casual skirts and pants; she had to go into debt in order to outfit herself for job hunting because she did the research to know that the industry she was interested in required suits.

Having a small wardrobe of high-quality clothes is much smarter than having a larger wardrobe of lesser quality. This is true whether you are male or female. You are making your first impression on the business world, and those first impressions will last.

If you're a woman and you wear a 4–6 dress size or a size 6 shoe, consider yourself lucky: you can take advantage of designers' samples and get designer-quality clothing at bargain basement prices. Samples are items that designers send to department stores as previews of their "look" for the upcoming season. Some stores sell their own samples at 50 percent or more off retail prices every few months; others send their sample wardrobes to be sold at discount stores. I suggest calling individual department stores to find out if and when they have samples available for sale.

Consignment shops, Junior League, and other nonprofit used-clothing stores, particularly in wealthy suburban areas, can also be gold mines for business attire. One of my former assistants lived in a resort town in the Rockies for a summer, and the secondhand clothing shop in town regularly had items such as Prada dresses and never-worn Ralph Lauren dress shirts and khakis for under $10.

Outlet malls, although they seem like a good idea, often cause you to spend more than you realize. Last year, an estimated fifty-five million Americans drove at least two hundred miles roundtrip to go outlet shopping—a distance equal to circling the Earth 440,000 times—so figure in the cost of gas when calculating the price of the clothing you are buying. In addition, because these malls generally house a large number of stores, it's easy to spend more than you originally intended because everything is such a "bargain."

Keep in mind that it never hurts to be conservative, especially in the first interview. Guys, take the studs out of your ears and take off any gold chains. Girls, get rid of your blue nail polish—you should wear clear only. Wear only one set of earrings, the smaller the better, and always carry a spare pair of stockings in your glove compartment. Based on the industry, you should have a good idea about what is appropriate to wear, but you can always go to the office building first to see how their employees are dressed.

Don't invest in too much clothing until you know what the corporate clothing culture will be in your new job. When you buy clothing, explain to the sales assistant that you are buying interview clothes for your first job and she can give you advice. I know of one young man who only bought his "first interview suit." When he was called back for a second interview, he went out and bought his "second interview suit," and so on.

☞ **Wake-up Call:** Before you walk out the door for an interview, look in the mirror and smile. One of the funniest stories I heard on my *Money Diet* tour was of a recent graduate interviewing at a major consulting firm. She made it through the first three interviews over a period of a few weeks, and then had to spend an entire morning doing consecutive interviews with partners at the firm. Of course, she smiled as much as she could and was very enthusiastic in every interview. Then she went home and happened to look in the mirror and see a huge poppy seed stuck in her front tooth from the bagel she had eaten for breakfast. Luckily, she got the job, but was teased at work about checking her smile every time before she went out to see a client—"Any poppy seeds today?"

Your job interviewer's first impression of you is based upon your appearance, and if that impression is positive you start the interview with an advantage and can probably get away with making a few mistakes. But if that impression is negative, you start at a distinct disadvantage and you may have to spend the entire interview trying to overcome it.

■ Know Thy Company ■

It would be great if a killer suit determined whether you got a job or not, but that is just step No. 2 (your résumé is the first step). Now comes the interview, and you need to be prepared. That means you have done some research on the organization and even have a list of ways in which you could be an asset to it.

You can do research on the Web, go to the library and look up its annual report if it is a publicly held company, and ask the reference librarian to help you get all the information you can. The more research you can prove you have done about the company for which you are interviewing, the more you are going to impress the interviewer: It shows that you take initiative, you have research skills, and you want the job. If you can rattle off a list of your prospective employer's top competitors and their strengths and weaknesses, you will distinguish yourself from your own competition (at least those who haven't yet read this book). Better yet, if you have a creative idea that might interest your prospective employer, present it in a humble manner: "This probably sounds naïve since I have just graduated from college, but when I was doing research on your company I got an idea— _____. Is this the kind of thinking you are looking for?" If it demonstrates an understanding of their organization, even if they never implement it, you will earn valuable points.

Registering with headhunter agencies that specialize in the field you want to pursue also may be a wise move. Nowadays, many companies hiring college-educated professionals don't use classified ads; instead, the company's job openings are released only to professional "headhunter" agencies, which still suffer from a bad rap because in the 1970s and 1980s they used to charge a placement fee to job seekers. Now, most agencies get you interviews for free, and their fees are paid by the companies that advertise their positions with them, because they know that the "best & brightest" job seekers are registered with one of these agencies.

If you can't find the job you are looking for right away, working for a temporary agency can also be a way to work yourself into a permanent position at a company you like or a way to check out the corporate culture of a number of potential employers. While you are looking for a job, be sure to ask everyone you know to refer you to people who might be willing to give you a fifteen-minute information interview. Make it clear that you are not asking for a job interview, but a chance for you to find out about an organization and its field. Be prepared to ask intelligent questions, and be sure and write a thank-you note afterward. The informational interview you have this year may result in the job of your dreams a few years down the road.

Practice interviewing with your guidance counselor, friends, and roommates, and demand honest feedback. Introduce yourself with a firm handshake (no dead fish handshakes!) and maintain eye contact. Be especially cognizant of how many times you say the word "like"—a real pet peeve for interviewers! When you practice interviewing, ask your audience to critique your vocabulary, body language, and every aspect of your "performance," because during a job interview, you are on center stage.

When going for an interview, always carry a couple of copies of your résumé with you—you may be interviewing with more than one person, or the interviewer may have misplaced her copy. Drink water, not coffee, during your interview in case you spill it, and because cold drinks make your voice clearer (heat can make your throat tissues swell a little).

■ Flexibility: It Doesn't Cost You and It May Pay Big Dividends ■

While it is certainly important to have strong convictions when you are looking for work, flexibility is also an asset because the job market keeps changing. If you were born in 1979, more than forty-three million jobs have been lost to downsizing since your birth. On the other hand, thirty million new jobs are created every year. So if you aspire to work in a field in which there is a shortage of jobs, try to keep yourself open to taking an alternative path. You never know where it might lead you.

After graduating from Smith College in 1995, my assistant, Karen, intended to pursue a career in event planning, which she had done part-time at Smith while she was a student and had enjoyed very much. Despite her extensive networking, upon graduation she couldn't find any entry level jobs in that field in Boston—they simply did not exist. She agreed instead to work for me on a temporary basis while she continued to look for a job in event management. Two years later, she is still working for me, has gotten her financial paraplanner designation, has appeared on "Oprah" with me, and has learned an incredible amount about managing money, which she will be able to personally use for the rest of her life. She also has decided to pursue a career in personal finance, which she would have never dreamed she would find interesting.

My own career path also shows that you cannot predict the future. I majored in political science and planned to take two years off before I returned to school to get my Ph.D. and teach. During those two years I married and became pregnant with my first child. At the time, I was working at a job I disliked, but I took advantage of all the educational opportunities it offered, including tuition reimbursement and time off during working hours for the CLU (Chartered Life Underwriter) and Certified Financial Planner programs. I only did this because I liked to study and loved school. Little did I know that it would become the basis for my career.

Five years later, I was accepted into Harvard's graduate program in Public Administration, but by that time I had a serious medical problem as well as two small children and could not handle a full-time course load, so I decided to withdraw my acceptance. It was one of the worst days of my life, and I could not possibly imagine what I was going to do with my future. My goal had been to spend one-third of my time teaching, one-third writing, and one-third consulting. Instead, I stayed in financial planning, and it turned out that I have more or less divided my time in that way—it's just a different career path from any I could have ever imagined wanting or enjoying.

If you work hard and become competent in one field, chances are that you can transfer your skills to other fields down the road. These days, people change careers an average of between seven and nine times in their lifetimes, and this trend shows no sign of disappearing, as Chapter 5, "Fresh Starts," will show you.

If you find that the entry-level positions in the field that you are interested in pay $5,000 less than many other fields and the pay scale for experienced employees is also well below others, there is nothing wrong with considering other professions. As I said before, there is value in flexibility. It is hard when you and/or your parents have spent so much money to educate you in a certain field in which you are then unable to find a job, but think of your schooling as a way to learn to think and to prepare yourself for life.

Also, of course, the value of what you give to society is not necessarily reflected in your paycheck. Teachers can make $20,000 a year and are responsible for molding young minds on a daily basis, while professional athletes can make $20 million a year. If you can make a comfortable living doing what you love, consider yourself lucky.

■ Salary: How Much Do You Need? ■

If you are passionate about work that isn't especially well-paying, make two budgets—your "Absolute Minimum Budget" to exist on, which would be the bare minimum for living expenses and loan repayments, and then a "Minimum Budget" that allows some leeway for savings, entertainment, etc. You can't evaluate a salary until you have both budgets, so that you know how much money you need to live on and how much you would be giving up in terms of lifestyle if you took a job that only covered your bare-bones budget. There is a section later in this chapter that will help you think through a budget once you have a steady income, and will give you tips on how to save money whatever your income. But during your job hunt you should shoot for a salary that will allow you to enjoy yourself as well as survive.

Financial independence doesn't come from relying on your parents or credit cards to bridge the gap. The stress of starting your career and a new job is bad enough without adding financial pressures to the mix right off the bat. Some young people whose dream is to work in publishing accept pitiful entry-level salaries, for instance, and then end up taking a second job or freelancing on the side to cover their rent.

Believe me, you won't be doing anyone any favors if you accept a salary that is unrealistically low. It's hard to concentrate on your work—even work you love—if you are worried about where your next meal is coming from or how you are going to pay your bills. One friend who works at a nonprofit organization explained her dilemma perfectly to me: "I want to save the world, but I can't do it if I can't sleep at night, and if I can't pay my bills I can't sleep at night. So I have to find a job that pays enough to keep me going, and I will use my spare time to try and save the world one person at a time."

Most students have student loans or loans from relatives to pay back, and they may have car payments as well. If you have credit card debt, that has to be factored in, too. If your new job requires you to move, who is going to pay for the move—you or your employer? You also need to find out what the cost of living is for the area in which you will be settling. It may be that by living thirty minutes away from work instead of fifteen you can save hundreds of dollars a month in rent and other costs will be less. For example, New York is a job mecca for recent graduates and twenty-somethings, but many of them live in outer boroughs like Brooklyn or commuter towns in New Jersey because the cost

Minimum and Absolute Minimum Budget

Expenditure	Minimum	Absolute Minimum
Alcohol		
Clothing		
Credit Card Payments		
Education/Student Loans		
Entertainment		
Food		
Furnishings		
Health Care		
Rent		
Miscellaneous		
Insurance		
Retirement Plan Contributions		
Taxes		
Transportation		
Utilities/Public Services		

of living is so much less than in Manhattan. Will you need a car? That alone could add several hundred dollars a month to your budget between car payments, auto insurance, gas, and repairs. Is there good public transportation, even if you have to work late at night? These are all questions that you need to answer.

If you are a member of Generation X or younger, however, you may be lucky enough to be job hunting during one of the strongest economies in a quarter century. Many of last year's college graduates who were considering a job in the financial services and computer industries, for instance, found themselves courted by rival employers. They were wined and dined, flown in to visit corporate headquarters, and offered salaries 10 to 15 percent higher than those hired the year before along with hefty signing bonuses.

Learning how to negotiate salary is an acquired skill, not an innate talent. It needs to be done with diplomacy, tact and confidence—and negotiation is not something you usually learn in school. Before you enter into salary negotiations, it is a good idea to practice negotiating with a job counselor or friend, especially if you are female. Unfortunately, negotiation is still a skill that seems to come harder for women than men, although the gap is narrowing. At age forty-five, after engaging in numerous business negotiations, I can say from experience that practicing ahead of time will help you build your confidence and think more systematically about what you want and what you need.

When you are evaluating a salary offer, compare it to similar jobs at other companies to make sure you are being offered the market rate. You'll look foolish trying to play hardball for a $30,000 salary when the going rate for an entry-level position in that field is only the low $20s. On the other hand, if the competition is fierce for someone with your qualifications and other companies are offering signing bonuses, make sure you get one, too. Don't hold back—some people double their bonuses simply by asking for more. It never hurts to ask, and I can give you example after example of a "yes" response—and the recruiter's admiration of the financial acuity and smarts of the job candidate. Your stock may actually rise just by asking!

If you have competing offers, sometimes it pays to let each prospective employer know you are in demand. There were two pharmaceutical companies who made offers to the same young woman for a sales position at virtually the same salary. Helen told each that she had also received an offer from another company and needed a few days to make a decision. Company X immediately threw in a $5,000 signing bonus and a company car, but it was not her first choice. Helen called her contact at company Y and reported the additional bonus and car, while simultaneously restating her desire to work for company Y. She also mentioned that she had a lot of student loans to pay back and would have to purchase a car in order to work for a company that did not give her one to use. The interviewer said he would call her back by the end of the day after he'd had a chance to discuss the situation with his boss.

Helen never demanded a higher bonus (or even a bonus at all) or a car—but she made it very clear, without being too aggressive, that she was going to have to turn down company Y if they didn't make her an offer exceeding that of Company X. At the end of the day, she received a call from Company Y with an offer of a $10,000 signing bonus and free use of a company car.

If you are lucky enough (or, more likely, have negotiated well enough) to get a signing bonus or a bonus to be paid after a few months, don't spend it! That money should go straight into a money-market account (we will talk about this shortly) to start your emergency fund. It will come in handy if you happen to lose your job, your car breaks down, you have unexpected medical expenses, or in any other of a dozen possible scenarios. That is what emergency funds are for—so if you get a bonus, consider it free funding of your financial cushion.

■ **Beyond Starting Salary** ■

Your starting salary is just that—a start. Before you accept a position, also consider the potential for advancement and pay at higher levels, as compared to other companies that are hiring.

Besides dollars and cents, make sure to consider the number of hours you will be working. Will you be given time off for lunch? Legally, you must be, but does this really happen? Ask seasoned employees whether you'll actually be able to fit it in. The average lunch hour has recently shrunk to twenty minutes, and nearly 40 percent of workers don't take any time off for lunch at all. Is this the kind of office where you have to stay until 8 P.M. every night just so the boss thinks you are working hard?

Another consideration is whether you will be gaining experience that will result in higher earning potential in the future. Is the experience transferable to other companies? To other industries? Would it be useful if you wanted to set up your own business? Are there educational reimbursement programs that will subsidize and perhaps allow time off for you to pursue classes related or even unrelated to your chosen line of work?

If your gut tells you this is the wrong job, or you do not like the person you would be working for even after just a thirty-minute interview, or if it is clear that the work is going to be boring or way over your head, unless you are desperate, you need to think twice. Remember, this is the first real job on your résumé and if it is not a good job fit for you, that will be reflected in your job performance, evaluations, and recommendations.

☞ **Wake-up Call:** Ask your potential new boss about opportunities for advancement and the time frame for those potential advancements. Take notes: later, if the time frame passes and you haven't received the advancement, you can show your boss your notes.

Before you take a job, ask for permission to talk to someone in a position similar to yours, and to maybe wander around the office. You may learn a few new things about your prospective employer that will help you determine whether this is the right position for you.

■ The Benefits of Benefits ■

The value of your benefits can add several thousand dollars to your salary. Of course, employer contributions to Social Security and unemployment insurance are required by law, but things such as medical insurance rarely are. Most important for anyone starting out is health-care coverage. If you are no longer a full-time student and/or are over a certain age, you can't be included on a parent's medical plan; if you were covered under your school plan, once you graduate, you lose that coverage as well.

Medical insurance is by far the most important benefit for anyone at any age, so be sure to ask whether it comes with the job. Don't assume that just because the company has more than a few employees, it offers medical coverage. Believe it or not, almost 40 percent of employers with more than nine employees do not offer health benefits, and the number that do is dropping. Thirty-nine million Americans don't have health insurance, and you certainly do not want to be one of them. It would be terrible to be spending all of your new salary paying off medical bills or getting yourself deeply in debt because you got sick or were in an accident.

If you are considering a job that does not offer a health-care plan, ask your interviewer what other employees in the company do about getting coverage; then ask how you can find out about cost. It may be that you have to get an individual policy on your own by purchasing it through an insurance agent or joining a health maintenance organization (HMO). Find out what it would cost you to insure yourself for a year and deduct that from your annual salary—because that cost is going to come right off the top of your paycheck.

If you are shopping for insurance on your own, find out when the "open enrollment" periods are for the insurance plans in your area. There are often certain times of the year (a month or so) when you can join without proving that you are healthy. For most people, this is not an issue, but if you have a medical condition such as diabetes or high blood pressure it can make the difference between being accepted and not.

If your company does offer insurance coverage, find out what kind of options exist. The health-care industry is evolving at warp speed, but there are a few basic types of medical insurance. The first is the HMO, in which you have a primary care physician who refers you to specialists as needed, and your only cost in addition to monthly premiums is a co-payment for each visit. The advantage is that you may pay much less; the disadvantage is that you have less control over which doctors you see and when you see them. If you already have health problems, often your best bet is to join an HMO because once you have been accepted, you cannot be terminated from insurance coverage if you get sick or your health-care costs increase. But make sure that the doctors you are already seeing can be covered under the HMO or that you can find doctors with the specialties you need.

Another popular form of insurance is the Participating Provider Organization (PPO), in which you choose your own physicians. The amount you pay for each visit is dependent upon whether the doctor is "in network" or "out of network." "In network" doctors have contracts with insurers to provide services at a fixed cost to the insurance companies. With a PPO, you pay a monthly premium and also have co-payments at each visit, with higher costs if you use out-of-network physicians because they do not have contracts with the insurers. In exchange for potentially higher costs, you have more control over who provides your care. Many people prefer this to an HMO—they consider the extra cost worth it. In response, some HMOs are now offering more freedom of choice, so you need to investigate your options carefully before you make a decision.

Traditional fee-for-service (indemnity) plans are by far the most expensive, but they allow you to select your own physicians. Generally, you pay a monthly premium and then are reimbursed for a certain percentage of your medical costs after a deductible is met. For example, if your employers' plan has a deductible of $300 a year, after you have paid medical bills equal to that amount, you will be reimbursed a set amount for each additional procedure, such as office visits, lab tests, etc. One of the primary disadvantages of the indemnity plan is that you have to pay the bills and then be reimbursed, and that can put a crimp on your cash flow. There also is a lot more paperwork to complete. Indemnity plans have become less and less common each year because insurance companies can control costs much more easily with HMOs and PPOs.

This information holds true whether you are buying fee-for-service insurance on your own or choosing among plans offered by your employer.

One of the most positive developments in corporate-sponsored medical care is that many insurance plans now also offer a wellness program that includes physicals, vaccinations, prenatal care, cholesterol, and blood pressure checks. If you like to work out, most also offer substantial discounts on health clubs in the area. If you have health problems already, or some run in your family, a health club membership may be very attractive to you now or later on in life.

Many companies also offer dental plans, vision care, maternity leave, and supplemental life insurance. These may not be critical to you now, but if there is any chance, however slim, that you will stay with this employer for a long period of time, put them in the plus column. A growing number of companies and government/nonprofit employers, especially the larger ones like Disney, also are extending medical coverage to partners of the same sex or of opposite sex who live together for a period of time. If you are gay, this may be important to you if your partner is planning not to work for a period of time, works for him- or herself, or has no coverage at work through his or her employer.

■ Life Insurance ■

A standard benefit at many companies is a free life insurance policy worth the value of one year's salary and the option to buy more. Unless you think that your parents or someone else will be depending on you for money later in life, or you have college or other loans to repay to your parents or other relatives, just take the free insurance, without buying additional life insurance. If you are single and don't owe loans to anyone else, you should probably name your parents as beneficiaries, especially if they paid some or all of your college expenses. Even if you did not go to college or got a full scholarship, they have raised you and no doubt your expenses kept them from saving as much as they could have for their own retirement. (The beneficiaries of your life insurance policies are not responsible for your debts, so you can name your parents and not have to worry about their having to repay your car loan, for instance.)

Sometimes a company's life insurance agent will meet with all new employees, in order to sell them additional insurance. Victor was offered a $50,000 whole life policy (with a premium he could not easily afford), which he was told he really needed because "your future is so bright that you are really going places." He resisted the sales pressure and decided to wait until he actually did need more insurance and had his budget under control. After all, he had just started working for the company and did not even know what his real cash flow situation was going to be—after clothing, commuting, and other miscellaneous work costs.

Wake-up Call: When you start working for a company, you may find that the corporate culture includes a constant parade of birthday lunches and gifts, baby showers, going away parties, etc., all to which you are expected to contribute. If it is putting a crimp in your budget, you can bet it is having the same effect on others. Quietly speak to one or two close colleagues and see if you can get some of these customs changed. For example, why shouldn't the company buy the going-away gift and the employees sign a card with personal messages?

■ Stock Options ■

Lots of people taking first jobs are offered stock options in lieu of competitive salaries or as a way to "sweeten the pot." You only have to look at all the Microsoft millionaires to know that stock options can pay off handsomely if a company goes public. If this is something you need to consider, please refer to Chapter 4 (page 180). In fact, six million workers are now offered stock options, and these can prove to be extremely lucrative. They are most often found in start-up high-tech companies, but don't discount their value. They are long shots, but they could become the biggest bonus you'll ever receive.

■ Why Save for Retirement Now? ■

Jennifer, a young woman who had worked part-time for me in high school, called with great excitement when she got her first "real" job. She was trying to look ahead, and had been told by her employee benefits manager that she could start participating in the company's retirement plan after she had been there a year. Her question to me—perfectly valid given her age, income and financial commitments—was, "Why should I bother putting money away in a retirement plan when I need it now?"

You are just starting out in your career, so retirement may seem like it is aeons away (and it is). But you will be better off putting even a tiny amount from every paycheck from your very first job into a retirement plan, rather than waiting until job number two or three, when you'll be making more money. Reason: You will not be taxed on the money you put into the plan until you withdraw it, and the sooner you start saving, the more chance your money will have to grow (remember the wonders of compound interest). Furthermore, thanks to recent tax law changes, many plans allow you to access retirement money a long time before retirement. For example, if you have a 401(k), you may borrow 50 percent of your balance or $50,000—whichever is less. You generally have five years to pay this money back, and the interest you'll pay on it must be considered "reasonable" by the IRS—usually prime plus 1 or 2 percent.

☞ **Wake-up Call:** Don't just assume you can borrow money from your 401(k) or other company retirement plan. Many plans offer this option, but some do not. If you do borrow money from your retirement plan, make sure you know what will happen if you leave your job before the loan is paid off. Most require you to immediately pay it back, so think about where you would get the money to do so.

If you choose to actually withdraw money (not borrow it) from your company retirement plan without paying it back, you may do so, but you must pay a 10 percent penalty plus taxes—which is a powerful incentive to leave it alone or at least borrow it.

Once you are eligible for your company plan, your employer may match your contribution up to a certain amount. This is a great deal because it "doubles your money," provided you stay with the company for a few years (until you are vested, which means you are entitled to take all company contributions with you if you leave the company). For example, your employer may match up to $3,000 of any money you put in your 401(k). (See Chapter 3, page 113, for more details on employer-sponsored retirement plans.)

If you can participate in your company's 401(k) plan, you can either put in 25 percent of your salary or $10,000, whichever is less. But if you can't save an amount this large, you're better off throwing $50 a month into a retirement plan than nothing at all, and each year you should increase your funding of your plan in accordance with your salary.

Whether or not you are eligible to participate in a company plan, you can still put away up to $2,000 a year in an IRA as long as your salary permits. So Jennifer didn't have to wait for a year to begin! At my recommendation, she opened an Individual Retirement Account (IRA) at her local bank the first month she started working and deposited $20 a week until she was eligible for the plan at work.

Just like Jennifer's company, many corporations require a year's employment before you can start participating in a retirement plan to which employees can contribute. But sign up as soon as you can. Don't hold off on signing up just because you don't think you will be at the company very long. You can't be sure. The most telling example was a few years ago with two clients who had both been at the same company for fifteen years (in fact, that's where they had met). Linda and Richard never signed up for the company's 401(k) plan that offered matching benefits because they thought they would soon be at different jobs. But fifteen years later, they were still driving to the same office building every day. I didn't want to do it, but they insisted that I calculate how much money they had lost because of their failure to take advantage of their company's retirement contribution on their behalf. Assuming no interest or increase in value, Linda and Richard had lost about $160,000. Taking the increase in the stock market and interest rates into consideration, their "opportunity cost" of not signing up was closer to $300,000. So don't delay!

Don't be afraid to sign up because you don't know where you should invest your money. Chapter 4 will give you the confidence to make those decisions, and you will get good information about your various investment options from your employee benefits manager or your company's retirement plan administrator.

■ Automatic Tax Deduction ■

You may be shocked when you see how much tax is taken out of your paycheck, even if you are working part-time or as a student. In fact, the Tax Foundation estimates that in 1998, the average taxpayer had to work two hours and fifty minutes of each eight-hour workday just to make enough to pay all federal, state, and local taxes (up from eleven minutes in 1988).

If you can have all your taxes deducted automatically from your paycheck, do so. You're going to have to pay them anyway, and it's much easier to adjust your lifestyle accordingly if the paycheck you bring home each week accurately reflects the money you have to spend. There's nothing worse than the nightmare of doing your taxes for the previous year and finding out that you owe big bucks to the IRS or the State Department of Revenue (or both). If you don't own property, and so do not need to itemize deductions, the W-4 you have to fill out for federal withholding (which includes instructions based on your situation) will probably bring you pretty close to the amount you should withhold. If you have any questions, your employee benefits manager at work, your parents, or an inexpensive tax preparation service such as H&R Block will be able to help you out.

If you deduct more than you need to just so you'll get a big refund at the end of the year, you'll in effect be giving the government a free loan, while you're probably paying interest on loans yourself! I had one client who found that this was the only way she could save. Finally, at my suggestion, Teresa arranged to have her payroll department make automatic deposits to a savings account instead of having extra-large automatic tax deductions taken from every paycheck. If your company won't do this (but most will), another way to avoid giving the government an interest-free loan is to have money transferred automatically each month from your checking account to a savings or money market account.

■ Mining the Books ■

If I could give you one absolute order, it would be to take every educational opportunity that's offered you. (Look what it did for me: I wouldn't be where I am today, or writing this book!) Actually, when you are looking for a job, education reimbursement expenses can be the deciding factor on which job to choose, depending on your future plans. These days, many people decide to pursue an undergraduate degree, an MBA, or a law degree at night while working during the day. Graduate tuition, books, and other costs can be just as expensive (and sometimes cost more) than undergraduate outlays. I know many successful business people and lawyers who obtained their education this way. As one client put it, "I sure am glad I got my MBA before I settled down with a spouse and children. It would have been absolutely impossible to go to class at night and study if I had waited."

■ Your First Raise ■

If all goes well, after six months or a year on the job, you will have earned a raise. When you get word of a salary increase, try to resist the temptation to spend it all in your head before it even shows up in your paycheck! This is a natural human response—and I say so because I have gotten numerous calls from clients of all ages who start the conversation this way: "I just got a raise! What would you think if I bought _____?"

Often, a performance review precedes any discussion of a raise.

Come prepared with a list of the ways in which you have met—better yet, exceeded—expectations, as well as areas in which you think you can show improvement. If your work is criticized, try not to take it personally. Unless you think the criticism is entirely off base, take it under advisement, and vow to spend the next six months improving your skills.

If you aren't offered a raise at your performance review, that's the best time to request one if you are unsatisfied with your salary. Make your case calmly, ready to back up any claims with facts and figures, such as the amount of money you have saved your company, or your paycheck compared to that of others in your field with your level of experience. If a raise is not forthcoming, perhaps you can ask for some other form of compensation, such as more time off, a more flexible schedule, or permission to attend (all expenses paid) that sales conference in Hawaii you've been daydreaming about and know you can learn a great deal from.

The best things to do if you get a raise are: Take the extra money and direct it to a savings plan, pay off high credit card debt, set up an emergency fund, or put it in a retirement plan. Unless you are getting a one-time bonus, your raise will come to you in dribbles over the next twelve months, so after taxes you may barely notice the difference. For instance, if you get a $100 per month raise, and get paid twice a month, each paycheck might only increase by about $35. A major employee benefits firm estimated average annual salary increases in 1998 for the workforce as a whole to be about 4 percent, but your first few pay raises are likely to be higher, depending on the company.

☞ **Wake-up Call:** If you rush out and buy a $1,500 surround-sound system because you got a $1,500 raise, you just made a bad move. Don't forget that your raise will be less than that once your taxes and other deductions are subtracted. Furthermore, if you spend a chunk of money now that will come to you over the next twelve months, you probably had to put it on a credit card, which means some of your raise will be frittered away on interest payments.

Make it part of your plan now to sock away all your raises (or as much as you can) into savings. My clients who are most successful at saving are those who have made this part of their self-discipline.

■ Don't Ask, Don't Tell ■

One thing *not* to do is to discuss your salary or raise with your co-workers. A few years ago a young woman who was a rising star in an architecture firm was fired because she happened to mention her salary to others in her office. She was making as much or more than some of the architects who had been there for ten years! It would be an understatement to say there was an office mutiny. She was incredibly talented, but incredibly stupid in revealing her salary. Discussing how much you make with your co-workers does nothing but cause trouble and create resentment, and it may even be a breach of company policy. Whether you discuss your salary with your friends is up to you, but I would advise against it as well for many of the same reasons.

Often, clients who are your parents' age ask me whether they should ask their children now living on their own how much they make. In fact, one long-time client called me in an absolute fury because his son refused to tell him. (This demonstrates why the son was so smart to refuse—trying to maintain control, the father would have made judgments about everything that poor young man did with his money.) My recommendation to parents is, "Don't ask." Even if you come from a family culture where it is common to share this type of information—everybody in the family knows every time Uncle Ralph gets a raise—I think it is up to you to decide whether or not you want to divulge that information to your parents. If you prefer to keep it to yourself, it's not their business. If you are making a good living, repaying your loans, and saving a little as well, you may want to point that out to your parents in general terms (without giving exact dollar figures) to prove that you have become a responsible adult.

■ A Second Job ■

As I said earlier, I don't recommend taking a job with a salary so low that you have to take a second job to make ends meet. But sometimes you don't have that choice, or your expenses rise faster (even if you are being very careful about your spending) than your income. If you just can't earn enough with one paycheck, it makes sense to take a second job on the weekends or in the evenings. It is exhausting, but better to get yourself in good financial shape now so that you can relax a bit more in the future. Jason took a job in a large city and made a major miscalculation in his budget—it seemed he had low-balled everything. He was good with people, and decided that a job that could bring in big tips was the answer to his financial troubles. So he looked around for a bartending course, took it, and says he sometimes makes more in seven hours on a Friday night than he does in two days at his regular job.

Decide whether it is easier for you to work at night or perhaps one day on the weekend. Then devote all your extra earnings to paying off your bills, saving for a car or apartment deposit and the first month's rent, or getting rid of those nagging credit card debts. Again, the time to do this is now, while you are young and unencumbered. There is nothing wrong with hard work, and when you go to interview for your next job, if your potential employer sees that you are motivated enough to work two jobs, that will be a great reference in and of itself.

SAVING

■ Saving for Its Own Sake ■

Saving regularly is a habit that I sincerely hope your parents were able to teach you as you were growing up. But if you did not learn about the importance of savings, you may feel so overwhelmed by student loans and the burden of impending financial responsibilities that you feel you may never get out of debt, learn how to live on a budget, or control your credit card spending. (If you continue to read, you will see that you are not alone in these sentiments; some people at all income levels feel overwhelmed and wonder whether it is worth it to save given their circumstances.) Furthermore, you may not know what you are saving for, so why even bother to start now? Why not just have a good time?

In addition, you may be truly on your own and have more control over your personal life than ever before, and you are probably surrounded by many temptations. As one recent college grad said to me, "I worked so hard all through high school and college to get good grades so I could get to this point at my life. Now I want to have some *fun!*"

The problem, of course, is that you don't know exactly what the future will bring. But it may bring something that requires a good hunk of change sooner than you think. You may decide that you are not going to marry until you are at least age thirty, but then at twenty-three you unexpectedly meet the person of your dreams and want to pay for a wedding or an engagement ring in a year. Or your siblings tell you that your share of your parents' twenty-fifth wedding anniversary party will be four times the original figure. No one can predict the future, so whether you think you know what you want to do with your life, or you don't even know what you want to do next week, you can make saving a goal for its own sake. In fact, that's what most of your peers are probably doing. One of every two twenty-year-olds have begun saving for retirement, compared to fewer than 40 percent of boomers who began saving before the age of thirty, according to a 1995 poll by Kemper Financial Services.

Beside saving for future prosperity, there are many other worthy goals for saving, such as:

- getting out of debt;
- putting $1,000 into your savings account for an emergency fund so you have a cushion in case of disaster;
- saving for a down payment on a condo, co-op or house in five years;
- saving for graduate school or other training; or
- any other goal that is important to you and motivates you to save—a trip, a car, etc.

■ Short-term Goals Pay Long-term Dividends ■

People hate goals because they are usually really big and really far away, and that stack of current bills or that tempting weekend away is always staring them right in the face. The trick is to break goals down into manageable chunks that have some relevance to your present life. Instead of saying, "I want to be rich when I retire" (who doesn't?), say something like, "This year I'm going to put $100 a month into my retirement plan."

The important thing is to set goals, even if they are not long term. Make the goals personally satisfying enough to motivate you to sacrifice a little today so that you can reach them in the future.

When you are twenty or twenty-five, it is hard to envision your life in forty years, so why try? Some of my young clients can't even think past their next vacation, much less to the stage in life when they won't be working anymore. If you have access to a retirement plan, forget thinking about retirement, just think about having your money grow without letting the U.S. and state tax departments siphon off their share of your hard earned savings. (And remember that under new tax laws, if you participate in a company retirement plan you can probably borrow money from it and pay interest to your account; if you have an Individual Retirement Account you can probably take that money out without penalty if you need a down payment on your first home or you need it for your own or your children's college education.) Hardly anyone really knows what they want to do with their lives at this point—and if they do, it is likely to change. One of the greatest things about money is that it gives you flexibility to follow your dreams and to make and change plans as you go along. And after twenty-five years as a financial planner, I cannot think of one client I have ever worked with whose life has followed the path he or she thought it would ten years beforehand.

To come up with a list of short-term goals, write down all the things you want to put money toward in a month, aside from things like food and rent. Ideally, the list should include primary savings goals such as one retirement plan, one emergency account, and then any secondary things such as a mutual fund or vacation fund. After you figure out what your primary savings goals are, decide how much per month you can contribute to each. I recommend saving 10 percent of your take-home pay if you can. If your monthly take-home pay is $2,000, for example, perhaps you can allocate $150 to a money market account (which has higher interest rates than a traditional savings account) for an emergency fund and $50 to your retirement fund. Once you have an emergency fund of $4,000 or $5,000, then you may want to start putting $200 in your retirement fund. For many people, especially those just starting out in life, 10 percent is too high a percentage to be able to save. So just figure out how much you can do, and do it.

For those secondary goals that require onetime expenditures, like a vacation or furniture, there are creative ways to save a little money at a time that can add up to a substantial sum. I have recommended to several couples, for example, that they schedule their weddings at least a year in advance and then put aside a certain amount every month so they can cover their share of the costs.

☞ **Wake-up Call:** Put a small box on your kitchen table or dresser, and every night put your change in it, and perhaps an extra dollar or two. If you start far enough in advance, you may end up with the spending money you need for your next vacation or other goal that gives you motivation to save. Be sure and label the box prominently for its purpose, such as "Vacation Fund." I know a couple who did this and completely financed a romantic weekend in Canada just by dropping in their spare change and extra money each day. (This also works great after you have children and you want to save for a vacation. They will appreciate it much more.)

■ Saving by Trimming Your Spending ■

Emily got a new job and made a very careful budget, because she had a lot of student loans to repay. She asked her employee benefits manager to help her figure out what her after-tax income would be (she could have also waited until her first paycheck to do so, but was anxious to start out on the right foot) and planned from there. There was not much "wiggle room" because she could not turn to her parents for help, so she knew that every dollar mattered. She made a basic budget that included onetime expenses such as her share of the security deposit and last month's rent on the apartment she was going to share with two room-mates, as well as ongoing expenses that she would be facing for the first time as an adult—utilities, transportation, etc. Emily then made a com-mitment to build up an emergency fund for three months' worth of expenses, and figured out how much she would have to save to do so. Any extra would go for savings for a down payment on an inexpensive used car.

Keep in mind that just as in starting a business, you have some "startup" expenses now that you are out in the real world, and you need to take those into account. Although these are primarily onetime costs, they make a big difference when you're factoring the total cost of your move.

Along with the more obvious expenses such as first (and possibly last) month's rent and a security deposit, come other, more hidden costs that will quickly deplete your resources if you aren't careful. For instance, setting up a kitchen can be expensive. In addition to purchasing day-to-day groceries, you will need to buy staples, such as sugar, flour, spices and condiments—everything you've taken for granted in Mom and/or Dad's kitchen. Do you need dishes? Silverware? Storage containers? Cleaning supplies? What about things like trash cans, light bulbs, and garbage bags? All of these can take a toll on your budget.

☞ **Wake-up Call:** Young, single adults eat out more than any other age group. Once you invest in setting up a kitchen, eating at home can save you a great deal of money.

Thrift shops, garage sales, and rummage sales are great sources for kitchen supplies, and often for appliances as well. Buy generic kitchen basics at the grocery store, rather than name brands. "Discount" gro-cery stores such as Sam's Club, BJ's, and Costco are smart destinations for large families, but be wary of "bargains" when you're shopping for yourself only, or even yourself and a roommate. The two-gallon jar of pickles for $20 may be cheaper per ounce than the smaller sizes sold at ordinary supermarkets. But if you buy it, you're still spending $20 on pickles, and you'll also be committing yourself to eating a pickle a day for the next year—just to get rid of them. Wholesale stores can be inexpensive sources for essential items such as toilet paper and paper towels—things you know you'll use quickly or will be able to store indefinitely, and that you will need to replenish as soon as you run out.

If you're lucky, your parents or family friends may have extra furniture for you to use. If not, or if you're lacking a few basic essentials, head back to the thrift store or scan the weekend paper for garage sales, particularly suburban ones if you live in a large city. If you're really broke and you're not picky, you can often find free curbside furniture the night before the weekly trash collection. The best time to find free throwaways is around the first of each month, when people are moving and often get rid of good, usable furniture simply because they don't want the hassle of transporting it. A word of caution: Picking up stuffed furniture, such as couches and mattresses, from the side of the road can be a questionable decision. I think it's best to stick to wooden or metal items, such as desks and bookcases, that are easy to examine for dirt, mildew, and bugs.

☞ **Wake-up Call:** Before you purchase any secondhand electrical items, make sure that they work. Usually, you'll be allowed to plug things in and check; if you aren't, or an outlet isn't available, I'd recommend passing on the item. And remember to check electrical cords for damage—if they are frayed or worn, they're a fire hazard that you cannot afford.

Generally, you can find a couch at a thrift shop or yard sale for $50 or less—if the price is higher, negotiate or look elsewhere. I actually bought a great, Victorian-looking rocking chair for $5 at Goodwill when I was twenty-one that I used for almost fifteen years. Unhappy about the brown and yellow floral pattern or torn armrest on your new purchase? Check out a large fabric store: Many have bins full of discounted drapery cloth (which is slightly heavier than average fabric) for as little as $4 or $5 per yard. Or hit Grandma's linen closet or a home decorating store—a bedspread for a full-size bed is big enough to cover a loveseat or easy chair, and chair slipcovers can be ordered by catalog for as little as $20. No one expects you to have a perfect-looking apartment straight out of a TV sitcom—so don't bust your budget trying to do so.

■ Save or Get Out of Debt? ■

One question I frequently get asked by clients who are in their twenties is whether they should pay off their student loans or other debts, or save for their retirement. If you can, I recommend you do both. If you can't do both, save (but make sure you get the interest rates on your credit cards down to a reasonable level; I will tell you how later in this chapter). The reason: No one but *you* will ever make you save, but your creditors will always make you pay those debts, even if it takes ten or twenty years to do so. I have seen people who have had more than a million dollars pass through their hands with not a penny of savings to show for it, and a load of debt as well. You are probably thinking, "This will never happen to me," but so did they when they were your age. Unfortunately, in this life it is up to you to develop your self-discipline for saving and spending—the savings police are not going to bang on your door demanding that you deposit $100 a month into your savings account. If you did not watch your parents save, or they were unable to for financial reasons, you are unfortunately going to have to develop those skills on your own.

☞ **Wake-up Call:** Start the lifetime habit now of arranging for all savings to be taken out of your paycheck or bank account automatically, because then you won't miss the extra money as much. You will get used to living on less, and it won't get spent on frivolous things.

■ Read Up ■

Educating yourself about financial matters is also very important, so start now. If you recently graduated from school, you are probably still in the "studying" frame of mind. (Reading this book is a great step in the right direction!) But the more you know, and the earlier you know it, the better decisions you will make all the way along in life. Some great material can be found on Internet websites, which are also a great way to learn about personal finance. There are even websites where kids as young as eight or nine can choose "virtual portfolios" of $100,000 and then buy and sell stocks and mutual funds. In addition to my weekly syndicated MoneyCentral radio show, I write a biweekly column for Microsoft MoneyCentral, an Internet financial magazine that includes newsgroups where readers can post their questions. I find that the site's users are overwhelmingly under age thirty-five and working hard to develop their financial savvy. The success stories they tell from just taking the time to learn about money are phenomenal. One managed to rid himself of credit card debt that totaled more than his income in just two years, and another developed a bare-bones budget so she could retire at age fifty-five: Even though she was still in her twenties, she was looking ahead. The great thing about Internet financial chat groups is that you don't just get advice from the experts who are running the groups, but you also get advice from lots of other participants. I have learned an enormous amount of tips and ideas from these people, who are all trying to do a good job financially on a day-to-day basis. From their postings, it sounds as if their strategies are working.

You, too, can have a phenomenal success story, but you need knowledge to begin. If you recently got out of school or find classroom experiences to be particularly rewarding, you might even consider taking a course in personal finance. Courses are now taught at thousands of high schools, colleges, and local community education programs around the country. I have taught a few of these courses, and the participants' ages range from early twenties to mid-eighties. So don't feel that you are too young to take advantage of a course if it will help you get your financial life in order.

COLLEGE LOANS

■ Payback Time ■

You may take comfort in knowing that the average debt from college loans carried by Generation Xers is $10,000. If you have a college loan on your balance sheet, the most important thing you can do is to send in those payments on time every month. Doing so will help you establish or keep a good credit report and may give you some leeway with lending agencies, should you fall short of money at some point in the future.

If you have other debts or are having a hard time saving, I usually recommend that college loans be repaid as slowly as possible because they usually have lower interest rates than most other debt. Be sure and keep track of the interest rates if your loan has a variable rate. You don't want to think you are paying 8 percent on a college loan when in fact, the rate went up to 11 percent. If, on the other hand, you took out a personal loan at a high interest rate to pay your tuition, then you should pay more than the minimum each month—in essence, treat it like a credit card debt. In general, however, student loans have lower loan rates than traditional loans, so you are better off paying the minimum amount each month and applying any extra money to credit card debt or other loans with higher rates.

Many colleges and universities now participate in the Federal Direct Loan Program. This program, begun in 1994, which allows students to borrow directly from the federal government, offers a variety of repayment options, so you can tailor the size and timing of your payments to fit your postcollege plans. In addition to the standard repayment plan, in which loans are repaid over a ten-year period in 120 monthly payments, the direct loan program offers three possible payment plans.

Income contingent repayment plans base the amount of your payments on your post-graduation income. They stipulate that your monthly loan payments cannot take up more than 20 percent of your monthly income. The idea behind this option is that as you gain work experience, your salary will grow—along with your payments.

Graduated repayment plans are similar to income contingent plans in that the initial monthly payments are low and the amount you pay each month slowly grows over time. However, your payments are designed to increase automatically over time, regardless of your income—which could leave you in trouble if you're out of work or change careers and take a pay cut.

Extended repayment plans are designed primarily for those with large amounts of debt. This type of plan reduces your monthly payments by simply stretching out your repayment schedule—from twelve to as many as thirty years, depending on the amount you owe.

One benefit of a college loan is that repayment on a timely basis can help you establish a good credit record, which will help you later when you apply for a car loan or a mortgage. I know more than one individual who was denied a mortgage because he got behind on his student loans, thinking that they didn't really matter because they were government loans rather than commercial loans—and he had been out of school for five years.

If you run into trouble making your payments, do not put off paying. Pay as much as you can on time, and follow up with a telephone call, preferably *before* the due date, to let the lender know what the trouble is and what your plan is for resuming full payments. Lenders will often work with you to make the monthly payments affordable. It's in their best interest to get you on a payment plan you can afford. Talk to them about getting a deferment or a forbearance, if, for example, you are un-employed during the summer after you graduate. Just as with any other lender, student loan organizations would much rather deal with you directly than have to turn your file over to a credit collection agency, where the lending organization only ends up with a small percentage of what is collected. And, frankly, you would probably rather not have a bill collector visiting you at your home, or calling you once every couple of weeks at work (which is legal in most states).

One young woman I know who found herself between jobs due to downsizing said, "I find that Sallie Mae is extremely helpful as long as you let them know what's going on. You're better off telling them that you need to lower your monthly payments, rather than being stuck with a payment that you're always paying late. I was able to lower my interest rates ¼ of 1 percent on *each* of my four loans just by having automatic payments every month from my checking account. It's worth it to call and ask." A quarter of a point may not sound like much, but it can add up to a substantial difference month to month. Plus, with automatic payments, your loans get paid on time, so your credit record looks better and better.

FINANCIAL FIRSTS

Budgeting, managing bank accounts, handling debt, and investing—these are all new skills you will need now that you are on your own, and for the rest of your life. The list may seem overwhelming at first, but if you tackle each task one at a time, you will be putting down financial roots that will sustain you for years to come.

■ Budgeting 101 ■

Once you have a steady income, whatever it is, you need a budget. Most people don't realize that even the very wealthy must have budgets or they will overspend as well—the only difference is you may be spending $800 a year on clothing while they are spending $8,000. So if *they* need a budget with that kind of income, then you *really* do! Regardless of your financial situation, you will always find a budget to be one of the most useful tools for staying on the right financial track.

As a teenager you may already have begun to establish poor money habits that you'll need to break. American teenagers had a combined income of $105 billion in 1996, $103 billion of which got spent—at a rate of roughly $67 a week. Fifty-three percent said they just got money from their parents as needed, but now that you're on your own, whether you are living at home or in your own apartment, it is unlikely that your parents are going to be giving you money—in fact, you may be repaying them for previous loans. So if you are used to having money in your pocket from parents or part-time jobs, you may find budgeting more difficult than you thought. You may have all sorts of new expenses you didn't have before—such as professional clothing and dry cleaning, commuting costs, lunches out, occasional entertaining, and gifts to office pools (those gifts, lunches, and parties I talked about earlier). It can all add up very quickly.

My long-time client Bruce is the best example of why you should start establishing sensible money habits so that you do not find yourself in the incredibly painful situation he had a few years ago while well into his fifties. He came to me because he had heard me give a speech, and he knew exactly what his problem was—overspending. Bruce said making the telephone call to me was one of the most humiliating experiences of his life, but after hearing me speak about the difficulties of changing money habits, he felt safe making the telephone call and, as he put it, "confessing my sins without being judged."

Bruce came to me right as his children were beginning to think about college. Up to this point he had managed to save a fair amount for retirement through his company's 401(k) plan (and because he was fortunate enough to be working for an employer who had a pension plan to which he did not have to contribute). But his children's education was in jeopardy because he hadn't saved for that, and in our sessions all he could talk about was what he called his "runaway spending." He didn't feel comfortable tackling any other financial issues, such as updating his will, until he resolved his financial demons. Belive it or not, it took him two and a half years to give me a list of where he had spent his money over the most recent three months, because he was so afraid of looking at the results and so worried about my response.

I will never forget walking into my office early one morning and seeing his expense breakdown sitting in my fax machine. The numbers were just about as bad as I had expected. But the numbers weren't important. The moment was as exciting to me as if one of my clients had won a $10 million lottery—because Bruce had finally "woken up" from years of financial denial. But he still bemoans all of the money he wasted over the years. So don't find yourself at age fifty beating yourself up about not having established good money habits earlier. Just do it!

Remember, 80 percent of American adults don't understand basic financial management, so you should be kind to yourself whenever you do make a mistake. It doesn't do any good to berate yourself, because then you'll continue to think negatively about your financial abilities and continue to make mistakes.

☞ **Wake-up Call:** Think positively. You can stay within a budget, even if you have never tried in your life. I have helped seventy-year-olds develop and stick to budgets, and they have fifty more years of ingrained habits than you do!

Use the categories in the Minimum Budget chart (page 65) to set up your personalized budget. Add any additional spending categories that come up regularly in your new life as a working person. Can you meet your expenses with your current income—as well as pay off those student loans, perhaps car loans, set up an emergency fund, and put money in a retirement plan? If you can't save enough to do at least some of these important things, then you need to try to trim your expenditures.

If you find you are having trouble sticking with your budget, use the strategy I suggested in "Beginnings": Take money out of your checking account with an ATM card and then write directly on the slip where you spent the cash. If you have not been keeping track of your money, it can be a real eye-opener.

Sometimes you will be surprised at what can bust your budget. Do you have a pet? I have been a pet owner all of my life, but I have noticed an increasing tendency among young adults to buy pets. The average pet will cost you over $3,000 during its lifetime; the first year of vet visits, shots, and pills alone is often around $400. And if you travel for your job or pleasure, you may have to pay someone to take care of your pet. With the recent advances in medicine, if your pet comes down with a serious illness, such as cancer or kidney disease, you may find that treatment costs thousands of dollars—money which you may feel emotionally obliged to spend, even if you cannot afford it. So be sure you understand the financial obligations you are undertaking before you buy that adorable puppy or kitten you have your heart set on.

☞ **Wake-up Call:** If you're a devoted pet owner, consider pet insurance to protect your budget. You can insure puppies and kittens, and even many adult pets (make sure you are aware of policy exclusions for any preexisting condition that Fluffy or Jake already has). See the Appendix for more resources.

■ Bank Accounts ■

You'll need two bank accounts right off the bat: a savings account and a checking account. Savings accounts give you a measure of emotional security and allow you to keep some of your money separate from your checking account, where you are more likely to spend it. Having a savings account also gives you extra points when you go through "credit scoring" for a new car loan, an apartment lease, or a mortgage. It counts against you if you don't have one. I know of a young man who made $50,000 a year, but who had to pay three extra percentage points on his new car loan because he did not have a savings account. Don't let that happen to you.

You'll need a checking account to conduct important transactions, such as paying your rent and utility bills, so you might consider a "companion" checking account. This means that both accounts have the same account number and are attached to each other, making it easy to transfer money between the two. It also makes putting away that recommended 10 percent savings each month (or whatever you can do) a little easier, because the transfers can be done automatically. The statements are combined and mailed once a month. If you are a spender, however, keep the accounts separate. That may reduce your temptation to move your savings into your checking account and then spend it.

Many banks offer free checking as long as you keep a certain balance in your savings account, so it is worth it to shop around to get the best deal. Another important issue to look at is whether a fee is charged whenever you use an ATM card, whether at machines belonging to your own bank or to another bank. These fees can really add up—I have seen clients with ATM charges on their statements of well over $100 a month—and they are not even aware of it because they never looked at the statements. Local community banks often offer free checking accounts with no minimum balance and free ATM usage at any ATM machine around the country.

Of course, you should balance your checking account each month to make sure that you know exactly how much money you have in it and to avoid bouncing a check. The best way to balance your checkbook is to keep a "running balance," which simply means figuring out how much is in your account after each transaction. Subtract the amount of each check at the time you write it, each debit card deduction at the time you spend it, and each ATM withdrawal from your current balance immediately after you put the money in your wallet. Similarly, add the amount of each deposit at the time of the deposit. And each time you get a bank statement, subtract the monthly fees. If you are using a computer software program such as Microsoft Money or Quicken to keep track of your checking account (which I highly recommend), you avoid having to do any math, which means you avoid making mistakes in your arithmetic that can cause bounced checks.

Save money by ordering your checks from an independent printer rather than from your bank. Two sources: Checks in the Mail and Current Checks (see the Appendix for information). If you are using a software program, the software packages will contain offers to buy computer checks. Make sure that any checks you buy are not only compatible with the brand of software you are using, but also with the version you have.

Choose an account that offers you overdraft protection if at all possible; you usually have to apply for this, but if you have a full-time job and can prove regular income, you can probably get overdraft protection of at least $500. This in effect acts as a loan, so if you've written a check that is over your limit and you do not have enough funds available in your account, the overdraft account will pay the check for you. In addition to avoiding bounced check charges, you avoid humiliation as well. You then pay interest on the amount that was advanced until you pay it off.

It is only logical that if you have extra money in your checking account, it should go to pay off your overdraft—but with many banks, this is not the case. Your overdraft is considered a separate loan, and you need to make payments on it. So make sure that you make those payments on time.

Don't get into the mind-set that the amount of money in your checking account, *plus* your overdraft, is the amount of money you actually have. I see this with clients who run up one overdraft as quickly as they pay off the last one; they are constantly in the hole.

If for some reason you do not get overdraft protection and you do bounce a check, don't panic. One bounded check will not show up on your credit report. Even millionaires bounce an occasional check. But I know from personal experience how embarrassing it can be. Not so long ago I bounced three checks because our office had been given incorrect information from our bank about how long it took for certain checks to clear. Even though it was not my fault, I felt foolish. I was appearing on television twice a week as a financial guru, after all!

If it happens to you, consider it a learning experience then vow to yourself that you will not let it happen again. In addition to subtracting it from your balance, write on a special page of your checkbook all the fees that your bounced check cost—both to yourself and to the recipient of your check. (Remember that you need to pay the fees charged to the recipient of your check—especially if it is a friend!)

■ Money Market Accounts ■

Money market accounts are like checking accounts, but they pay higher interest and usually restrict the number of checks you can write in a given period of time. These are a good option if you need a temporary spot for your savings—say you've saved $1,000 but you need $2,500 to make an initial investment in a mutual fund. Most money market accounts require you to maintain a minimum balance to avoid higher fees, however, so remember to close it promptly if you can't maintain a balance above that level.

■ Plastic ■

You may have already been using a credit card for years; 59 percent of college students carry credit cards, many of which have been co-signed by one or more of their parents. But now you need one in your own name, especially if you hope to rent a car or buy tickets to a concert through Ticketmaster. But beware! It's easy to get in financial trouble with a credit card. The average interest rate on credit cards in 1998 was almost 19 percent: the Consumer Federation of America calculated that if you have a balance of $7,000–$8,000, you will pay close to $1,000 in interest in just one year. A large percentage of college students max out their cards—charge them up to the limit—within a year after getting them. If you don't pay your bills on time you can really wreak havoc with your credit report, which can hinder you for years.

Once you are on your own, there are all kinds of incentives—such as free gym workout bags and watches—to encourage you to sign up for various cards. Stick with the major cards—brands like MasterCard, Visa, or American Express—and avoid store cards, which usually have high interest rates and deluge you with "special sale" circulars that tempt you to spend even more. "Save 50%!" the circulars scream. But of course, if you buy the item, you will be spending 50 percent more than you would have if you had simply not purchased it! Most stores will accept either a major credit card or a personal check to make a purchase.

☞ **Wake-up Call:** Many stores ask for your telephone number or Social Security number when you are using a credit card as a way to track your purchases. Most states prohibit stores from requesting this information. Don't give it out: Someone may take advantage of you by using it to access your credit card number, enabling them to make purchases with your card!

A good way to build up your credit rating is to charge $25 or $50 worth of purchases each month, and then pay it off in full each time. If the only way you can afford something that is not absolutely necessary is by putting it on a credit card, then you shouldn't be buying it in the first place. Deferred gratification is actually a very satisfying feeling. Did you know that outstanding credit card debt accounts for almost 20 percent of the disposable personal income of Americans? Don't fall into the credit card trap.

One mistake many people make when they are first using credit cards is to fail to pay the minimum on time each month, rationalizing that they will send in a big check when they can—perhaps two or three months later. They do not realize that this will affect their credit rating in major negative ways. *Paying on time is always more important than how much you pay.*

If you do run up debt that you can't pay off when the bill comes, pay it back as quickly as possible. One trick is to round up your payment from the minimum amount to the next hundred dollars. For example, if the minimum payment is $71, send in $100. This will help you pay off your debt more quickly and save you significant sums in interest.

☞ **Wake-up Call:** If you do not need to carry a balance for a lengthy period, call the credit card issuers and tell them you are thinking of moving your balance to a card with a lower rate, and ask that they lower your rate. That's usually all it takes. (Even if you don't get an offer right then, you are likely to receive one in the mail shortly.)

Sending in biweekly payments, rather than paying monthly, also can reduce your interest costs. The Pocket Change Investor calculated that if you owed $3,500 on a credit card that charged a 17 percent interest rate and required a minimum payment of $70, it would cost you $7,000 in interest over the thirty years it would take to pay off the debt. But if you sent in $35 every two weeks, it would take only seven years to pay off the debt and your interest charges would be reduced to $2,000. The minimum balance is usually about two percent, so if you pay the minimum, you are mainly paying interest every month. Assuming you pay just 2 percent on a $2,000 debt, guess how long it will take to pay it off—40 years! Double that payment to 4 percent, and you are still talking about 10 years. That is a long time to pay for the dinner you had out last week with your friends!

To evaluate a credit card, look at the application fees, late fees, and the point at which interest gets charged (is it from the date of purchase, or when you fail to make your next payment in full?). Different states have different maximum interest rates that can be charged, which explains why you may get offers from faraway states that allow higher rates.

If you have a card that offers bonuses such as frequent flyer miles, you usually cannot negotiate the interest rate or annual fee. Since an airline ticket usually requires you to accumulate twenty-five thousand miles, if you earn one mile for every $1, that means you need to charge $25,000 on your credit card, so for most people just starting out, these cards are not worth it.

Sign up for a card without an annual fee. Or if they have one, ask them to waive it. Often they will because there is so much competition for cardholders.

You always have to read the fine print. Some cards offer you cash back at the end of the year based on a percentage of how much you charge, or credit toward merchandise or a car. Others advertise fee-free cash advances as long as you pay them back by the next billing date. But when I looked into that offer further, I found that it was actually going to cost me more than $100 for a $1,000 cash advance. There are numerous websites that track the best credit card offers (see appendix for a list).

So much of our spending is connected to our emotions—we spend to make ourselves feel better when we are down, and we spend to celebrate

$1500 Credit-Card Charges
Monthly Minimum Payment Only

Interest Rate	Years Until Paid Off	Total Interest Paid
5%	7	$305
10%	9	$713
15%	12	$1500
20%	20	$3745

when something great has happened. So where do we go? The mall! There is nothing wrong with that, but running off to the mall with charge cards in your wallet is a recipe for disaster. The solution is to set a budget and to take only cash with you, leaving your checks, ATM card, and charge cards at home. That way you can only spend what is in your pocket. Carolyn had a real spending problem that ruined every trip she took to a mall—because she always overspent and then regretted it. After using this technique, she told me that her anxiety level virtually disappeared when she went shopping, because she knew she could not get herself into trouble.

☞ **Wake-up Call:** Millions of consumers are sending their credit card payments in late, indicating that they are having trouble paying their bills. If you find you just can't handle a credit card, don't use it anymore. Cut it up if you have to.

■ Credit Reports ■

Credit reports are issued by independent companies that track and record how many cards you have, what your monthly balances are and whether you've paid on time. They also track how many times you have applied for credit or an increase in credit and when you have been turned down. Additionally, credit checks are often run when you apply for a job or for an apartment, and these all show up on your report as well. When you apply for a loan or additional credit, these reports are the basis for whatever decision is made, so you should keep them in mind every time you make a credit-related transaction.

Too much activity of any kind is always considered suspicious. An example: I recently worked with a young woman who was turned down for a condominium loan, even after we had run the numbers and it was clear that she could afford it. It turned out that Suzanne had looked at seven or eight apartments before she had decided to apply for a condominium, and each apartment complex had run a credit report on her. So in the space of six months, there were seven different credit checks—a statistical fact that makes credit bureaus and lenders suspicious. Once we identified the problem, she was able to explain the situation to the lender, and the condominium loan went through without a hitch.

Most important are the transactions you have made in the last two years, but any credit problems you've had will sully your report much longer than that. Information about unpaid debt is included in the report for seven years. Personal bankruptcy is listed for ten years.

☞ **Wake-up Call:** A less-than-perfect report doesn't mean you can't get credit. You'll just have to pay more for it. For example, if you have had problems paying credit cards on time or not paying them at all, you may only be able to get a "secured" credit card (where you keep a special bank account with the credit card company that is equal to your spending limits). Or, you may end up on a list of higher-risk credit card holders, and be deluged with offers that are terrible financial deals. One client showed me a credit card offer "guaranteeing" him a minimum of a $300 spending limit. All he had to do was pay $90 in a first year fee (30 percent of his credit limit; compared to many cards with no annual fees) and then, depending upon how timely his payments were, his annual fee thereafter could drop to "as low as $45 a year" (15 percent of his credit limit).

Because the credit reporting companies are keeping track of so much information, mostly provided by creditors, and there is no penalty to them if there are mistakes, errors are not uncommon. A *Consumer Reports* study found that 42 percent of all credit reports had errors in them. That's why it's a good idea to request a copy of your credit report every year or so from each of the three big credit companies—Equifax, Experian, and Transunion. Usually there's a nominal fee (under $10). If you get turned down for credit based on a report, you are entitled to a free copy. In Massachusetts, Colorado, Maryland, New Jersey, Vermont, and Georgia, residents are entitled to one free copy of their credit report each year. You also are entitled to a free credit report:

- if you have been denied credit within the last sixty days,
- if you have been denied employment or insurance based on your credit report,
- if you are a welfare recipient,
- if you are unemployed and looking for a job within the next sixty days.

If you do find false information, such as a defaulted loan listed that is not even yours, write the credit bureau and ask for an explanation; they are required by law to follow up and verify your claim. Even if you disagree with the result, you have the right to have an explanation included at the bottom of your credit report. You also can ask the bureau to add your own 100-word explanation of why you were behind in payments—if you lost your job or had a medical emergency, for instance. The key is to look responsible on your credit report. If you got behind on your credit card or mortgage payments five years ago, for instance, because you were seriously ill and that is noted on your report, if you have been reliable in meeting payment schedules since then, you will probably get credit. See the Appendix for information regarding obtaining your credit report.

■ Emergency Fund ■

Unless you already have money in the bank, one of the very first things you need to do is set up an emergency fund. Even in a terrific job market, it may take you a few months to find just the right job for you: This fund gives you the luxury of being able to wait for the right offer. It also will come in handy when the old car you are driving needs new tires, or you suddenly need to come up with a deposit on an apartment or new car. I typically recommend that clients have an emergency fund equivalent to three to six months' worth of expenses. At this stage of life, however, it is going to be hard enough to save three months' worth. Make that your goal, and then do the best you can.

☞ **Wake-up Call:** What happens if you are hit with an emergency but you don't have any funds set aside? Don't despair. You can consider using the credit available on your credit card or overdraft allowance to cover your expenses. But once you are back on your feet and have paid off your credit line, make sure to build up your fund as soon as you can.

■ First Investments ■

You don't have to wait until you are a middle-aged millionaire equipped with a cell phone, a laptop, and your own personal broker to invest. Even if you can't devote more than a few dollars a month to investing, get started now. You will reap real rewards down the line. You can set up a program where as little as $50 a month goes into a mutual fund in a retirement plan or a fund you invest in on your own. If you invested $50 a month for ten years and earned 10 percent after taxes (or 10 percent before taxes in a retirement plan), you would have $10,242.

If you don't have $50 a month to spare, save what you can in a savings account until you have enough for a minimum investment in a fund, usually $1,500. Start with one mutual fund and go from there. Confused about how to select a fund? So is just about everyone else, even though they may talk a good game. Read about investing in detail in "Building Up" (Chapter 4).

■ Computerized Financial Planning ■

If you own a personal computer, or have access to one at work or through your family or friends, I highly recommend purchasing a personal financial management software program, such as Microsoft Money or Quicken. You can enter data, such as your budget, checkbook register, or investments, for example, and apply it to a financial planning program. These programs also connect to the Internet. You can usually download your credit card and bank account statements, make electronic payments (instead of mailing checks) and update your investment portfolio. You can then transfer the data to a tax software program such as Tax Cut or Turbo Tax, and your taxes are virtually done for you.

Even if you don't have a computer at home, perhaps you can use the one at work to start paying all your bills online. (If you are allowed to do that, make sure you feel comfortable putting all your personal financial information on the company server, and you have a special personal-use password). Another, better alternative is to store all your information on a disk, so you don't have to leave it at the office. It is easier to keep track of your financial picture on a computer, and my clients (as well as I) find it extremely motivating to get great reports, which you can issue yourself as often as you want. By using the Web or direct banking options available with these computer programs, you also can see which checks have cleared, what your current balance is, and you can automatically schedule future bill payments. Talk about streamlining your life! This is a great habit to get into as soon as possible.

YOUR HOME LIFE

■ Living at Home Versus Striking Out on Your Own ■

If you are still living at home even after you start a full-time job, you probably won't feel any peer pressure to get your own place. Currently 30 percent of adults in their twenties live at home. The benefit is that you will probably spend less money this way. The downside is that you are giving up some measure of freedom.

If you decide to stay home, or return home after a period away, sit down with your parents and reassess living arrangements. There should be clear rules about who pays for what as well as what the house rules are. But make sure the rules are fair. Recently a client of mine who prided herself on her open-mindedness was bemoaning the fact that sometimes her adult daughter did not come home at night. She was very disapproving of this until I reminded her that her adult son was living at home and often did not come home either, but that did not seem to bother her. Her subconscious double standard was causing enormous friction, and it was clear that the family needed to agree upon house rules that would apply to both young adults.

Your parents may charge you a nominal rent for the privilege of living at home after you're out of school. They also could legitimately charge you for laundry or food, unless you work out some type of deal with them where you do grocery shopping or other chores in exchange. Still, you will be spending less money than if you had moved out. Use this opportunity to sock away money into an emergency fund or to save for a security deposit and first month's rent on an apartment, or to pay off credit card bills or student loans.

Some parents place a time limit on this arrangement. This is actually a good idea for both of you. If so, ask them to help you set up a savings program so you can save a certain amount every month for an apartment's down payment and rent. In fact, they can make that part of your weekly or monthly rent and just set it aside in a checking or savings account for you. You will reap the benefits of this automatic savings plan when you move out.

Renting an apartment can be expensive. In fact, the largest part of a recent graduate's paycheck goes to rent. One great solution is to get roommates. If you do, make sure that all roommates are listed on the lease and on all utility bills so that you cannot get stuck with hundreds of dollars' worth of bills.

In addition to paying rent, you will need renters' insurance. This usually does not cost more than a couple of hundred dollars a year, and it may seem frivolous, but it's not. It will protect you if your roommate has a party and someone gets drunk, falls down your stairs, and holds you responsible for his medical bills. Renters' insurance will also protect you against theft.

Strapped for cash? Do what my assistant Karen did, and find a roommate who is already set up in a furnished apartment and who is willing to share her computer. Karen was able to use her roommate's computer while she was job hunting as long as she supplied her own diskettes, which she took to the local copy shop every time she had to print something out.

☞ **Wake-up Call:** *Never* fall for the rent-to-own offers and advertisements for furniture and appliances that will come your way. You can end up spending three times as much for your furniture or your television, and those bills can haunt you for years.

Here are two examples of "Early Risers" and their budgets:

Ken is a twenty-four-year-old living at home with his father in a large northeastern city. Although Ken majored in history in college, he also took courses in computer programming and made it a priority to have a working understanding of today's developing technology. When he graduated two years ago, his computer knowledge enabled him to land a job as a computer help-desk technician at a large consulting firm. His salary is $32,000 per year, and it includes full health benefits. Most of the employees dress in an "office casual" style: For men, this means khakis and button-down shirts.

After graduation, Ken decided to sacrifice the freedom of an apartment for a few years in order to save money, because his college loans totaled over $40,000. He moved into his father's apartment in the city, where public transportation was convenient and inexpensive. His job was fifteen minutes away by subway, and the amount he saved on parking, gas, insurance, and car payments was enormous.

Because he lived at home, Ken did not have any of the start-up costs that come with a first apartment: His father's place was furnished, the kitchen was stocked, and his old bedroom was right there waiting for him. Ken pays his father $100 per month in "rent," and in exchange, his father pays all the utility bills and buys all the groceries. Ken is responsible solely for his long-distance bills, which are relatively high because the majority of his college friends live on the West Coast.

Let's take a look at Jamie's situation, which is very different:

Jamie is a twenty-three-year-old woman sharing a two-bedroom apartment with a roommate in a medium-sized midwestern city. She works as a copy editor at a textbook publisher in the suburbs, and she drives thirty minutes to get to work every day. She loves her job and is trying to get experience in the industry so she can soon qualify for a higher-paying position. Jamie's yearly salary is $24,000, including health benefits.

Jamie's job requires "professional" attire every day but Friday, so she must spend more money on suits and appropriate work clothes than Ken. She chose to live in an apartment rather than move home because her parents live in a rural area where the job opportunities are few. The cost of living in her city is relatively low when compared to that in other parts of the country. However, the area lacks a convenient public transportation system, so for Jamie a car is necessary—not just for commuting to work, but for getting around in general.

Jamie couldn't afford a one-bedroom apartment, so she moved in with a friend. The two of them split all of the household expenses, groceries, and cleaning supplies. Jamie's roommate's family lives in the area, so it was easy for them to give the young adults some of their old furniture, towels, and kitchenware.

Jamie doesn't drink or smoke, which saves her a lot of money—one night at a bar can blow your entire budget! She is also very careful about long-distance phone calls, making them only at night or on her phone company's designated "saver" day. In the winter, when heating costs skyrocket, she and her roommate put plastic over the insides of all the windows in their apartment. This prevents heat from escaping and saves them big bucks at bill-paying time.

Jamie's and Ken's incomes, expenses, and the amounts they save each month are outlined in the table on the next page.

■ Bill-Paying Techniques ■

Whether you've got your own place or not, handle bills as they come in. Separate your bills from regular mail right away—have a special basket or bin just for bills that need to be paid. Throw out the outside envelope and any other stuff and put it in its mailing envelope. If you are not paying bills electronically, write the check right away and add that to the envelope. If the bill isn't due immediately, set it aside until a week or so before it's due. There may be a temptation to let utility bills slide because there are no interest charges if they are late. Don't—you may incur a late fee, and you could damage your credit rating. Some people attach a Post-it note with the due date to remind them when each bill should be mailed.

Others go a step further and write out all their checks for an entire year (leaving the amount blank if necessary), date them, and then file

Jamie and Ken Chart

Monthly Gross	Jamie	Ken
Income	$2,000	$2,670

Minus: Monthly Expenses	Jamie	Ken
Alcohol	0	20
Clothing	125	30
Education	200	250
Entertainment	50	100
Food	175	30
Furnishings	30	0
Health Care	10	20
Health Insurance	0	50
Household Supplies	20	0
Credit Card Payments	50	100
Miscellaneous	30	25
Retirement Plan	50	50
Rent	350	100
Transportation	325	30
Utilities	50	40
Total Expenses	**$1,465**	**$845**

Minus: Taxes	Jamie	Ken
FICA (Social Security)	$150	$200
Federal Taxes	$240	$630
State Taxes*	$100	$130
Total Taxes	**$490**	**$960**

Amount Saved Each Month	Jamie	Ken
	$45	$865

*Although state tax varies from stat to state, this example assumes 5 percent state tax on gross income.

them all chronologically together. That way you can just mail the check on top of the pile each month.

■ Ginger's Quick Filing System ■

If you are not a naturally organized person, let me suggest that you try my "Quick Filing System," which I included in *The Money Diet* and was a big hit with readers, based on their letters and comments. The only equipment you'll need is a small filing cabinet or a large filing box and a couple dozen hanging or manila folders. Set up a separate folder for each of the items listed in the chart below. One for each credit card or bank account you have, for instance. For taxes, set up a current-year income tax file with envelopes for your pay stubs and deductions, if you have any. You can also make a file for bills to be paid, if you haven't already designated another spot. I also suggest making twelve monthly files for miscellaneous bills that are paid during the year, a general "to-do" file, and a "pending" file for things that require action by someone else.

Keep track of warranty cards, instructions, and purchase receipts, and set up one file for each type of household expense: kitchen items, major appliances, audio/video/TV equipment, sports gear, pets, etc. Also, set up one file for insurance policies and another for employee benefits.

ON THE ROAD

■ Getting Wheels ■

Buying a car is a rite of passage for many people because it's their first big-ticket purchase. If you've never owned a car before, you may not realize how much cars cost. Along with car payments come insurance (which can be high depending on the type of car and where you live), gas, repairs, and parking (if you live in a big city). That can add up to quite a bit more than your monthly payment.

If you have a bad credit record already and you need a car loan, you'll be in for big payments because you'll be charged a high interest rate. If you have had a bad driving record (and if you do, you're not alone; it's a sad statistical fact that every year, more than 40 percent of sixteen-year-old drivers have crashes serious enough to generate a police report), your insurance rate will be high, too.

Quick Filing System

Taxes
Current year

Next year

Household Files
Kitchen

Major appliances

Small appliances

Audio/video/TV

Lawn and garden

Home furnishings

Miscellaneous

Financial Files (one for each individual item)
Credit cards

Bank accounts

Investment accounts

Retirement plans

Real estate

Automobile

Employee benefits

Insurance

Annual Files (one for each person in your household)
Current year

Next year

Ongoing File (with lined paper to keep ongoing records)
House capital improvements

House repairs

Current Files
Bills to be paid

12 monthly files for miscellaneous bills

Pending

To do

The smartest approach to owning a car is holding onto it as long as possible. More and more people are doing this; the median age of a vehicle on the road today is eight years, the oldest it has been since the 1950s. And no wonder—the average car now sells for $21,840, up from $16,350 in 1990.

Tackle shopping for a new car the same way you would approach writing a research report for your toughest high school teacher or college professor. If you do your homework before you set foot in the showroom, you will end up saving money and getting the car you want. Plan to spend at least a week or two on your search; don't be rushed.

Start by identifying two or three car models that meet your needs. Find out dealer cost on base models and options by calling the Consumer Reports New and Used Car Price Service (see the Appendix for more information). There's a small fee but it is well worth it. Check out your local library's copy of *Consumer Reports* to evaluate the different cars on safety, reliability, and other features. Also figure out the upper limit amount that you will pay.

Even if you don't intend to buy from a showroom, visit one to test-drive all of your possible models. If you know exactly what you want, you can order it (and negotiate the price) from the dealership, or even buy over the Internet. Once you select the car you want, start bidding at just above dealer cost. One source that claims to offer competitive prices is Auto-by-Tel (www.onlineauto.com). You can also buy a car over the Internet through competitive bidding by using Carpoint (www.carpoint.com). Don't wait more than fifteen minutes for "manager approval" of your offer—a sales tactic designed to keep you waiting so you are too tired to go anywhere else and you have no time. Get the final offer in writing and take it to another dealer. You can play one against the other.

Three more notes of caution:

1. Don't get roped into buying factory options—things like a sunroof and leather seats—that you don't want. The dealer can search the region for a car that meets your needs.
2. There are also packages such as the "decor group" (exterior decoration, special mats, etc.) and "protection packages" (rustproofing, for example, which is no longer needed) that just add dollars to your cost. These options are added by the dealer, so they can be avoided.
3. Never say you are trading in your old car until you have completed negotiations on the new one.

4. Don't accept dealer financing before checking with your credit union or bank to see if they have a better deal.

Throughout life you may find that you'll be tempted to buy new cars, because it's one way you can feel richer than you are. The average consumer may spend close to $100,000 on cars by the time he or she turns sixty. Even if you are of modest means, you can buy an expensive car by stretching out the payments over five or more years. As you age and as the amount you want to spend on a car increases, so do the opportunity costs. If, for instance, you are trying to decide between two models, one of which costs $15,000 more than another, you should consider the cost of choosing to spend that extra money on a car rather than saving it.

■ **New or Used?** ■

New cars depreciate in value so quickly (they drop as much as 30 percent in value as soon as you drive them off the lot), that it's worth considering buying a used car before you invest in a brand-new one. You can get really good used cars that don't have many miles on them for less than you would pay for a new car. One source is rental car companies, which sell the cars they rent out after a couple of years of service. The advantage to this is that usually, these cars have been well-maintained.

☞ **Wake-up Call:** Don't ever buy a car from a used car lot, especially if it is your first purchase. You don't have a factory-authorized repair garage on the

True Cost: Choosing to Spend $15,000 More on a Car

	8%	10%	12%
After 10 Years	$30,000	$35,400	$41,600
After 20 Years	$64,800	$91,800	$129,200
After 30 Years	$139,800	$237,900	$401,300

True cost is how much less you would have if you spent the money instead of saving and investing it at 8%, 10%, or 12%. If you had taken out an auto loan, "true cost" would be much higher because it would include all those interest payments.

premises, and chances are the warranty is very limited. Plus, as a younger buyer you are more likely to be taken advantage of, and your warranty is going to be better with an established dealership. Finally, a dealership has much more to lose in reputation than a used car lot if you are not dealt with fairly.

Another possibility is to buy a car that has been leased, or after you have leased it. Because of the increase in popularity of leasing over the last few years, the market has been flooded with preleased cars, and these are often good deals. They can't be leased again as new cars, and their prices have dropped, because the number of these cars out there far exceeds the market demand for them. This may be a terrific alternative to a new car, and you may even get the equivalent of a new car warranty as well.

Before you buy a used car, take it to a mechanic to check it out. It's also important to investigate your state's lemon laws so you know how long you can wait before you change your mind—even if you bought it from a private party—and get your money back.

Don't buy extended warranties. I have bought them—nothing I've needed has ever been covered, even when I've had big problems like entire door-locking systems that failed, transmission problems, bad brakes, and more. Car experts tell me my experience is typical.

If you are a woman trying to buy a car on your own, either brush up on your negotiating skills or be prepared to bring along a man to shop—the salespeople will take you more seriously and won't try to play as many games. One study cited in *Women Pay More (and How to Put a Stop to It)* by Frances Cerra Whittelsey and Marcia Carroll found that women were quoted higher initial prices than men and ended up paying 40 percent higher markups. I have a woman friend who earns a six-figure salary and negotiates multimillion-dollar contracts on a regular basis at work, yet when she tried to buy a car on her own, she gave up in disgust at the sales tactics and patronizing attitude toward women. She'd been called "honey" one too many times. If you are female and anyone treats you in a patronizing manner, touches you, or seems to be trying to sell at a higher price because you are a woman, tell the manager and walk out. There are plenty of good dealerships that don't resort to these tactics, so make it your business to identify and do business with them.

When you need to get your car serviced, it also pays to shop around until you find a good local mechanic to whom you can return to over and over. For warranty work, you must take your car to a dealer, but it doesn't have to be the one who sold you the car, if you find a mechanic you prefer at another dealership. Any dealer you choose will be paid by the car manufacturer. Do your best to develop a relationship with your mechanic, so he gets to know you and your car. This will make your car last longer. I have a 1994 Jeep, and I actually bake pies (and I hate to cook) to take to my mechanic as a thank-you for staying late, under-charging me, diagnosing a problem, and then scrounging around for a used part ("Why should you have to pay for a new part when a used one in this case will do just fine?" he says). My car has eighty thousand miles on it and he knows I want to keep it forever, even if I decide to use it as a second car to tackle four-wheel-drive roads in Vermont or keep it for my kids to use when they graduate from college.

If your car is in the shop and you get a call telling you it will cost $2,000 to fix it, is it worth it to get it repaired, or are you better off trad-ing it in, or buying or leasing another car? Unless you are worried about your current car's safety and reliability, think hard before junking it.

Total up your repair costs and your insurance payments for the last two years to help you estimate your costs for the next two years. If you've spent roughly $600 a year on insurance and $400 on repairs, then your total costs for the next two years (including the big $2,000 re-pair) will be roughly $4,000. Then total up the costs of a new car for the next two years, including monthly payments and higher insurance rates. If you are thinking of buying a new car that will cost you $250 a month plus $800 in insurance, your total cost for the next two years would be $7,600. Look at both totals, and then decide if you should junk your current car. Usually the best thing to do is to drive your car until it dies. Buying a used car and driving it until the end was a common character-istic of the people profiled in the best-selling book *The Millionaire Next Door*.

If you don't need a car every day, look into the cost of renting a car on the weekends when you need one. That may be a much more eco-nomical option.

■ How About Leasing? ■

Leasing a car, which means "renting" it for a few years, is another op-tion to consider. You put money down up front, maybe $1,000, and then make monthly payments. At the end of the lease, you can either turn the car in or buy it. Leasing allows you to feel really wealthy, be-cause you can usually lease a much more expensive car than you can buy. However, keep in mind that counting depreciation, insurance, maintenance, and gas, an expensive car costs about $1 per mile to operate. Understand that a "luxury" car is exactly that: a luxury.

I don't recommend leasing unless you're only going to need the car for a couple of years. Then it makes sense, because you may end up paying less money to lease than you will lose if you bought a new car and then sold it only a couple of years later. For instance, if you spend $15,000 on a new car but can only get $10,000 for it two years later, you would be better off spending $3,000 to lease a car for two years. In that example, you would be saving $2,000.

Leases come in two types, open-end and closed-end. Open-end means that the renter bears some responsibility for the car's worth at the end of the lease. If the car is worth more than anticipated (this rarely happens because the market has been flooded beyond expectation with leased cars, so prices have dropped), you will share the profit. If it is worth less (far more likely), you must pay the difference. Closed-end leases put the responsibility for the value of the car totally on the lessor, and not on you.

Avoid open-ended leases because you may have to come up with big bucks when your lease ends. Also avoid leases with annual mileage caps of below 12,000 miles; that number or above is fine. Watch out for built-in disability and life insurance premiums in the contract—don't buy them because the cost for the coverage is prohibitive. If you need disability and life insurance, you need it for more than just your car lease. Go to the section on life and disability insurance in Chapter 4 and learn how to buy coverage that will last as long as you need it—not just as long as your car's lease does.

Many people get caught up in the habit of leasing time after time, which means that they never get to own anything in return for their payments. Just as buying a house makes sense over time, so, too, does owning a car.

☞ **Wake-up Call:** For a modest fee, *Consumer Reports* provides a service that gives you information about the cost of buying any car you could want. They provide lots of information, from the number of cylinders to dealer transportation costs, and a base price which you can use to bargain. AAA's Auto Insiders Service, Inc. offers a similar service to members. Call your local office or see the Appendix for details.

■ Auto Insurance: What You Need to Know ■

Protecting yourself through your auto insurance policy is just as important as driving a safe vehicle. All states require that car owners carry a minimum amount of insurance, but frequently that is not enough to protect yourself in case of an unfortunate accident. Even if your state offers "no-fault" insurance, you can be sued by an injured party if you caused the accident, and that is not at all unusual.

An auto insurance policy can be written to offer several types of coverage. Because you are younger, you could get away with lower amounts, but if you are in an accident and it is your fault, your wages could be attached to pay any court settlement damages for years and years to come—not a great way to start off your adult life. Even if you drive an old beater, I recommend the following insurance minimums to my clients:

To help you pay for all this extra auto insurance coverage, you can save money by increasing your deductibles (how much you have to pay before insurance kicks in) on collision and comprehensive coverage. People typically have deductibles of $100—and sometimes no deductible at all. Raise your deductible to $500 or even $1,000. Paying that extra deductible if you get into an accident is nothing compared to the extra protection you are getting by increasing your other coverage.

If your car is more than five years old, consider dropping collision and comprehensive altogether because even if you total it, all you will get back is its actual cash value (basically what a car dealer would pay you).

☞ **Wake-up Call:** Your auto insurance coverage is too important to trust to just anyone. Use an agent who has the initials CPCU (Chartered Property Casualty Underwriter) after his or her name, which indicates that he or she is experienced and knowledgeable. Even though you are young, a good agent will know that you can be a client for life, and that as your needs grow, your need for an agent will grow as well, so you can expect the same quality of service as someone twice your age. One hole in your auto insurance can literally bankrupt you.

Auto Insurance

Type of Coverage	Mandatory?	Recommended Amount	Characteristics		You May Not Need It If . . .
			What It Does	
Bodily injury to others	Yes	$250,000/person $500,000/accident	Covers medical bills for people injured by your car.		
Bodily injury caused by an uninsured auto	No	$250,000/person $500,000/accident	Covers your medical bills if the person who hit you is uninsured.		
Bodily injury caused by an underinsured auto	No	$250,000/person $500,000/accident	Covers your medical expenses if the person who hit you is underinsured.		
Optional bodily injury to others	Yes	$250,000/person $500,000/accident	Covers you if you are sued by the person you hit.		
Collision	No		Covers the cost of repairs if your car is damaged while it is moving.		The premiums you pay for the insurance cost more than 10% of the car's value.
Comprehensive	No		Covers the cost of repairs if your car is damaged while it's parked.		See above.
Property damage	Yes	$25,000/person $50,000/accident	Covers you if you damage someone's property or if you hit a car parked in a driveway.		

JUST IN CASE

■ Why You Need a Will (and Your Parents Need One, Too) ■

Even if you only own an old beat-up Honda, or a TV, VCR, and a stereo system, you need a will. Every adult needs a will, because everybody has assets. If you die without a will, your so-called "estate" will have to pass through probate court. (The same is true for your parents, so if they—like 60 percent of the American population—don't have a will, now is the time to urge them to get one.) Having a will makes the process much easier and saves loved ones enormous grief.

If you are like most people, you probably assume that your nearest living relative inherits your assets when you die. Unfortunately, it's not nearly that simple. Your insurance policies and retirement plans automatically go to the beneficiaries you've named. In addition, any trusts being held for you go to the beneficiaries named in the trust. But everything else that you own is part of "probate" property, meaning it has to pass through an elaborate legal process to be transferred from you to your loved ones. If you have a will, the language in that document controls who gets what. If you don't, the laws of the state legislature where you have legal residence determine who gets your assets. When James Dean died at twenty-four in a car accident, he did not have a will. As a result, his entire estate (including the legal rights to his likeness) automatically went to his only living relative, his father, who had abandoned James and his mother and whom James openly detested.

Wills can be simple several-paragraph declarations of your wishes, or a complicated book-length document that set up multiple trusts, trustees, and guardians. At this stage of the game, unless you have substantial assets, a one-pager may be all you need. If you have an attorney draft one, typically the charge for a simple will would be no more than a couple hundred dollars. You can use will-writing software, and I recommend Kiplinger's Home Legal Advisor or WillMaker, but it doesn't hurt to have your will reviewed by an attorney. And don't forget to have it properly signed by witnesses, according to the laws of your state.

You should also have a living will, health-care directive, and durable power of attorney. (See Chapter 3 for more details.) The number one killer of young adults under twenty-five is automobile accidents, and someone will have to make decisions about your health care if you are injured—these documents make this possible. These documents can also be obtained from a lawyer or through some of the will-writing software available that takes your state laws into account.

GROWING SEASON

"Money doesn't grow on trees" is probably one of those sayings you heard a few thousand too many times while you were growing up. You've probably also heard that money cannot buy happiness, but sometimes today's consumer-driven society makes us wonder if that statement still holds true. What's most important when it comes to money is expanding your knowledge as you go along. That way you'll be able to take advantage of every opportunity you see coming your way. In future chapters, you'll read about those unfortunate clients who weren't as savvy about money as you are today—just because they never bothered to pick up a personal finance book. Already you are ahead of them.

Of course it's true that money does not buy happiness, but the more money and the more knowledge you have, the more flexibility you have to take control of your own financial and personal destiny. That means being able to take a chance on a job at a small start-up company with huge prospects; or take time off to travel or to have children; or being able to buy that first house when an incredible deal comes along. The one saying that is always true is that "knowledge is power." The sooner you start to acquire that financial knowledge, the more financial power you will have.

✔ **Taking Root Checklist**

Signs that you are financially alert:
— I got a job that pays more than my "absolute minimum budget."
— I'm saving _____ % (ideal: 10%) of my take-home pay.
— I found out when I am eligible to contribute to my retirement plan and marked it on my calendar.
— I signed up for the company retirement plan at work.
— I opened an IRA.
— I wrote up a budget and usually stick with it.
— If I'm having trouble paying my student loan, I call the loan agency to make new payment arrangements.

__ I have an emergency fund equivalent to two or three months' worth of expenses.

__ I have a box to save my extra change. I'm looking forward to using it for _____.

__ Before I bought a new car, I calculated and compared the costs over two years of keeping and repairing my old one vs. buying a new one on credit.

__ I made sure I have adequate car insurance.

__ I have one credit card, and I pay my bills in full on time.

__ When I go to the mall, I only spend the cash I bring.

__ I wrote a will and had it reviewed by a lawyer and notarized.

__ I read one financial magazine or website this month.

3

Settling Down

If you are like most people, you have attended quite a few weddings in your lifetime, and some have a lot more personal meaning to you than others do. A couple of years ago I sat in a church pew and watched the wedding of friends whom I had known for ten years. Andrew and Donna are now in their late twenties, but they started dating in high school. They went to different colleges, broke up and reunited, got out of college, and were determined to live together in the same city. They both wanted to go to graduate school, so one went while the other worked long hours with a horrendous travel schedule in order to pay the bills—with the idea that when one graduated, the other would start. Money was always an issue because Andrew had family money and Donna did not, so they were used to different standards of living, but they were determined to work it out. About every six months I would get a call from one of them with some financial question, large or small—Is this too much to pay for an apartment? What kind of student loan should I take? Our old car just died, should we buy a used or new one? At one point they even had to live apart for a period of time, but their ultimate goal was marriage. Andrew and Donna were lucky because they found each other relatively early in life, so they knew what they were working for before most of us do—they wanted to settle down and make a life together. I just heard from them recently, and they are now contemplating their next step, which is buying a home.

Many of the wedding attendees, unaware of all that had preceded the wedding day, talked about how "lucky" the happy couple had been to find each other—it had certainly been "fate" that had brought them together. I am a great believer in fate, but over the years I had seen the effort these two had put into making each phase of their relationship work. I watched them learn how to live without, then with, and then without each other, while juggling careers and school. They argued over money (because each had such different money styles, and Donna didn't want to live off Andrew's income), and struggled through nights when important plans had to be canceled because one or the other had to stay late at work, or school, or had missed a plane.

At the end of the ceremony, as they passed my pew and walked down the aisle together as husband and wife, it all looked so easy. But life is never smooth sailing all the time (and for a lot of us, it is rarely smooth sailing), and usually there is some major struggle and soul-searching before we make big decisions like getting married or selecting a career (and if not, there should be!).

At some point, however, each and every one of us reaches that stage in life when we feel ready to make momentous decisions such as these. Sometimes it happens at twenty-five, sometimes at thirty, and sometimes at fifty.

How do you know when you have arrived at the "Settling Down" phase of your life? Ask yourself these questions:

- Do you love your work and find it easy to imagine yourself doing it for the rest of your life?
- Do you find yourself evaluating your current boyfriend or girlfriend as spouse or permanent partner material, and have you even been discussing marriage?
- Have you begun thinking about owning a place of your own (or is your CPA telling you that you are committing tax suicide by continuing to rent)?
- Are you thinking about starting a family?

If yes is your answer to even one of these questions, you may have reached the beginning of the "Settling Down" season of your life. In today's society, the term "settling down" does not mean that your youth has ended or you are getting old. What it does mean is that you've had

enough life experience to develop the confidence to make some big decisions, many of which can—and will—shape the course of the rest of
your life. This is an exciting time of transition, in which you are taking
on more responsibility, but it can also be terrifying as well. Even after all
their years together, and the absolute certainty that getting married was
the right thing to do, both Andrew and Donna had major cases of
"prewedding jitters." In fact, Donna was such a wreck that she did not
get one sentence right during the wedding rehearsal!

Financially, the "Settling Down" stage is a watershed, because it
probably feels as if you are finally "grown up!" A typical consumer
makes 1,000 significant financial decisions in his lifetime. Even if you've
made a few hundred already, you no doubt have the bulk and most important of them ahead of you. And just about any major life decision
you make during this season of your life will have profound implications not just for your financial bottom line, but for your happiness as
well.

☞ **Wake-up Call:** In this society we often create an artificial dichotomy between the romantic and the practical sides of life. For example, we marry for
love and devote months to planning a storybook wedding, yet rarely spend much
time discussing with our intended how we'll jointly manage our finances during
married life. I remember reading one study that ranked topics discussed by engaged couples in the year prior to their wedding. Out of ten topics, money was
dead last. In the first year after the marriage, it was the number one topic. That
is a sad commentary on romance vs. practicality because money should never be
the number one topic in a marriage—ever. But if it's completely ignored for too
long, it does become a primary issue when at last the couple is forced to "wake
up" and deal with it.

Nearly one of every two marriages ends in divorce, and nearly half of
those breakups are due to disputes over money. Similarly, many first-time
home buyers spend more time shopping for furniture than for a mortgage, even though the latter will probably do more to affect their comfort
in terms of their standard of living and even their day-to-day happiness
(because too high a mortgage can result in bitter arguments with a partner over cash flow) for the next 30 years. The reality is that in this season
of growth—and during the rest of your life—*happy endings depend on
smart beginnings*. And smart beginnings require considering—and planning for—the financial consequences of your choices.

It is so much more fun to be romantic than to be practical. The most
extreme but true example I can cite are my clients who fell in love with

the exterior of a home in a "hot" neighborhood. They sat in their broker's car and wrote out a check for a 10 percent ($25,000) down payment on a $250,000 home they had not even set foot in, because they loved the "front porch with all its ferns," and because they knew that four more couples were scheduled to see the house that day, and they did not want to get into a bidding war. They were even ready to sign a purchase and sales agreement (which is very hard to get out of) just to lock in ownership of their so-called dream home (which, by the way, needed a $20,000 roof job, a new kitchen, and was already over their budget). And this after months of my working with them on their financial planning!

My clients aside, most people are less inclined to act impulsively after working closely with a financial professional, which is why I think professional financial planning is a good idea when you begin to think seriously about settling down—and making major financial decisions.

Many people believe you only need financial planning if you are rich or you are over age fifty, but nothing could be further from the truth. I am not saying that you need a $3,000 financial plan—but I fervently believe that a $300 financial plan, or one you can do yourself with software such as Microsoft Money or Quicken (as we talked about in "Taking Root" on page 89, is the best investment you can make in yourself and your financial future. When I ask clients from twenty to fifty why they have not seen a financial planner before they came to me, a frequent response is that they did not feel that they were "grown-up" enough to need one. But we are all responsible for our own financial futures, even if we were born with silver spoons in our mouths. At the end of this chapter, I will give you advice on how to find a good financial planner for this—and any—season of your life.

CAREER

▪ Moving Up ▪

Remember the wedding I told you about at the beginning of this chapter? One of the most fascinating conversations at the reception was not about silver patterns but about jobs. A group of people between the ages of twenty-five and thirty-five were comparing notes about where they were in their careers. Their levels of happiness and apparent compensation were all over the map. John had gone to law school and found that he hated working for his big, prestigious law firm, but felt trapped by student loans. Frances had started as an entry-level assistant at a software company, but her career was on an upward path. Maria was frustrated because she felt that her talents were not being appreciated at her job, but she couldn't seem to get up the nerve to look for another one or to fight for advancement at her own company; she didn't have enough confidence in her own abilities. As the friends exchanged experiences and advice, I applauded the things they seemed to agree on: find work that makes you happy, and make sure you are adequately compensated. As a planner and as someone with twenty-five years of work experience and career decisions behind me, what pleased me about this conversation was that as it went on, each participant—even Maria—became more determined to take charge of their work instead of having their work take charge of their lives. They seemed to take inspiration from one another, and vowed to provide encouragement and support to each other—all they had to do was send an E-mail or pick up the phone.

Once you select a career, you'll have more and more job-related financial decisions to make. If you join a start-up company, for example, do stock options make up for a low salary? Should you make the maximum allowable contribution to your 401(k) plan? Does it make sense to switch jobs for a small pay increase?

The good news is that in 1997, 64 percent of working age people had jobs—an all-time high. Furthermore, most Americans got a pay raise that beat inflation. On the other hand, we seem to be working harder than ever. The proportion of professionals and managers who work more than forty-nine hours a week has risen by 73 percent since 1985, according to the Bureau of Labor Statistics.

Most of us focus first on our level of compensation. How does your salary compare to the national average, which was $26,156 in 1997? And how about your profession's average pay for someone with your amount of expertise? Usually, an organization of professionals in your field can give you data that will help you compare your income with national averages.

As you move along in your career, you'll often find that you have to be your own best advocate when it comes to getting pay increases. But don't despair: A recent survey found that nearly 65 percent of companies say that job candidates have the advantage in salary negotiations. Don't be afraid to ask for an increase that you feel you deserve.

To prepare for the time when you ask for a raise, keep a running document recording each time you add value to your company or organization, either by bringing in new business, keeping clients happy, improving organizational procedures, managing difficult people, or whatever fits your situation. Don't be too shy to showcase your talents at salary review time. Make it clear that you are anxious to take on new projects and become more and more valuable to the company by cross-training for other jobs in case of an emergency or if someone leaves.

One thing you should never do is threaten to leave your job—unless you are sure you plan to follow through with it. Brad had a new baby and a wife who had quit her job to stay home full-time, but he used this tactic to try to get a higher salary, and it failed. It took him six months to find a new job, and in the meantime they had to deplete all of their savings just to make ends meet.

It can be very difficult to stay calm and emotionless throughout your performance review and any salary negotiations. I have one dear friend who cries easily. I keep reminding her that crying can be a purely physical response and not a sign of professional weakness. But sometimes the tiniest criticism puts her in tears, which she finds humiliating. If you have this problem, visualize in advance the worst potential criticisms you might receive and how you will respond to them. My friend found that this reduces the "crying factor" enormously—she is not caught off guard and has plenty of ammunition to gracefully fire back, or she accepts it calmly and explains how she will change her behavior. This is not just a "woman problem;" I know several men who have the same physical response, and it is even more embarrassing for them.

☞ **Wake-up Call:** Remember that some employers never *offer* a pay raise; they wait for an employee to request one. Be prepared for this possibility and do your homework. Practice what you will say and how much you will ask for. Always ask for more than you think you can get; you may be pleasantly surprised, and if your boss is the kind who never offers a raise, he may also be the kind of person who always feels compelled to negotiate down from whatever the employee asks.

If you are offered a better paying job, don't forget to factor in other expenses that may come along with your new position. If you have to relocate, for instance, who will pay your moving expenses? How do living costs in the new location compare to your current costs? If you are being offered a 20 percent increase in a town where costs are 35 percent higher, you had better think twice—or ask for an even higher salary. The opposite can be true as well—I know someone who moved from New York City to a much smaller city in the midwest and automatically expected to be paid the same amount she was receiving at her high-paying executive job. It took blank stares from two to three prospective employers when she started talking money before she realized that she needed to adjust her expectations to the local economy. A little research in the library and at the Chamber of Commerce gave her a better idea of the compensation package she should be looking for. And she still came out ahead because the cost of living was lower in her new city.

Another formula that I recommend to my clients is to figure out the dollar amount of your raise or potential increase and then multiply it by a factor of 0.6. This takes taxes into account and shows you what your net annual increase will be in your paycheck. You can then divide that by twelve if you are paid monthly, twenty-four if you are paid twice a month, etc. Sometimes the results are a bit disappointing because that huge raise gets whittled down by Uncle Sam and Social Security, but keep the big picture in mind and realize that you must have done a good job to have earned a raise at all.

▪ Finding and Cultivating a Mentor ▪

These days, the word "mentor" is a common part of the lexicon of business words, but when I started out in the working world in 1974, the only female in a sea of male faces at every conference, I did not know what a mentor was. I desperately could have used career advice in negotiating raises, planning a career strategy, and dealing with difficult situations at work (like the time a female secretary openly resented me because I was a woman in a higher position). A lot of the mistakes I made in the first couple of years at work could have been avoided if I had had someone to turn to for advice.

But you can't just count on someone to look out for you; you need to find and cultivate a mentor yourself. And you don't have to limit yourself to just one. The best mentor for you is someone who is at a much higher level than you in your organization, whom you admire and who has the power to help you advance in your career at that company. Of course, your mentor may take a new job, then see an opportunity for you at their new company as well. Your relationship with your mentor can last a lifetime.

How do you cultivate a mentor? Julio, who is in his early thirties and works for a software company, put it best: "Treat your mentor with the utmost respect and keep all conversations between you absolutely confidential. Ask advice where appropriate, but do not gossip or whine about unimportant matters." When you see a job that may be opening up at your company, get your mentor's advice about whether it is a smart career move for you to apply for it. If your mentor is powerful enough, he may already know that the job has been unofficially filled, but that it had to be posted for all employees due to company regulations. In that case, why let your current boss know that you want to move on when you don't have to?

☞ **Wake-up Call:** It is not appropriate for you to shower your mentor with gifts. However, a small thank-you gift at holiday time or after your mentor has helped you in some particularly important way is just fine, as is taking her out to lunch occasionally.

■ Employer-Sponsored Retirement Plans ■

Companies are not required to have retirement plans, and in 1998 only 50 percent of the nation's employees were covered by one. So if you are fortunate enough to work for a company that offers the option of participating in a retirement plan, find out when you are eligible and write the date in big red letters on your calendar. Sign up the minute you can.

Twenty-five years ago, 75 percent of retirement plans were fully funded by the employer and were not dependent upon the vagaries of the stock market—they were based upon what your income was during your work career, with heavier emphasis on your last few years of earnings before retirement. Employees were not expected to contribute to their retirement plans at all. How times have changed!

These days, retirement plans come in many varieties: Some accept employee contributions, and others do not. With some plans, the employer pays. With others, you pay. With matching plans, the employer will match a certain percentage of what you put in.

These plans come in several basic types (which are described below), but they can be called just about anything, which sometimes caused confusion. Some of the names I've come across are "retirement savings program," "pension savings plan," and "save and invest plan." Regardless of the name, your employer is required to give you a document that explains in straightforward language all the basic information you need to know about your plan, including how it is set up, how the money is invested, and what contributions will be made on your behalf. If you feel you are not being given all of the information you are entitled to, you should ask for it from your company, and if you still can't get it, contact the Department of Labor.

Here is a list of the most common types of plans:

Pension Plans

In the past, pension plans were the standard way in which employers provided retirement income for their employees. They are set up and funded by employers and generate a monthly income for employees upon retirement. The company takes full responsibility for investing the money. Typically, before you are given entry into the plan, you have to work at a company a certain number of years, generally one or two, and fulfill a few basic requirements such as working a certain number of hours per week. Voluntary contributions by employees are not allowed.

The amount of money contributed each year to your pension plan depends on the type of plan and your income. A defined benefit plan is set up to provide you with a certain percentage of your annual income, such as 50 percent of your salary (usually calculated by taking your average salary during the last three to five years before retirement). For instance, if your average annual salary before retirement was $60,000 and the plan guarantees 50 percent, your annual retirement benefit would be $30,000. Most annual pension plan statements give the value of the pension in terms of monthly income at retirement.

Defined contribution plans base your retirement benefits on how much money is actually contributed to the plan, not on your annual income. Your employer sets aside a certain percentage of your income every year, subject to certain limitations. A defined contribution statement usually gives two estimates—the amount of annual income at retirement, and the total lump sum that would be available if you decided to take it all out at once. Don't get confused and think you get both amounts!

One benefit of any type of pension plan is that company contributions must be made even in unprofitable years, unless the company petitions the Internal Revenue Service and receives permission to skip or reduce its annual contribution. This is why profit-sharing and other more flexible plans have become so much more popular over the years.

Profit-Sharing Plans

In this type of plan, each year the employer decides how much to contribute to the fund. For example, one year the employer may kick in 6 percent of each employee's income, 2 percent the next year, and none the following year. The same percentage is contributed for each employee, regardless of compensation level. Sometimes profit-sharing plans are offered in addition to 401(k) and/or pensions.

☞ **Wake-up Call:** If a profit-sharing plan is the only one available for a job you are considering, think twice before you take the position—you may go for years without receiving any contributions. Find out the percentage that has been contributed in each of the last five years for a clue to your future benefits.

401(k) Plans

Unlike the previously described retirement programs, 401(k)s are partially or fully funded by employees, who also take all of the responsibility for investing the money. These plans have become increasingly popular over the last decade, growing from 30,000 plans in 1985 to 150,000 in 1995.

Contributions to these plans are tax-deductible and free from state and federal taxes (but you still have to pay Social Security taxes). In 1998, you were allowed to save the lesser of two figures: 25 percent of your income or $10,000, and this amount will increase each year. Some companies contribute even if an employee doesn't. Others match employee contributions dollar-for-dollar up to a set limit. Still others are funded entirely by employee contributions.

Typically, participants in 401(k) plans must select from several investment options. Usually you can choose among a number of mutual and money market funds, which vary widely in their degree of risk. (If you need to make selections for a 401(k), see the section on investing in Chapter 4, page 180). Until a couple of years ago, companies couldn't give anything even remotely resembling "investment advice" to their employees. However, under today's Labor Department guidelines, companies can provide their 401(k) participants with three categories of information. They are:

- General financial and investment information with no direct relationship to investment alternatives available to participants
- Materials to help employees relate hypothetical investment advice to their financial situations
- Interactive information that allows employees to design their own asset-allocation models

Should You Borrow from Your 401(k)?

The more money you put into your 401(k), the more likely you are going to want to take it out at some point before retirement—perhaps for a down payment on a new home, to buy a new car, or to pay for your own or your children's college education. Clients ask me all the time, "Is this a good idea?"

First of all, find out if your plan allows employees to take out loans; not all plans do. If it is an option, usually you will be able to borrow 50 percent of your account balance, or $50,000, which is less. You'll have five years to pay the money back, and the interest you pay must be considered "reasonable," typically the prime rate plus 1 or 2 percent. If the prime rate is, 6 percent, for instance, your interest rate might be 7.5 percent.

Borrowing money from your 401(k) is certainly preferable to taking the money out as a regular distribution before you reach retirement age. In that case you would have to pay income taxes plus a 10 percent penalty. Some people think that borrowing from your retirement plan is the same as taking money out of your savings account and then paying it back. But the reality is that you do have to pay interest. Furthermore, the interest is not tax deductible, as it is with a mortgage or home equity loan, so you should definitely consider those sources first.

The drawback is that if you leave your job for any reason (get laid off, take another job, or retire, etc.) when you still have a loan out-standing, most plans require you to immediately repay the balance. If you don't have the money on hand, your options are to borrow it from somewhere else, probably at higher interest rates, to take it out of sav-ings earmarked for other uses, or to take that amount out of your 401(k) as a regular distribution—which means taxes and the penalty kick in. So find out what your plan requires if you take a loan and then leave the company unexpectedly—just in case.

403(b) Plans
Similar to 401(k)s, these plans are offered by nonprofit organizations to their employees. They are often called tax-sheltered annuities because that was the original type of investment used. Employees are allowed to contribute up to $9,500 or 20 percent of their salary each year, depend-ing on a number of factors. (Some veteran employees may be able to contribute more.)

Vesting
Companies have time requirements that you must fulfill before you are fully *vested* in the money that your company has put into your plan. This means you are entitled to take the company's contribution with you if you leave the company, or you are entitled to a monthly benefit when you retire. This is a vast improvement over years past, however, when people had to work twenty years at a company before they were

entitled to any of the money in their retirement plan. In those days, it was not uncommon for an employee to work for eighteen or nineteen years and then get fired, leaving him without any rights to his pension. To prevent such abuses, laws now guarantee that an employee must get at least some portion of his employer's contributions after three years of employment.

SEPs

Congress created the Simplified Employee Pension Plan to cut through the complex IRS reporting requirements that prevented many companies from establishing other types of retirement plans. Companies who set up a SEP are not obligated to begin coverage for employees until they work for three years. Employer contributions are not required, but they can be as high as 25 percent of your taxable salary, or up to $30,000. Employees (except employee-owners) cannot contribute to a SEP, but once they are eligible to participate, they are fully vested.

SIMPLEs

The Simplified Incentive Match Plan for Employees, or SIMPLE, also was created by Congress. This type of plan is designed for employers with fewer than one hundred workers. Unlike other plans that limit your contribution to a percentage of your income, with a SIMPLE you can contribute up to $6,000 or 100 percent of your income, whichever is less.

The best place to invest your money is through your company retirement plan or an IRA (Individual Retirement Account) because it is tax-sheltered. The problem is that there is real discrimination against lower paid workers when it comes to access to a 401(k). For example, in 1993, 70 percent of the 2.2 million workers earning over $75,000 had access to a 401(k) plan, but only 10 percent of the fifteen million workers earning under $10,000 could put money in such a plan. IRA plans have been available for quite some time, but until the laws changed starting in 1998, very few people took advantage of them. For example, only 3 percent of the sixty-eight million Americans with incomes under $30,000 in 1995 had opened IRA's.

The good news is that the Roth IRA, introduced in January of 1998, has fueled interest in IRAs in general. In fact, in the first quarter of 1998, Fidelity reported that more people had put money into IRA plans than in *all* of 1997!

How Much Can You Contribute to Your Retirement Plan?

You may be able to contribute to more than one of these plans in the same year.

	Who Can Contribute	Employee Contribution Limits
401(k)	Employer and employee	15% of earned income up to $10,000
403(b)	Employer and employee	3 possible formulas, but generally the lesser of $10,000 or 25% of earned income
Keogh	Employer and employee	The lesser of 25% of earned income or $30,000
SEP	Employer and employee	The lesser of 15% of earned income or $30,000
Simple IRA and Simple 401(k)	Employer and employee	The lesser of $6000 or 100% of earned income
Traditional or Roth IRA	Any individual with an income	The lesser of $2000 or 100% of earned income

Is the Roth or the Traditional IRA Right for You?

If you want to invest money outside of your retirement plan at work, you have two options: the traditional IRA and the new Roth IRA. Each offers different advantages to investors.

The tax laws changed in 1997 to increase the income limits for contributing to a tax-deductible IRA, making it possible to contribute $2,000 to an IRA if you are a nonworking spouse. The new laws also state that you can contribute to a Roth IRA if your income is too high for a traditional IRA, or if you simply choose a Roth instead. In 1999, you can make a traditional IRA deduction of $2,000 if you are single and your income is $31,000 or less, or $51,000 or less if you are married filing jointly. With both plans, all earnings and appreciation of the accounts grow without taxes being taken out each year.

The Roth IRA differs from the traditional IRA in one key way: You pay your taxes *before* you put your money in, so the money is tax-free at retirement. With the traditional tax-deductible IRA, you get to deduct your contribution now, but everything is taxable at retirement.

Most people are eligible for the Roth, even those who make too much to qualify for a traditional IRA. If you are single or the head of a household, your adjusted gross income can be as much as $95,000. If you are married filing jointly, your adjusted gross income can be as much as $150,000. If you are participating in another retirement plan, you can still make a $2,000 contribution to a Roth. If you are a non-working spouse, you also can make a $2,000 contribution. (The amount you can contribute is phased out if your income is over these amounts.)

Contributions are limited to $2,000 each year per person. You can also move your existing traditional IRA into a Roth IRA account in any year in which your adjusted gross income (not including the rollover amount) is under $100,000. The catch is that you must pay income tax on the full amount of the rollover in the year you do so. All growth and earnings in subsequent years are tax-free, however, because they are now protected in a Roth IRA.

The advantages of a Roth over a traditional IRA are:
- Income tax-free withdrawals after age fifty-nine and one-half
- Income tax-free benefits to your heirs at death
- You can keep making contributions after age 70 ½ if you are working
- You never have to take distributions at retirement; the money can just sit there and accumulate for your heirs

The disadvantages are:
- You can't take a tax deduction each year on your contributions
- Tax laws are constantly changing and the Roth tax-free provisions may be changed later, just as the taxation of Social Security benefits did (which was added after years of promises that they would never be taxed)

You should choose a Roth over a tax-deductible IRA:
- If your tax bracket is 15 percent now (in 1998, if your income is less than $25,350 for singles and $42,350 if you are married filing jointly
- If you expect to be in a higher tax bracket at retirement
- If you expect an inheritance or other windfall so you will have much more income later in life
- If you never expect to touch the money, so it will go income-tax-free to your heirs

☞ **Wake-up Call:** Run the numbers before you make a decision. Visit the MoneyCentral.com website for a Roth calculator.

LOVE

■ Morals Aside: Marriage Versus Living Together ■

The term "living together" is emotionally charged for lots of reasons. For one thing, it raises its own moral and religious issues, which are extremely personal. Still, it is common enough that clients frequently ask me about its financial implications: Over half of couples who eventually marry live together first. My first question is always, "What kind of living together are you talking about? Is this someone you are serious about and see as a potential spouse or life partner, or someone who would be fun to live with for another year, or a chance to see whether you can stand to be around each other day-to-day before you make a bigger commitment?" It is rarely a decision that is made lightly. And I do understand why some people are gun-shy about getting married—between 1966 and 1977, the divorce rate doubled, and 40 percent of today's young adults lived with a single parent by the time they were age sixteen. That's a far cry from the sitcom family of the 1950s.

Looking at it from an entirely economic point of view, there are lots of advantages to living with someone else, whether you are married or not. Obviously, you will only have one set of housing expenses (rent, utilities, etc.) instead of two, which is always a plus.

Generally, if people move in together without plans to get married, it is probably wise to keep separate checking accounts and simply split all the bills (rent, food, etc.). Then, if you break up and one person moves out, neither one owes the other money. As I talked about in "Taking Root" (Chapter 2), no matter whom you are living with, always make sure that both names are on the lease and on all utility bills. But if you do plan to get married, this is a great trial period for trying to manage your money together. This will save a lot of emotional negotiations and pain your first year of marriage.

If, for whatever reason, you plan on living permanently with someone but not marrying, only you can decide whether you should combine your money. In my professional experience, I have found that in the early years of living together, most couples keep their money separate and split the household expenses. After a couple of years, things tend to loosen up. But be sure to check the laws in your state, because in many states if you live together for a certain period of time, you are said to have a "common law marriage" and are considered legally married.

☞ **Wake-up Call:** If you are not married and buy a home together, make sure that each of you owns enough insurance on your partner's life to pay off his or her share (or all) of the mortgage in case of death. Otherwise, you may end up owning the entire house, but if you have unmanageable mortgage payments you'll have to sell it. And a precohabitation agreement (similar to a prenuptial agreement), which specifies how you will divide your property if you split up, is a terrific idea—one that I recommend to every couple who plans to live together without getting married in the near future.

■ Wedding Bill Blues ■

In my day, kids got out of college and were married by the end of the summer after graduation—perhaps at ages twenty-one or twenty-two. Now, the average age at which Generation Xers marry is twenty-eight. I don't know whether this means marriages last longer, but I do know from working with young clients that they are much more realistic about the problems they will face in the future. They recognize the importance of trying to meet their goals, and of working with each other to reconcile differences in the way they manage money. All of these are good signs. The problem is that too many marriages start off on the wrong foot because of the day they began—the wedding day.

Today, the average wedding costs over $17,000. If that doesn't give you cold feet, you must be in love! But with good planning, there is no reason why your wedding should cost that much, unless you want it to.

A wedding should be one of the happiest occasions of your life. But don't plan one without regard for the cost. Paying the bills shouldn't ruin you—or your parents or in-laws, for that matter, if they are footing the bill. The key is to set a budget up front, otherwise the spending gets out of control all too easily. It's easy to see how it happens: You set a $1,000 limit on a wedding dress, but when you try on a $3,000 one at the bridal store, it makes you look like a Hollywood star. Or you try to keep the cost per guest for the caterer at $30, but then you taste a caterer's food that is twice as expensive and think, "This is the most special day in our lives. Why not have the best food?" I attended one wedding that ended up costing $75,000, which meant both the bride and groom had to dip into their 401(k) plans to pay for it. It was a wonderful day, but every quarter thereafter when they got their plan statements, they wondered whether all the extra expense was worth it.

To help you keep within a reasonable budget, consider the spreads in national bridal magazines as "fantasy weddings" (they tend to hype the most expensive and lavish options) and rely on regional bridal magazines for more realistic suggestions. An added bonus is that they will have a list of local reception sites, caterers, musicians, and other services. Also ask friends for referrals. You can save big-time on reception costs by using the church or synagogue hall, or a friend's home, and having it decorated with beautiful flowers. Another way to trim wedding costs is to hire a disc jockey rather than a live band. If you must have live music, hire a duo or trio instead of a dance band. Flowers can be expensive, too. For a friend's wedding, her parents bought plants instead of cut flowers and planted them outside their Cape Cod house after the wedding. They are still thriving 14 years later—and are a nice memory of the day.

☞ **Wake-up Call:** Talk to both sets of parents ASAP and clarify who will be paying for what. Remember that different areas of the country have different wedding customs: for example, weddings in New England traditionally include a sit-down dinner, while those in the South may only involve hors d'oeuvres.

One of the great things about bridal magazines is that they have checklists of things you need to remember to do. I know of one couple who tried so hard to cut costs that they forgot quite a few of the essentials. The problem was that the wedding was in another state. The future parents-in-law had never met, and had planned to spend a few leisurely days getting to know each other. Instead, they spent their time frantically running around trying to rent tables, chairs, tablecloths, silverware, and plates—and making sure they were delivered on time! I guess it was a bonding experience, but not one that I would choose for my family.

■ **Sharing the Wealth** ■

After the wedding, one of the best ways to build a strong marriage is to share the financial responsibilities. Yet surveys show that this is often not the case. A Microsoft Money Survey found that only 14 percent of couples surveyed share the responsibility for day-to-day and long term financial planning. Over 60 percent of the women were responsible for long-term planning; over 75 percent were responsible for day-to-day decisions.

If you are already married, check out the following chart, "Who Handles the Money Now?" to see how well you share the responsibilities. If it turns out that one partner does substantially more than the other, use the next chart, "Who Will Handle the Money from Now On" to discuss how to divide up the money-related tasks more evenly. If you are about to get married, use these charts to help you plan ahead.

To give your marriage a better chance of survival, make discussing money with your spouse one of your priorities. Americans only spend an average of *three and a half hours every month* discussing financial issues with their partners—compared with an average of *six hours a day* watching TV!

Make a weekly date (preferably the same time each week) to sit down together at the kitchen table and talk about what money came in, what went out, and where it went. That way neither one of you will be surprised by a zinger (such as a big luxury purchase or unexpected bill) the other one "forgot" to mention.

For example, two of my clients, Carey and Dennis, ended up springing a big bill on the other—that neither one thought would be a problem because of their emergency fund. But the problem was that both bills needed to be paid at once. The plumber had come to look at the furnace and told Carey that it was on its last legs and needed to be replaced at a cost of about $3,000. At the same time, Dennis had taken the car into the shop and then found out that the transmission and brake jobs were going to be about $2,000. Each spouse was stunned at not being told by the other, but their schedules were so busy they had barely seen each other to talk about weekend plans, much less furnaces and auto repair bills. They realized that if they had not sat down to talk, each would have written a check and their account would have been severely overdrawn, with major bank fees and even more major embarrassment. At the end of each weekly meeting, discuss how you are doing in terms of your saving goals, and talk about anything you think needs adjusting in the coming weeks or months.

Love is a many-splendored thing, but just one overspender can ruin a marriage. If you are having disagreements about how either you or your spouse is spending money, try my "No-Argument Plan," with which I have helped countless couples stop picking on each other—and a few stop threatening each other with divorce. The only tools you need are three checking accounts—a joint one and one for each of you. Use the joint account as the place where you deposit all of your income. It is also the account you should use to pay for household expenses, debt pay-

Who Handles the Money Now?

Task	(Name)	(Name)	Both	Nobody
Opens bills				
Sorts or piles up bills				
Pays bills				
Collects bank statements				
Records checks in register				
Balances own checking account				
Balances joint checking account				
Researches investments				
Makes investment decisions				
Reviews monthly spending results				
Reviews yearly spending results				
Makes homeowners insurance decisions				
Makes car insurance decisions				
Deals with insurance agent				
Deals with estate planning lawyer				
Gives children allowance				
Makes children's financial decisions				
Initiates major financial decisions				
Plans ahead for purchases				
Tax planning/deals with CPA				

Who Will Handle the Money from Now On?

Task	(Name)	(Name)	Both	Nobody
Opens bills				
Sorts or piles up bills				
Pays bills				
Collects bank statements				
Records checks in register				
Balances own checking account				
Balances joint checking account				
Researches investments				
Makes investment decisions				
Reviews monthly spending results				
Reviews yearly spending results				
Makes homeowners insurance decisions				
Makes car insurance decisions				
Deals with insurance agent				
Deals with estate planning lawyer				
Gives children allowance				
Makes children's financial decisions				
Initiates major financial decisions				
Plans ahead for purchases				
Tax planning/deals with CPA				

ments, and savings. Every month deduct a personal allowance for you and your spouse. (Usually it makes sense for them to be the same amount, but that may vary depending on your situation.) That allowance is then yours alone; spend it as you see fit. If you want to indulge in a massage or a night out with your friends, feel free. But don't forget, the same is true for your spouse. He or she can spend that money however it pleases him or her, no questions asked, no derogatory comments allowed. Period.

■ Deciding to Stay Single ■

One of the good things about the changes in our society over the last twenty years is that there is no longer any stigma attached to staying single. You don't get pressured into marrying too early in life or to the wrong person, or at all if you don't want to. But that means that your financial responsibilities are totally your own; you don't have someone else's income to fall back on if necessary. It also means that you can't count on a partner or spouse to write those checks to pay the bills, help you make investment decisions, or know all about money so that you don't need to know anything.

A friend of mine who is a television producer in New York tells me that this is the only drawback she sees to being single. Anna's life and schedule are so unpredictable and crazed that she says she does not have time to take care of her financial matters—so bills go unpaid, 401(k) money sits in money market accounts, she neglects to refinance her mortgage at a 3 percent lower rate when it is available, and so on. She asks for my advice, so I reminded her that she was able to find time to go out to dinner at least three or more times a week and also considered herself a real movie buff. I suggested that although she did have a tight schedule, the issue may be less about time and more that she was not interested in dealing with her money, or had an aversion to it. This was a real eye-opener for her, and she thought about it over the next few weeks.

When we met again on my next trip to New York, she told me I was absolutely right and that she realized she hated dealing with money. "Let's face it," she said, "I'm as creative as it comes when putting together a sitcom, but a total loser when it comes to money. If only I had a husband or partner who could deal with this for me." We both laughed and agreed that was not a good enough reason to get married, but I told her that she needed a bookkeeper and a good financial planner in New

The No-Argument Plan

_____'s
MONTHLY TAKE-
HOME INCOME
$ _____

_____'s
MONTHLY TAKE-
HOME INCOME
$ _____

JOINT CHECKING ACCOUNT
HOUSEHOLD EXPENSES/DEBT
PAYMENTS/SAVINGS
$ _____

_____'s
PERSONAL
ALLOWANCE
$ _____

_____'s
PERSONAL
ALLOWANCE
$ _____

Personal allowances are just that—you can spend it on whatever you want, and you do not have to account for it to your spouse.

York. The lesson is that when you are living on your own, it is easy to postpone making financial decisions and taking action, because you are not accountable to anyone except yourself. So build some accountability into your life—and you may actually find that you enjoy having control over your money.

☞ **Wake-up Call:** If you are single, pick another single friend who you think is probably a good match for you in helping to address each other's financial issues. When you do have those dinners out several times a week (or even better and cheaper, when you eat at home) make one weekly dinner with your friend to review what has happened financially in the last week and what you have to do in the upcoming few weeks. Just having moral support may launch you on your own path to financial independence. After all, you have decided to remain socially independent, so why sabotage yourself by not having the financial independence to match?

■ Wills and Living Wills ■

If you do not already have a will, now is the time to write one. We talked about it in the last chapter, "Taking Root," but now, with added responsibilities, you have even more reason to have one in place. If you have one you wrote before you were married, you should update it to reflect your new status.

A will is even more important as your family grows. If you don't have a will and you have children, you won't have any control over the way your assets are divided up. If you are married with children, for instance, you probably want your spouse to get all of your assets so he can provide for himself or herself and your kids. But without a will, your spouse will get only a third of your assets, while an individual named by the probate court (typically a lawyer) to represent the interests of your children will control the rest. That can make life very difficult for the surviving spouse, who may have to petition the court to use some of your money to pay bills and provide necessities. If you are single and have a child, your offspring may only get half of your assets; the rest may go to your siblings or your parents.

You can also use your will to bequeath real estate, antiques, family heirlooms, or items of sentimental value to the individuals or charitable organizations you choose. You can even provide for the care of your pets, with any money left over once your beloved animal dies going to the next beneficiary in line.

Wills can be designed to guard against the personal flaws of your loved ones. Perhaps you want to give your spendthrift daughter a fixed amount of money each year. Or you might give your nieces and nephews control of their assets in stages. For example, the first one-half of their inheritance becomes available at age twenty with the remainder available in equal disbursements at ages thirty and forty. Usually goals like these are accomplished by using a will to set up trusts. (For more information on trusts, see Chapter 6.)

While you can still change your will, you should be sure to discuss your intentions for the trust with your heirs and hear their feedback. Otherwise, your heirs may abuse the fund and circumvent your wishes. For example, the son of the founder of a successful manufacturing company was left a substantial trust that would pay him a fixed annual amount—except in the event that he got married. In that case, the trust stipulated that it would give him a wedding gift of $250,000—so he married thirteen times!

A will is also the document in which you can name a guardian or guardians for your children in case both parents die. Otherwise the court will decide their fate. You also name the executor of your will, who should be someone you can trust to shepherd your assets through the probate process, and help your beneficiaries with the other aspects of your estate, such as insurance policies and retirement accounts.

Finally, a will can also be used to express your last wishes, and to put conditions on inheritances. I've seen some wills that require spouses to forfeit their inheritances if they remarry, and others that, in a very loving tone, encourage a spouse to remarry. You can disinherit a relative who might otherwise be entitled to part of your estate, such as the spouse of a deceased child, preferring to leave the money to your grandchildren instead. No state, however, allows you to disinherit your spouse. (Prenuptial agreements, which we will talk about in Chapter 5, "Fresh Starts," are a way around this.)

Whatever your will says, make sure to have it reviewed by a lawyer and notarized as well.

■ Living Wills ■

Living wills also are important once you are married, because in the event that you are ever struck with a life-threatening illness or injury, your spouse will not have to agonize over how you would like your health care to be handled at the same time he or she is struggling with profound grief.

It's rare to die peacefully at home these days. You are far more likely to die in a health-care facility, where you will be subjected to all the benefits and drawbacks that attend the latest medical advances. On the one hand, you may live longer; on the other hand, you may not wish to be subjected to a great deal of expensive and emotionally draining medical intervention. To exercise some control over the kind of care you receive, and to save your relatives the agony of trying to decide what you would have wanted, it is best to state your wishes clearly in three important documents *before* an emergency strikes.

The first two documents—the living will and the health-care proxy—together are called our *health care directive.* The living will states under what conditions you are to be kept alive. Some simply state that you don't want extraordinary measures used if you are likely to die within a few days or will be permanently unconscious. Other versions offer more detailed instructions about specific aspects of care. You can also include your preference about organ donation. In some states you are required to sign a living will, also known as a "health-care proxy" or "declaration of intentions," when you check into a hospital. This relieves a hospital of legal responsibility for terminating care at your request.

In 1998, a new living will form that is valid in most states was created. Called "Five Wishes," it can be downloaded from Aging with Dignity's website (www.agingwithdignity.org) or send four dollars for postage and handling to Aging with Dignity, P.O. Box 1661, Tallahassee FL 32302-1661.

The second piece of the health care directive is the *health care power of attorney,* also known as the "health care proxy." The power of attorney allows you to select someone to make critical medical decisions on your behalf in the event that you cannot make them for yourself. It can cover either all matters or specific issues such as permission to operate.

The third document, *the durable power of attorney,* turns over financial decisions to someone you appoint in the event that you become mentally incapacitated but are not dying. It may help your relatives avoid unpleasant legal battles over who is responsible for your affairs, which unfortunately is a common occurrence. You can give "your agent" power over as many financial decisions as you desire, including signing checks, handling your taxes, and managing your assets. I recommend making it as broad as possible. If you recover your mental abilities later on, the durable power of attorney will no longer be in effect.

It's unpleasant to think about needing any of these documents. But it's far worse to imagine your loved ones agonizing over decisions about your care because they never had any indication of your thoughts on these matters. With these three documents, you have a far greater chance of having your wishes carried out, and you will save your family a great deal of additional and avoidable emotional pain.

HOUSING

■ Renting Versus Buying ■

One young couple I know pays more for rent than most people pay for mortgages. When it came time to sign another year's lease, they struggled with whether they should buy a condominium so they could begin to build up equity. After thinking it over, they decided to hold off on buying anything for another year. The reason: The young man was starting a new business, and he wasn't sure exactly when it would be up and running, or in what city his office would be based. Based on their situation, it made financial sense to wait on buying a home.

Owning your own home is part of the American dream. But it may not be the right thing for your future, depending on your circumstances. When does it make sense to keep renting instead of buying a home or condominium? When does it make sense to buy?

When housing prices are going up, real estate looks like a good investment, particularly if you are spending more than 25 percent of your before-tax income on rent. Some people get afraid and say, "If I don't get into the housing market now, I never will, because the prices will go up faster than I can afford to buy." But this is usually not true over the long run.

The most important factor to consider when you are thinking about buying is how long you expect to stay in one general area. You should not buy a house unless you expect to live in it for at least five years. This is because it takes an average of four years to recoup your moving and closing costs. Other extra costs include real estate taxes, higher insurance, and maintenance costs on a house or condominium that you would generally avoid on a rental. You also lose the investment return on whatever down payment you put into the house, and when you sell it, you usually have to pay a broker's commission of 5 or 6 percent. So, to come out even, you need to count on selling for perhaps 15 percent more than you paid for it. For example, if you buy a house for $250,000, you would have to sell it for at least $287,500 to break even.

If you are investing during a period of price increases, such as we had during the spring of '98 or during the early 1980s, and you try to sell too soon, you risk selling at a time after the market has peaked. In the end of the 1980s, many people who wanted to sell could not find buyers at all or could only find buyers who would pay less than their mortgage, which meant the sellers would have to come up with cash to sell their houses. One couple I had as clients wanted to sell their house for $175,000, but had a mortgage of $200,000: They had to come up with another $25,000 to pay off the mortgage so they could get those payments off their backs.

During the last five years of the 1980s, over two million homes were foreclosed on (ownership was taken over) by mortgage lenders. That translates into more than two million home owners losing their down payments and all the equity they had in their homes, not to mention adding a black mark to their credit reports for at least seven years.

So, you may want to continue renting if:

- You cannot afford the kind of home you want because you don't have a large enough down payment or because you can't qualify for a large enough mortgage. The way to find out is to go to a bank and ask to be prequalified for a mortgage. A loan officer will tell you how much you can afford to pay. You can even check out moneyinsider.com, fanniemae.com, or bankrate.com to figure it out using a standard formula.
- You need your down payment money for something else important, such as graduate school tuition for yourself or your spouse. Don't even assume you can buy a house and then borrow on your down payment through a home equity loan in the next few years. Reason: If the value of your house decreases, you probably won't find a bank that will give you a home equity loan. Reputable banks will only allow total mortgages of 80 percent of the fair market value of your home.
- You enjoy renting and do not want the hassle of house maintenance or paying a condominium fee every month.
- Your job or your spouse's job is unstable. You can always move to a less expensive apartment, but you can't reduce your mortgage payments and real estate taxes just because you lost your job.
- The urge to buy is based on something you don't like about your current rental house or apartment. You can always look for another one.

☞ **Wake-up Call:** The old rule of thumb, that you should buy a house as soon as you can, and buy as much as you can afford doesn't hold true anymore. More than anything else, a house is a place to live. Even though it certainly can be a valuable asset, it is better not to think of a house as an investment, at least one that can easily be bought and sold. Why? Because you just can't assume that housing prices are going to go up and that you will find a buyer when you need one. And you may decide to live in it forever, too.

■ Jumping In ■

Purchasing a home may be the single biggest financial decision you make. If you are scared by the magnitude of the decision, take courage from the fact that millions of average Americans have done it and survived—most of them more than once. Two big advantages to owning a home are that you build up equity as you pay off your mortgage, and you qualify for significant tax breaks.

Once you decide to take the plunge into ownership, the next question usually is how big a house can you handle? You can answer that by determining how much money you have for a down payment and how large a mortgage you can afford.

First, let's look at your down payment. Twenty percent of the purchase price is considered the standard. But the required amount depends on the mortgage program you use. Some lenders allow down payments of 10 percent or even as low as 5 percent. If you put down less than 20 percent, you will incur an extra cost for private mortgage insurance (PMI), which covers the mortgage in case of default. It is not tax-deductible and can be expensive, so I recommend putting down 20 percent if you can swing it.

Several government agencies offer special programs for low-income and first-time buyers and veterans. They generally require lower down payments than conventional lenders. For information about whether you qualify, contact the Federal Housing Administration (FHA).

If you are having trouble coming up with a down payment, this is an excellent time to set up a savings plan so you can accumulate what you need over a number of months or years. Another possibility is to get a gift from a family member. But to qualify for a mortgage, in most instances, you must prove that you came up with at least 5 percent of the down payment on your own. Sometimes, if a seller is desperate, he might be willing to lend you the part of the down payment you need as a short-term loan to help you qualify for a mortgage. If you do this, hire an attorney to draw up the papers. *Do not* rely on a broker who, after all, represents the seller.

The good news is that there are new zero down payment and 3 percent down payment programs for qualified buyers. For example, if you have excellent credit and you are buying a property that is located in a low-income area (defined by the U.S. Census tract) you may get a loan regardless of your income. You may also be eligible for a 3 percent down payment program if you have excellent credit, regardless of your property's location. The entire down payment can be made to you as a gift or you can borrow it as a regular loan, to be repaid in installments. And the 3/2 down payment program means that you must come up with 3 percent of the down payment from your own savings and 2 percent can come from someone else.

Government FHA loans allow you to have a lower credit rating, but you have to come up with 3 to 5 percent of the loan amount. The good news is that you can get this down payment as a gift; you do not have to have saved it yourself, and all of the closing costs can be financed into the loan. As you can see, there are many new mortgage options available for people with low income, and who have little or no money for down payments, so you owe it to yourself to check them out now.

What if you have more than enough for a down payment? Should you plunk down, say, 35 percent of the purchase price? I usually recommend sticking to 20 percent, so you can avoid private mortgage insurance as long as your cash flow can handle the mortgage payments. That way, you'll have more savings to invest and to maintain as an emergency fund.

■ Taking on a Mortgage ■

The size of a mortgage loan you can qualify for depends on your income, the interest rate of the loan, your other debts, and your credit rating. Generally, your mortgage payment can be no more than 28 percent of your gross monthly income, and your total monthly debt payments including student loans, credit cards, and mortgage/insurance/real estate taxes cannot be more than 33 percent of your income.

If interest rates go up slightly while you are shopping for a mortgage, don't panic. The increase in your monthly payments does not increase by very much if the rate rises $1/2$ or even 1 percent. If you need a thirty-year mortgage of $100,000, for instance, and the rate rises $1/2$ percentage point, it will cost you $35 a month more *before taxes*. If you are in a

28 percent tax bracket, (as are the majority of Americans) your after-tax monthly cost is only about $25.

One way to get a lower interest rate is to pay "points," which is the name for an up front one-time fee paid in return for securing a lower rate. Points are also charged by lenders to compensate for a low down payment. A point is equal to 1 percent of the mortgage amount, so in the case of a $100,000 mortgage, a point is $1,000.

Mortgages are available directly from the lenders themselves, banks, and government agencies such as Fannie Mae, or from mortgage brokers (professionals whose only business is matching buyers and lenders).

There are three basic types of mortgages:

- Traditional fixed rate mortgages (75 percent of homeowners choose these)
- Adjustable rate mortgages (ARM), in which the rate floats with prevailing mortgage market
- Hybrid loans, which start out with a stable rate, usually for three, five, or seven years, and then turn into an ARM

I recommend a thirty-year mortgage for many reasons. First, if you end up staying in your house until you retire, you have given yourself the maximum amount of flexibility. Why pay off a mortgage in fifteen years and have a mortgage-free home with no cash to live on? At that point, your only options are to take a reverse mortgage (see Chapter 6) or to sell your house. Second, you can invest those extra mortgage payments you saved by not taking a fifteen-year mortgage. Over time, if you do invest them in diversified-stock mutual funds, you are much more likely to do better. Third, you are taking advantage of one of the last great tax deductions—mortgage interest. Fourth, the cost of every payment you make decreases each year as inflation increases, so that the $1,000 payment you make this year may only be worth $300 in purchasing power in twenty years.

Adjustable-rate mortgages make sense if you think you may be moving in the next few years or if you think the rates will be coming down and you plan on refinancing to lock in a lower rate. They are also useful because their first-year rates are usually low, and if you know your income is going up substantially next year, you can take advantage of the lower mortgage payments this year.

Hybrid loans are a combination of first and second mortgages. They are used as a way to get around the higher cost of a "jumbo" mortgage, which is a larger mortgage and therefore has a higher interest rate. If your total mortgage is high enough, you may actually save money by taking out a first mortgage that is below the "jumbo size" and then taking out a second mortgage that has a slightly higher interest rate for the rest.

Even though a lender may qualify you for a mortgage, you should consider your own cash flow situation before you agree to a monthly obligation that can add a great deal of stress to your life. You may have monthly expenses—like child care, for instance, or care of an elderly parent—that the lender does not take into account when qualifying you.

☞ **Wake-up Call:** To calculate your monthly mortgage payments, use a mortgage calculator found at web sites of your local real estate broker, Fannie Mae (www.fanniemae.com) or Bankrate monitor (www.bankrate.com).

Closing costs usually range from 3 to 6 percent of the purchase price. These costs are the fees for expenses like title insurance (required by law to protect you if there are defects in the title and your ownership is challenged), attorneys' fees, appraisal fees (an appraisal must be done of the property you intend to buy), and loan origination fees (a processing fee charged by the lender).

If you are worried about how you are going to come up with closing costs, talk to your mortgage broker or banker about including them in the loan. This can often be arranged ahead of time, and can relieve you from some major financial anxiety at closing time.

■ Bidding on a House ■

Once you know what you can afford, it's time to start shopping. Choosing a neighborhood is just as important as choosing the right house for you. The old adage in the real estate business is that there are three things that determine the value of a property: "location, location, location." In other words, if you buy a mansion next to a garbage dump, don't expect to wake up and smell the money!

☞ **Wake-up Call:** Take a good walk around the property to see what your views will be in all seasons. I know of a beautiful house in the northeast that sold for a premium price in the summer. The new owners (two busy executives) had no idea that after the leaves fell, their backyard directly overlooked an abandoned strip mine.

Another rule of thumb says not to buy the best house on the block or even in a neighborhood, because the surrounding homes may bring your property's value down. On the other hand, if you move into an up-and-coming neighborhood in which lots of young people are moving in and fixing up the houses, you may be poised to see your property's value rise rapidly.

When considering a neighborhood, ask yourself these two questions: How desirable is the location for you? How desirable might it be to potential buyers when you are ready to sell? The average American lives in a home six years before selling it.

How convenient is it to places you need to go—work, public transportation, shopping, parks, schools? If you have children, how good are the schools? Even if you don't have children, you should check out the schools because they may be of interest to buyers if you end up selling your house later. Find out about test scores, the percentage of high school students who go on to college, and the district's expenditures per pupil. If you can't get this information from the local school board, check the local library for reports or stories about area schools in local newspapers. If you have children with special needs, do they have programs to accommodate those needs? If not, does the law require the school system to pay for private schooling that does?

It's not uncommon to be charged for local services like garbage removal and water. If you are deciding between two towns—one which charges $750 a year for services, the other which offers them for free—figure that you could afford a house that costs $7,500 more in the town which offers free services. An added advantage is that the additional mortgage interest you'll pay on the more expensive house is tax deductible, while the service fees are not.

In general, how expensive and exclusive is the area? How likely is it to appreciate over time? How do the taxes and services offered compare to those of other nearby towns? My advice always is to buy in the best location you can afford, even if it means buying a smaller house. Before you make any final decision, find out how much housing prices have increased—or decreased—over the last decade in the neighborhood you are considering.

You can either look for a house on your own, or work with a broker. The advantage of using a broker is that the good ones have tremendous knowledge about their area's housing market, and they can alert you as soon as something that meets your needs and is in your price range comes on the market. But remember, brokers usually earn their commissions from the sellers, so they work for them. If you are being shown too many homes that don't fit your needs and tastes, or you are feeling pressured to make a purchase, find a new broker.

☞ **Wake-up Call:** *Never* (this is a tip I must repeat from *The Money Diet*) tell a broker your upper limit. Otherwise that information will get conveyed to the seller, who will hold out for your top price. I know, because it happened to me.

Most houses are listed with a Multiple Listing Service, which means that the listing broker coordinates the showings, but any broker can show the property. If your broker sells you a house that he hasn't listed, his office will split the commission with that of the listing broker, with a portion going to each broker. The commission is usually between 5 and 7 percent.

Contrary to popular perception, brokers' fees are sometimes negotiable. Try to negotiate up front. If you aren't successful, look to the broker for some flexibility. Sometimes a realtor will trim his fees if it will affect the price enough to guarantee a sale.

If you fall in love with a house that is being sold by its owner, you can try to purchase it on your own. If it's an especially tight housing market, or you want help negotiating, however, consider hiring a buyer's broker, someone who will work for you. They typically charge 2.5 percent to 3 percent. To find the names of buyers' brokers in your area, consult the Yellow Pages or call your local realtors' association. But make sure to hire an experienced attorney whom you trust to guide you through the legal and financial issues, which can be confusing.

When you find a home that you love in your price range, it's time to bid. But before you bid, do your homework. It always pays off. Overbidding based on your heart is a common mistake home buyers, especially first-time home buyers, often make.

A general rule of thumb is to bid 10 percent below the asking price. But first make sure the house is priced right by checking what homes of similar size in the same neighborhood have recently sold for. (These are called "comparables.") Lists of recent residential sales are usually printed from time to time in local newspapers, and are now usually available on the Web. They are also available at any local realtor or town hall.

One of my more savvy clients fell in love with a condominium that was for sale. But before he bid, he took a contractor with him to check it out. As they went from room to room accompanied by the seller, the contractor kept shaking his head and pointing out all of the flaws—small cracks in the walls, a leaky tub, broken floorboards. The owner, who had never tried to sell a piece of property before, was so shaken that he agreed to accept a price much lower than what he had originally asked for, even though the cost of the repairs was minimal.

Unfortunately, paying real estate taxes is part of owning a home. But you may get some relief if you appeal your real estate taxes. You can do that by filing an appeal of your property assessment with your local assessor. If the assessment is lowered, your tax bill will drop. Nearly half of those nationwide that appeal get a tax reduction. The only time *not* to appeal is when you're in the process of selling your house, because buyers will think it's worth less.

■ Homeowners' Insurance ■

Your house is likely to be your largest asset, so it's very important that you insure it properly. Homeowners' insurance actually insures more than your home. It is a package of coverage that protects not only your house or condominium, but also its contents, including china, silver, furniture, stereos, and computer equipment. It also provides liability coverage to protect you if there is an accident in your home and someone sues you.

How do you figure out how much insurance you need? Many people think it should depend on the market value of your home. But that has nothing to do with it because market value includes the value of your land. Homeowners' insurance is designed primarily to protect your house and its contents. The amount you need depends on the cost of rebuilding your house if it were damaged or destroyed, which varies according to the construction costs in your area, the size of your house, and special features, such as antique molding, marble fireplaces, and top-of-the-line appliances.

☞ **Wake-up Call:** Use a camera or camcorder to record all the rooms and exterior of your house, especially any unique architectural features. Also, get out your silver, china, jewelry, etc. and capture it on film, along with 360-degree views of any antique furniture you have. Then put the images in your safe-deposit box. That way, you have a record of your property—out of the line of fire or water damage. (Even if you do have an appraisal, it may be outdated if and when items are destroyed or stolen.)

The value of the insurance should be based on replacement cost because the market value of identical houses can vary by hundreds of thousands of dollars, depending on the towns where they are located—remember that "market value" includes land. Make sure you buy "guaranteed replacement cost coverage," which means the insurance company must rebuild your house no matter how much it costs.

Usually your contents are automatically insured for up to half of what your house is insured for. The problem is that there are "internal limits": the maximum amounts you can collect for certain types of valuables such as jewelry, silver, and boats. It can be confusing, so ask questions until you understand exactly what the language in the policy means. If you see that the limit on reimbursement for theft or loss of jewelry is $1,000, for instance, you may think that means $1,000 per item. But it may really mean that $1,000 is the total reimbursement figure even though you have five items that are each worth $1,000. In that case, you may need to list valuable property, such as your diamond wedding ring, antiques, silverware, individually in your policy so you can be reimbursed for each one. The cost of this extra coverage is generally very small.

Again, you want to buy guaranteed replacement cost coverage. You may have paid $3,000 for your big screen TV and surround-sound system two years ago, but it is only worth about $1,000 now—you want to be able to go out and replace the items you lost at their current prices.

Even if you are renting an apartment, you need renters' insurance for the liability coverage. Let's say someone trips on your rug, breaks his arm and decides to sue you for $250,000. Believe it or not, this is very common. Your liability coverage would pay for whatever damages you owe if you settle out of court or if you lose a lawsuit. Liability coverage protects you if your dog bites the mail carrier, or your child leaves a skateboard on the sidewalk and someone steps on it, or there is a baseball game in your backyard and one of the kids smashes a line drive through your neighbor's window. I recommend that everyone carry liability coverage of at least $300,000.

If you live on a flood plain, be wiser than 80 percent of your neighbors and get flood insurance. It's provided by the government because private firms won't offer it, and generally the waiting period is thirty days, so don't wait until you see the river rising to buy it. It usually doesn't cost more than a few hundred dollars. Also, check to see if you live in an earthquake-prone area: Earthquake damage is excluded from homeowners' policies. It's not just Californians who should consider this option: Believe it or not, unexpected places such as Massachusetts also have a high potential for earthquakes. Earthquake insurance is either sold as a rider to your home owners' policy or as a separate policy altogether. My friends laugh when I tell them I have earthquake insurance, but when I envision an old Victorian house full of damage, a large mortgage, and no insurance to pay for repairs, the $200 I pay yearly seems like a bargain.

When you buy property casualty insurance, use an insurance agent who has the letters CPCU after his or her name—a designation that indicates a specialization in property casualty. Have the agent come to your house and tell you how much you should insure it for by looking around for special features, measuring square footage, and looking at your valuables to see if they should be listed individually on your policy. This way, the insurance agent and company are responsible if you end up with too little insurance, because you bought what was recommended. And if the company is reputable, usually you will be reimbursed without much of a hassle.

☞ **Wake-up Call:** It doesn't do any good to overinsure, because the insurance company will not pay you that extra money if it costs $20,000 less to repair or rebuild your house than the amount of insurance you have.

FAMILY

■ Planning for Parenthood ■

Children are precious and priceless—but anything that is precious and priceless comes at a cost, and with children come big-time expenses.

The average cost from birth to the first birthday is $5,900, not counting prenatal care or the delivery bill, according to Denise and Alan Fields, authors of *Baby Bargains* (1997, Windsor Peak Press). The average cost of raising a child to age eighteen, assuming she was born in 1990, is $210,000. After you get done paying for diapers, cribs, baby food, strollers, car seats, and baby clothes, you're on to tricycles, sports equipment, piano lessons, video games, and more clothes. Then there are those preteen and teenage costs. And then comes college!

My best advice is to start a college fund (see chart below to figure how much you'll need to save) as soon as your child is born and do your best to put in a small amount, even $20 a month, from then on. Let your relatives know you have started this fund and invite them to contribute to it on birthdays and other special occasions, even if that means spending less on toys or other gifts. As soon as you have enough for a minimum deposit in a stock mutual fund, invest it. (See the section on stock mutual funds in "Building Up," Chapter 4, page 221.) The money will grow because you will have seventeen years until your child's high school graduation. If he doesn't go to college, you will have a nice nest egg to help him out with his first apartment rental or housing purchase, travel, a vocational training class, or whatever he needs at the time.

☞ **Wake-up Call:** If you are about to give birth and you are considering breast-feeding, you no doubt are weighing the health benefits, convenience, and other factors. One benefit that you might not realize is economic. Breast-feeding for more than six months saves families over $1,400 in health care costs during the first year of a child's life—and that's not including the cost of formula, bottles, and other feeding supplies—according to a recent study by HMO Kaiser Permanente.

■ Should Mommy (or Daddy) Work or Stay at Home? ■

My friend Alice recently faced this dilemma when she gave birth to her first child. Should she keep working or stay at home with her new baby? Alice was lucky because she worked for a company with more than fifty employees, so she was covered under the Family and Medical Leave Act. The law has changed a great deal since it was first passed, but currently you can take up to twelve weeks of unpaid leave to take care of a new baby (by birth or adoption), care for a spouse or parent, or recover from an illness or accident of your own. This meant that Alice had three months in which to make a decision, although she had certainly thought about it all throughout her pregnancy and had even investigated day-care options.

But you never really know until after your child is born whether you want to go back to work full-time, part-time, or not at all. One of my closest friends swore she would be back at work four weeks after her first child was born—and she is still a full-time, at-home parent nineteen years later. The smart thing to do is to look at the financial implications of working full-time, part-time, or not at all—so that when you do hold that baby in your arms, you don't find yourself making an emotional decision that you cannot financially manage or will feel horrible about every day when you leave for work. And this is not a problem exclusive to new parents; very often parents decided to cut back hours on the job or take time off when their children are in preschool, elementary school, or even high school.

Let's face it—giving up work means giving up income that your family may need. On the other hand, continuing to work incurs a set of expenses of its own. Let's look at Alice's example and then you can fill in your own chart based on your own situation. Right now Alice's husband is making $45,000 a year and Alice is making $30,000 a year, so her income is providing a substantial portion of their monthly cash flow (and is what is making it possible to save). Rick feels strongly that Alice

Yearly Estimated College Costs

Including room and board, assuming 7.37 percent yearly inflation rate.

	Public	Private	Ivy League
1999	$10,737	$23,621	$25,769
2000	$11,528	$25,362	$27,668
2001	$12,378	$27,231	$29,707
2002	$13,290	$29,238	$31,898
2003	$14,269	$31,393	$34,249
2004	$15,321	$33,707	$36,773
2005	$16,450	$36,191	$39,483
2006	$17,662	$38,858	$42,393
2007	$18,964	$41,722	$45,517
2008	$20,362	$44,797	$48,872
2009	$21,863	$48,098	$52,474
2010	$23,474	$51,643	$56,341
2011	$25,204	$55,449	$60,493
2012	$27,062	$59,539	$64,951
2013	$29,056	$63,927	$69,738
2014	$31,197	$68,638	$74,878
2015	$33,496	$73,697	$80,396

should return to work because he thinks they need the money, and he is also worried that her job skills will be rusty by the time she reenters the job market because of the way computers and software are changing at warp speed. He feels more comfortable leaving the baby with a baby-sitter or in a day-care center than Alice does.

Rick and Alice decide to attack this from the rational point of view, by "looking at the numbers" first. That is always the best way to approach a complex decision with financial implications. Otherwise you may make a purely emotional decision, and then find out later that it is financially impossible to carry out. Not having an accurate picture of your finances before you make a decision is the equivalent of touring million-dollar houses with a real estate agent, when the maximum you can afford is a $200,000. You are setting yourself up for disappoint-ment, instead of being thrilled at having a house of your own. The chart below shows the costs of Alice's working full-time vs. the costs of stay-ing at home. This way she has an idea and knows the bottom-line cost of making one choice over another. Remember that "choosing wealth" is about making deliberate choices about your future, and this is a major one because it is probably the biggest lifestyle vs. financial dilemma you will ever face if you have children. And keep in mind that choosing wealth is not always about having the most money. It is about what is important to *you* and how you can manage to meet your goals while making lifestyle decisions.

Rick and Alice looked at their situation with and without her income. The first thing they had to take into account was taxes, which took a big bite out of Alice's paycheck. Her income would be taxed at 28 percent for federal and 5 percent for state. Additionally, Social Security and other payroll taxes would eat up 7.65 percent of her income. The good news is that they would be eligible for the child care credit of $480. So out of her total annual income of $30,000, she would bring home $18,885.

Next came the cost of day care for the new baby. There was a day-care center nearby they had toured and liked a great deal (they had looked at ten), and had gotten recommendations for it. The annual cost for children under two years old was $7,800. Some of this was recouped in the child care credit, so it is not as expensive as it seems.

If Alice kept working, she would continue to have the same work ex-penses as usual, and she could estimate them fairly well. She had to spend about $1,500 on new work clothing and shoes every year, be-cause as a customer service representative, she must always be dressed appropriately. Alice had been taking the bus to work, but with picking up and dropping off the new baby at the day-care center she would have to use their car, so they estimated that her additional auto expenses would be about $1,000 a year for gas and wear and tear. Rick and Alice were realistic and knew she would not be able to pack a lunch every day anymore because things would be so hectic at home, so they figured she would be spending an extra $500 a year on food at work. Finally, be-tween office birthdays and goodbye parties, they threw in an extra $200 to be safe.

Rick also had to look good at his job, and with the new baby, neither one was going to have time to iron their clothes every day from now on if Alice worked. They also knew they would eat more meals out because both would be too tired to cook, and because both would be working full-time, they wanted to spend their free time with the baby. That meant hiring someone to clean the house every other week and do some of the yard work in their huge back yard. All of these costs would add up. When they totaled them, the amount came to $13,340. You can see these numbers on the chart below.

Rick and Alice were then able to see the bottom-line effect of her working full-time vs. staying home with the baby. Of course they could make an emotional decision, but it was based on financial facts. Rick and Alice "woke up" in time to make the right decision for them.

If you look at the bottom line, you'll see that Alice's income, minus all their child-related expenses, gave their household an additional $5,545 yearly, or $462 per month. Once Alice saw these figures, the decision was clear to her. She felt it was well worth it to take time off to spend with the baby. She thought she could economize in their budget enough to make up for the shortfall caused by her lack of income, even though they had new expenses with the baby's arrival. Alice also knew that the stress on all their lives would be dramatically lessened if she were at home, instead of both Rick and her working full-time jobs while trying to provide child care at night and on the weekends.

But Rick had other issues to point out. In this day and age, the decision to stay with or quit a job depends on other factors besides salary: the availability of company employee benefits, especially pension and 401(k) matching plans. Rick's additional concerns were the rapid obsolescence of current work skills in the rapidly developing technological world, and the unfortunate discrimination that still exists against mothers trying to obtain employment. (Of course, whether or not a woman has children is an illegal question to ask, and it's also illegal to make a hiring decision based upon her answer, but it still happens—just ask any mother looking for a job.) Companies are becoming more family-friendly, but discrimination is still a factor that working mothers must contend with.

Finally, although he could not admit it to Alice, Rick was worried that if his wife were at home with the baby full-time, he would feel left out. This shows how financial and emotional factors are always intertwined. We are constantly making sacrifices in one area to achieve success in another—and the goal is to find balance.

Alice's employer was actually putting about $5,000 a year into her pension and 401(k) plans, and her benefits package (life insurance, disability insurance, etc.) was worth another $1,000. He pointed this out to Alice. After Alice's three-month family leave had ended, she decided to approach her company and ask for a leave of absence, which would not disqualify her from future participation in the retirement plan, with an understanding that she would return in one year. This way, Rick's fears that her skills would become obsolete were allayed, because Alice would only be absent from the workforce for a year. Frankly, they also both thought it would be nice for the baby's first year to have one parent around full time. They made a vow to stick to their budget, and Alice decided to take the year off. Of course, a lot of things can happen in a year, so their situation may well change appreciably: Rick may get a raise, for instance, or Alice may be able to negotiate part-time work.

If you need to or make the choice to work, you certainly have plenty of company. More than twenty-three million moms work, including 70 percent of married moms, 57 percent of single moms, and 75 percent of widowed, divorced, or separated moms. To decide if it's worth it for you, take your income and then subtract the expenses incurred from working. Your list of expenses should include: income taxes, employment costs (dues, co-worker birthdays, etc.), child care, commuting, clothing, dry cleaning, lunches out, family dinners out, and other time-saving expenses (house cleaner, yard care).

If a father is considering staying at home, he too should do these calculations. If he is earning less than his wife, it may make financial sense for him to stay at home at least when the children are very young. Of course, another factor to consider is how that might hinder his future earnings, because the sad reality is that in the workplace, men are typically penalized more than women are for taking time off.

Once you have figured out the monetary advantage (or loss) associated with working, it's time to consider non-monetary issues. Make a list of the advantages of working, which might include career advancement, security of having an income if your spouse loses a job, personal satisfaction, and growth. Then make a list of the disadvantages. It might include added family stress, less time with children, less time with spouse, and less personal leisure time.

Every working mother and father should do these calculations, no matter how much you make. Fifty-five percent of Americans say they'd be willing to reduce their material possessions and earnings either "some" or "a lot" to gain time with family and experience less stress. Even high-income moms may decide that what they bring home is not worth what they lose at home. In the end it is a very personal decision. Take your time to make it, and realize that, either way, it's reversible.

Back to Work: Is It Worth It?

	Alice's gross income	**$30,000**	
Minus	Federal taxes[1]	(−) $8,400	
Minus	State taxes[2]	(−) $900	
Minus	Payroll taxes[3]	(−) $2,295	
Equals	**Alice's total after-tax income**	**$18,405**	
Plus	Child care credit[4]	(+) $480	
Equals	**Alice's total net income**	**$18,885**	
Minus	Child care	(−) $7,800	
Minus	Clothing	(−) $1,500	
Minus	Car/commuting costs	(−) $1,000	WORK EXPENSES
Minus	Extra lunches, office gifts, unreimbursed expenses, etc.	(−) $700	
Minus	Dry cleaning	(−) $360	
Minus	Restaurant meals	(−) $900	TIME-SAVING EXPENSES
Minus	Cleaning service for house/yard	(−) $1,080	
Equals	**Alice's Total Net Pay**	**$5,545**	

[1]Federal taxes equal income times your tax bracket—here, 28%. Marginal tax rate is the rate at which income is taxed. Tax brackets start at 15% and cap off at 39.6%.

[2]State taxes equal income times your state tax bracket—here, 3%.

[3]Payroll taxes equal income times 15.3%—you pay 7.65% and your employer pays 7.65%.

[4]The maximum child care tax credit is $480 for one child and $960 for two children.

■ Flexible Spending Accounts ■

A flexible spending account (FSA) is a valuable benefit because it cuts your taxes. An FSA allows you to set aside up to $5,000 of your pretax paycheck to use for either child-care or health-care expenses. Let's say you anticipate spending $300 a month on day care for your child. Then you can request that every month $300 of your salary—*before* any taxes are taken out (but after Social Security)—is deposited into your flexible spending account. To receive that money, you simply need to submit documentation of your expenses.

The downside is that you must project your expenses for the entire year. If, for some reason, you do not spend $3,600 during the year on day care (if we return to our example), you forfeit the difference between what you actually spent and what you put aside. With this type of account, you can't take child care credit, but you will still come out ahead.

■ Trimming Child-Care Costs ■

Child care can be one of your largest expenses when your children are little. I have one friend whose monthly nanny bill plus preschool costs equals her monthly mortgage payment. She'd love to move into a house that's twice as nice when her three-year-old starts first grade, but I reminded her that would be an ideal opportunity to step up her saving for her daughter's college. And for many people, child-care costs extend well past kindergarten, because you may need to pay for after-school care and summer programs to cover the hours when you are working and school is out.

Before hiring a nanny to take care of your children in your home, you should check his or her credentials and training, and require references. If Mary Poppins is your image of the ideal babysitter, consider first that nannies who provide care in your home are generally the most expensive child-care option. The most experienced nannies demand an hourly rate well above minimum wage, a couple of weeks of paid vacation, and sometimes money for carfare or gas, if they are required to drive your children to music lessons or nursery school. On top of that, if you want to avoid a personal "nannygate," you are required to report their income to the IRS and pay .0765 percent of their social security income, as well as meet any state tax requirements. Illinois, for example, requires a quarterly payment to cover unemployment insurance. Of course, you may get what you pay for—a steady, loving person to focus on your child, even when she gets sick.

Less expensive options include family day care (in someone's home) and child-care centers. Family day cares are often run by mothers who want to stay home with their own children while simultaneously earning some extra income. Often you can obtain lists of the ones in your area from your local government. If you select a home that is licensed, you will have some assurance that they are inspected on a regular basis.

The advantage of the best family day-care homes is that they can provide a warm and loving environment in a homelike setting without costing an arm and a leg. Your child also will get regular exposure to other children. One drawback: If your child is sick, you will have to stay home or make other arrangements for her care.

Child-care centers vary so widely in size and quality that it is hard to make generalizations about them. The best thing to do is to visit in person on several occasions and see if you feel comfortable with the way the children are treated. How much one-on-one interaction do they have with caregivers? Are the children safe at all times? How do the caregivers handle discipline issues? What do other parents say about the quality of care? Ask about child-to-adult ratios, staff turnover, daily routines, and safety measures.

Sometimes the least expensive option can turn out to provide the highest quality care: an arrangement in which you and/or your spouse share the responsibility between yourselves or with neighbors. Can you and your spouse arrange your work schedules so that you can split child care? If at least one of you can work part-time or job share, this can actually work out. I know two police officers who do that: He works during the week and she works on weekends. These parents rarely see each other, which is certainly a drawback, but they are satisfied that their children are receiving the best possible care. Or perhaps you can trade off care with one or two neighborhood families. Another possibility is to join a babysitting co-op, in which you earn credits for caring for other peoples' children that can then be cashed in for free care for your own kids. To find out about babysitting co-ops in your area simply call local nursery schools or ask parents of young children in your neighborhood.

Try to be as creative as possible when thinking about your options. Can grandma or your favorite aunt help out two or three days a week? That may make the difference between your working part-time or leaving the workforce altogether. Then, be as discriminating as you can when it comes to making a decision. When you find a good person or day-care staff to take care of your child, you will find that your family life will be enriched by their experience and love for your child. And of course, that will be worth far more than you will ever pay for it.

■ Get Your Kids to Wake Up and Smell the Pennies ■

It's hard enough to be a parent these days given all the time constraints of work—there's music lessons, soccer practice, and nighttime reading together—and simultaneously trying to avoid hitting the hamburger drive-through more than two or three times a week. Trying to teach your children about managing their money may seem like one of those "it would be nice if I had the time" life lessons that can fall by the wayside.

☞ **Wake-up Call:** My clients with the biggest spending problems are often those whose parents never taught them how to save and how not to spend.

If you start when your kids are still young, good money habits will come to them almost naturally by the time they are adults. An image that vividly comes to my mind is a well-known media celebrity with a huge salary, sitting with his face buried in his hands and telling me, "My parents never taught me to save a dime, and I haven't. But my profession has planned obsolescence—the older I get, the less valuable I am, and I could kill myself for having frittered away all of that money over the years." Too few parents coach their children in this area.

Even toddlers are targeted by television advertising—today's cartoons have characters based on action figures that were designed before the cartoons! Businesses are in business to sell products to children, and schools and other social institutions have been slow to step into the area of educating kids about money, so it is up to *you* as a parent to take the lead. And ultimately, your kids' ability to manage money will directly affect their happiness as adults and their ability to reach their goals. What could be more important to their long-term happiness—a Sony PlayStation now or learning the value of saving for that PlayStation? Or how about putting the money in a savings account for college instead?

Start young, as early as age four or five, by giving a child a small allowance. As your kids get older, gradually increase the amount, making clear what you expect them to pay for (toys, treats after school, baseball cards, whatever), and what you will cover (cost of school lunch, bus money, clothes). You may find this hard to believe, but studies have shown that kids who get allowances are substantially happier about their money situation than kids whose parents dole out money as the need arises, *even when they end up with less money!* Plus, if you just hand out money when asked or begged, you are not teaching them anything except how to ask you in such a way that you will give it to them. And you may end up parting with more money than if they had an allowance.

If you are not sure how much allowance is appropriate, call the parents of your children's closest friends and ask how they handle it. Also inquire about what their children are expected to pay for out of their allowances.

To encourage saving, request that your child save 10 percent of his money. Go with him to the bank and open up a savings account—you can even do this with very young children—and ask for a passbook savings or statement savings account, if possible. This way, he can see the balance increase, which is tangible evidence of his efforts. Every week when he gets his allowance, make it a condition that he go to the bank and deposit his savings, or put it in a piggy bank or jar. Starting early may help your kids to beat the current habits of average American teenagers: 68 percent of them have savings accounts, but they save less than 2 percent of their allowances.

If your daughter wants to buy an expensive toy, help her figure out how much she has to save each week in order to do so. If it is too much or too overwhelming, you could offer to pay half as long as she saves the rest. Have faith that you are doing right by your child by making her wait. If she has to save for a toy or a school trip or a special treat, it will mean even more to her and she will get more pleasure out of it.

Another condition you should impose when you begin giving older children an allowance is that they keep track of where they spend it. This is how John Rockefeller taught his children about money. Each one got a weekly allowance and a small account book; each child had to show him the book every week and account for every penny. Just as adults who see where they are spending their money do, your children will gain insight if they see they are blowing it on items they could do without—fast food and candy, for instance—when they really want to buy those $100 in-line skates. They will learn the important lesson of watching where their money goes.

One caveat, and this is going to be hard from your point of view: *When they show you where they spent their money, you have to be totally nonjudgmental or you risk that they will start lying to you about it.* Remember that it is their money and they can do what they want with it. The only exception is if they are supposed to be buying lunch at school and they are skipping lunches to save money. Then you have to intervene: Take away the money and make them pack their lunches.

■ When Your Child Earns Money ■

What about money that your child earns working for the neighbors or at the local drugstore? Is it hers to keep, or do you need to take control of that as well?

You should follow the same principles as you do for allowance, or she will spend every penny, or most of it. Furthermore, if your child is a teenager, she should be saving closer to 20 or even 40 percent, because by now she should be saving for part of her college expenses. The reality of the old days, when you could afford to pay for all of your children's college, while funding your own retirement, are over. You have to protect your own retirement fund first, which means that your children are going to have to shoulder some of the burden of their own college education themselves.

You need to negotiate with your children what percentage will be set aside for college, because every student's, as well as every family's situation is different—but it is not unreasonable that as much as 40 percent be put in a special college savings account. Whatever your financial situation, I still believe that college students should be responsible for at least 10 percent of their tuition, room, and board—even if their parents are multimillionaires. I agree with one of my wealthiest clients who said, "If my son is paying for part of that 8 A.M. class [and the money was earned in a summer construction job], he is more likely to show up instead of sleeping in."

I feel very strongly about this, and I will give you a personal example of how it can actually benefit your child. During my daughter Rickey's first semester at college, she did very well in school, but did not look for a job because I wanted her to get settled in. During the second semester, she decided to get a job so that I would have to send her as little money as possible—and she got even higher grades. As Rickey said, "My schedule was so tight that I knew I had to plan my studying carefully and it made me work more efficiently. First semester, I just had too much time on my hands."

☞ **Wake-up Call:** Remember that they watch how you deal with money, and you are teaching them by your own actions. So practice what you preach!

■ College Saving Strategies ■

One of the most frequently asked question I hear is "How can I do both—save for college and retirement?" There are a number of things you can do, both from your children's perspective and from yours. First, make it clear to your children early on that they are going to have to pay for part of their college expenses themselves. As soon as you think they can understand, explain that you need to plan for your own retirement so that you do not become a burden to them when you get older.

When I wrote *The Money Diet* and traveled around the country on my book tour, I had the opportunity to meet hundreds of readers, many with very personal stories to tell about their own financial experiences. I will never forget the young woman is St. Louis who begged me to include her story in my next book because it is a classic example of where the best intentions can produce the worst results.

Shana had a full scholarship, including room and board and a stipend, at a state university in Missouri, but instead she chose to go to a four-year private college thinking it would make a major difference in her job prospects. Shana has been out of school now for about five years and she has concluded that the extra $80,000 she and her parents spent for the private school education was just not worth it, especially when she could have gotten a college education for free. As she said, unless the private school had been an Ivy League one, it would not have mattered.

Her parents spent their savings and also have a second mortgage on their house that will not be paid off until they are eighty, and her own student loan repayments are over $500 a month. She introduced me at a book signing to her new husband, and they both told me that they desperately wanted to buy a home but couldn't because they were in a "double trap." As her husband said, "We are stuck with huge student loan payments and we know that we are going to have to take care of Shana's parents when they retire. The way we see it, it will be at least ten years before we can afford to buy a house—and what does that mean about our ability to have a child?"

If your children are young, explain to them that from now on, their paper routes and other income needs to be partially allocated to a college fund. (A bonus here is that you'll be teaching them great savings habits!) Many planners recommend that children set aside 25 percent of their earnings for college, but you know what's best in your own situation.

Many parents report that when children are actively involved in the college financing process, their grades start to improve and they take school more seriously, even at the elementary level. They also are less apt to spend their money foolishly. One ten-year-old boy I know whose parents talked to him about saving for college surprised them by being appalled when a friend spent $40 in one day on Warheads, a popular sour candy.

Enlist your relatives and close friends—anyone who regularly gives your children gifts—in the effort as well. Ask them to spend whatever they like on birthdays, Christmas, or special events like Confirmations or Bar Mitzvahs. But ask them to use only half of the money they plan to spend on a gift; and say you'd like the rest in the form of a check to be deposited into your child's college account.

☞ **Wake-up Call:** Show your children their account statements on a regular basis so they'll know how much money they have for school and how it's growing.

When your children reach high school age, explain to them that college tuition has quadrupled in the last twenty years. Many private colleges run $30,000, including all expenses; many public colleges are well over $12,000. Tell them that you expect them to have jobs in the summer and to contribute half of that amount to the college account. Finally, tell your children that they will be expected to take out college loans. It's not uncommon for recent college graduates to have student loans of $15,000 or more. Time has proven this isn't an undue hardship for college graduates whose incomes rise sharply during their first several years after graduation.

■ Investing for Education ■

Starting in 1998, you can sock away $500 each year in a new education IRA for any child under age eighteen. There are income limits, however: If you are single, you must have an adjusted gross income of under $95,000, or if you're filing jointly, it must be less than $150,000. If you are not eligible, perhaps the child's grandparents are. Actually, anyone can contribute to an education IRA on behalf of your child, as long as they are eligible to do so. The chart on the next page shows the income limits for eligibility to contribute to an education IRA.

If you take advantage of this opportunity for fifteen years and earn a 10 percent annual return, you'll have $15,900, which you can then withdraw tax-free to pay for college.

There are some drawbacks. You (and anybody else) are prohibited from putting money into a prepaid-tuition plan for the same child in the same year that you make a contribution to the educational IRA. Certain colleges have developed *prepaid tuition plans* which allow parents to pay significantly reduced tuition by paying it years before their children are old enough to attend. If your child decides not to attend the college for which you have prepaid tuition, it often can be used at another college.

These educational accounts also may cut into your financial aid eligibility. And once your child is a college student, you can't claim the new Hope Scholarship (a tax credit of 100 percent of tuition and related expenses for your child's first two years of college) or Lifetime Learning credit (a tax credit of 20 percent of college-related expenses, up to $20,000) during the same year you withdraw money tax-free. The full amount of these last two programs is available to joint filers with an adjusted gross income of $80,000 or less, or single filers with an adjusted gross income of $40,000 or less. The amounts you get from these programs are not phased out until your income reaches $100,000 if you're married filing jointly, or $50,000 if you're single.

Except for the education IRA, which must be in your child's name, keep all college expense money in your name, or else your child's chances of getting financial aid will be reduced (35 percent of your child's assets are considered available for college expenses every year, versus 6 percent of yours.) By putting college money in your children's names, you also create the possibility that when they become adults, they may not decide to use the money for college but for new sports cars or trips to Europe—especially if they are among the 27 percent of college freshmen who drop out or transfer during the first year of college.

Liz and Ed, for example, had saved carefully over the years for their three daughters' education. They were fortunate in that they had been able to accumulate over half of what they expected the girls' college costs to be. The problem was that they had saved these funds in Unified Gifts to Minors Act (UGMA) accounts in their daughters' names, and under their state law, children are considered adults at age eighteen and allowed access to that money. This worked well for their oldest daughter, Betsy, who knew that every penny was to be used for educational expenses. But when Janet, their middle child, decided to take a couple of years off before she went to college—which is not uncommon these days—she did not work during that time. She ended up spending nearly all of her educational funds—over $60,000. Now if Janet decides to go

Maximum Education IRA Contributions

Single Filers		Joint Filers	
Adjusted Gross Income	Maximum Contribution	Adjusted Gross Income	Maximum Contribution
$500–$95,000	$500	$500–$150,000	$500
$98,000	$400	$152,000	$400
$101,000	$300	$154,000	$300
$104,000	$200	$156,000	$200
$107,000	$100	$158,000	$100
$110,000 and up	$0	$160,000 and up	$0

to college, she will be starting at square one. This may sound like an extreme example, but I've seen it happen many times. No matter how well you think you know your children at five, eight, ten, twelve, even fifteen, you can't predict what they'll do with the money if you put them in control of their college funds.

If, at the time college begins, you want to take out a loan for your child's college expenses but your credit isn't good enough to get it in your own name, have your child take out a loan, and then you can repay it on behalf of the child. This is one way to get college funding at a low rate of interest because in 1998 Congress passed a bill that reduced the interest-rate on student loans held by students and grads.

■ Go for the Tax Deduction ■

If you are not financially capable of contributing the maximum to your retirement and a separate college account, put every dollar you can into tax-deductible retirement plans. This strategy has multiple benefits. First, your contribution is tax deductible, so you won't pay tax on the earnings until you begin to make withdrawals. If you invest even reasonably well, even if you have to withdraw some of the money for college expenses after seven years, you'll probably be better off than if you had invested it in something else. You'll have to pay taxes on the amount you take out, but if you can prove you spent the money on higher education, you won't have to pay the standard 10 percent penalty for early withdrawal.

Financial aid is much more dependent upon your *income* than your *assets*. So, one added benefit of putting your savings into retirement plans is that financial aid calculations will not take those dollars— considered assets—into account. Your chances for financial aid, therefore, are greater if you have money in a retirement plan or even invested in your own home (because home equity isn't taken into account either) than in a bank account.

■ Negotiating Financial Aid ■

There are four sources of financial aid: federal, state, college, and private. Most financial aid packages include at least federal and college aid. These days, financial aid packages tend to include college grants (which don't have to be repaid) and federal student loans (which do have to be repaid). Often, students are offered work-study jobs on campus as well. State aid is usually offered for state colleges.

Let's say you have financial aid offers from three different colleges. Do you automatically accept the highest one?

Absolutely not. First, you and your child must rank your college choices. One may be worth going to even if the cost is higher. Do not automatically assume that your total cost for a public college will be less than a private one. You may be able to negotiate an aid package at the private college that makes the costs about equal.

Consider your financial aid offers to be first offers—just like bidding on a house, except that your child is the house that the college wants. The more the college wants your child, the better a deal you will get. Remember that applying early decision (which is more and more popular these days) severely limits your negotiating abilities for financial aid.

My friend Hugh was returning to school for a Ph.D. He received five acceptances, four of which were free rides, including tuition and living stipends. But his first choice was number five. So he copied his letters of awards from the other four and mailed them to his first choice. Number five then came through with a generous aid package.

Over 10 percent of college students contest their financial aid awards, and a significant proportion get an increase. Don't be belligerent with financial aid officers; simply explain that your child has gotten a better financial aid package from another college and ask the officer to see if he or she can match it. Be prepared to back up your claim with written documentation. Try to negotiate with all the colleges that accepted your child. Even a college that did not offer financial aid initially may come back with an attractive package. Be sure to tell your child's first choice college that it *is* her first choice—the college is more likely to offer a better deal because it knows the student will accept.

☞ **Wake-up Call:** If your child needs help with choosing the "right" college, consider hiring an education consultant—a counselor specializing in college placement who works with you and your child to ensure a good academic, emotional, and financial match. But be prepared to spend anywhere from $500 to $2,000, especially if the consultant feels additional testing is needed.

TAXES

There is one difference between a tax collector and a taxidermist—the taxidermist leaves the hide.

—Mortimer Caplin,
Director of the Bureau of Internal Revenue, 1963

■ April Is the Cruelest Month ■

T. S. Eliot wasn't thinking about taxes when he penned that famous line, but it's certainly apt from a financial point of view. The median-income family pays between 26 and 30 percent of its income in federal, state, and local taxes, according to the Center on Budget and Policy Privatization. You will find April much more pleasant if you take steps *all year* to keep organized. The result: You will pay as little tax as possible.

Think of doing your taxes in three stages:

- planning the attack
- executing the attack
- reviewing the damage

(If you use a tax preparer, you still have to do the organization work, but not all of the computations. And if you used personal financial management software such as Microsoft Money or Quicken, your job is very easy because your data can be easily imported into a number of tax preparation programs). My rule of thumb is to give yourself at least a week for each stage, so you are not rushed. I don't know about you, but when it comes to math, when I am rushed I make big mistakes even with calculators—and I miss big deductions as a result. Begin by making a 1999 tax file and make one for 2000 at the same time (if you haven't already done so in the Quick Filing System).

■ **Planning the Attack** ■

The best time to start is in February. By then you are supposed to have received all of the tax statements you need from your employers, banks, etc. See if you are missing any W-2s, 1099s, or other documents that were supposed to be mailed to you by January 31st. If you don't have them by the beginning of the following week, call. You don't want anything to hold up filing your taxes if you are going to get a refund, or to hold up figuring out how much money you are going to have to come up with on April 15th.

Most people hate working on their taxes. In fact, I can't name one person I know who enjoys it—it's kind of like going to the dentist, but you are drilling on yourself! Getting the paperwork together is the worst part and that's why it's so much easier if you can be organized throughout the year with my filing system! Because you are starting early, in February, you can work in two-hour chunks to avoid frustration and mistakes, and you should give yourself a small reward when you have gotten all your papers in order. (For a lot of people, just giving themselves a week off between gathering papers and doing their taxes is reward enough.) The good news: 73 percent of all taxpayers got a refund in 1996, and 1997 refunds were even higher. If you are lucky, the government will give you money instead of vice versa.

Here are the documents you need to gather before you begin:

- W-2 statements of wages, salaries, and tips
- 1099s—these are generated by most other forms of income, such as 1099-INT for interest income and 1099-MISC for miscellaneous income
- canceled checks and account statements
- credit card statements
- receipts for charitable donations (cash and noncash items like clothes)
- investment account statements
- ATM slips (if you have written deductible expenses on them)
- last year's tax return

Organize these items by putting each category in a different envelope or in a different pocket of an accordion file (available at your local stationery store), or you will miss deductions.

Common Income Tax Categories

Income

Wages and salaries	
Tips	
Scholarships and fellowships	
Interest	
Dividends	
Pension, annuity, or IRA income	
Unemployment compensation	
Social Security and Railroad retirement benefits	
Self-employment income	
Partnership income	
Rents and royalties	
State and local tax refunds	
Capital gains	
Gain from sale of house	
Alimony	

Adjustments to Income

IRA contributions	
Keogh contributions	
Alimony paid	

Itemized Deductions

Taxes	
Home mortgage interest and points	
Charitable contributions	
Moving expenses for business purposes	
Unreimbursed employee expenses	
Medical/dental expenses	
Investment interest expenses	
Personal casualty losses	
Gambling losses	

Tax Credits

Earned income	
Credit for child and dependent care expenses	
Credit for the elderly or disabled	

A couple of years ago I missed a big deduction in a year when I had a lot of medical expenses because I skipped looking at just one month's credit card statement. That month, I'd charged a tax-deductible, prescription-ordered orthopedic brace to my card. If you make a mistake like this, your option is to amend your return, or if the amount is not large enough to warrant the effort, to just forget about taking the deduction altogether. Either way, it leaves a bad taste in your mouth.

The next step is to divide this information into four key categories that correspond to those on your tax return: Income, Adjustments to Income, Itemized Deductions, and Tax Credits. See the chart below for the items that come under each key category.

☞ **Wake-up Call:** Take advantage of getting out all that paperwork to do your tax return as an opportunity to clean house as well. You can throw out checking account statements after three years and tax returns after seven years. You don't have to keep tax returns for years in which you have bought and sold houses anymore, because it doesn't matter what you bought or sold your previous house at and what its cost basis was.

■ Tax Saving Strategies ■

Minimizing your taxes means thinking about them all year, not just at tax time. There are several strategies that might help trim your tax bill. Read through all of them to determine which ones fit your situation:

Strategy 1: Deferring Income
If you expect next year's taxable income to be the same or lower than this year's, see if you can receive taxable income after January 1 that you might otherwise get in December. This is easier for those who are self-employed, who can delay sending invoices, though it's worth asking your employer to delay the payment of a bonus, for instance, until after the first of the year if it will make a difference taxwise.

Similarly, if you expect to be in a higher tax bracket next year, try to be paid as much as you can this year. It's better to pay 15 percent ($150) on $1,000 this year than 28 percent ($280) on $1,000 next year. If your state has an income tax, you will save there as well.

Strategy 2: Time the Sale of Investments
The same strategy holds true if you are planning on selling investments. Sell investments that will produce a gain next year (if you are try-

ing to reduce this year's income); sell those that will produce a loss this year.

Reverse the strategy if you are trying to increase this year's income and reduce next year's.

Strategy 3: Time Your Payment of Expenses
The same strategy holds true for expenses that you know you can deduct. Prepay those that will count as this year's deductions, such as tax preparation fees, investment-related expenses, and other miscellaneous deductions. To qualify, they must total more than 2 percent of your adjusted gross income (AGI). Also pay (and perhaps even prepay) medical expenses if you know you can deduct them. In order to do so, they must amount to more than 7.5 percent of your AGI.

Strategy 4: Sign Up for a Flexible Spending Account
Using pretax dollars for medical and child-care expenses can reduce your taxes. Most medical expenses end up not being deductible because the total has to exceed 7.5 percent of your adjusted gross income. So if your medical expenses are $2,000 and you are in a 28 percent federal tax bracket, you have just saved yourself $560 by using flexible spending account dollars.

Strategy 5: Make Contributions to Retirement Plans
I also talk about this in Chapters 2 and 4, but you should contribute as close to the maximum as you can afford to your retirement plans. You will reduce your taxes now and in the future, because you are not taxed on the plan's earnings until you take the money out. Some plans even allow you to contribute until April 15 and apply the deduction to the previous year's taxes.

Strategy 6: Convert Nondeductible Interest into a Tax Deduction
Paying off your credit card and auto loans with money from a home equity loan or even a first mortgage may make the interest payments tax deductible. In general, a home equity loan cannot be more then $100,000 more than the original mortgage and is subject to other limitations as well. Just don't automatically assume that you can deduct the interest, as all those sports figures on TV promoting their refinancing plans imply. Check with the IRS or your tax preparer before you take out one of these loans.

Strategy 7: Mileage Plus

If you drive for business or for a charitable cause, your miles are tax deductible. Current allowances are $.315 a mile for business, and $.12 a mile for a community group or other charitable outing.

■ Executing the Attack ■

Believe it or not, there is a method to the madness of doing your federal taxes. (State taxes vary so much by state that there is no method at all to their madness, so I am not even going to try.) The key is to understand the process—step by step. Then you can use your federal return to complete your state return.

The steps in the tax return process:

STEP 1: FILING STATUS

Determine your filing status: single, head-of-household, married filing jointly, or married filing separately. If you are single and have no dependents, your filing status is obvious. If you are married or have dependents, you have a more complicated choice to make, because the amount of tax you owe will depend on your filing status. You must determine whether you should file jointly or separately.

If you are single and have a child, usually you will pay fewer taxes if you file as head of household. Even if your child is not a dependent, you can qualify for his status if the child lives with you.

If you are married, it is usually advantageous to file jointly. However, common circumstances in which you may save money by filing separately include: when one spouse makes most of the money, one spouse incurs most of the medical deductions, or your combined income is over $110,000. In these cases, run the numbers both ways (or have your tax preparer do so) and pick the one which results in your owing less.

STEP 2: EXEMPTIONS

Determine the number of exemptions to which you are entitled. In 1998, each exemption was worth an estimated $2,700. You always get one for yourself; two if you are married and filing jointly. In addition, one exemption is allowed for each person you support. The person doesn't have to live with you if he or she is a close family member (such as your elderly mother) and you meet certain IRS rules which have to do with the amount of financial support you provide. The person does have to live with you if not a family member (such as your daughter's unemployed boyfriend).

If your income is high (over $124,500 if you're single; $186,800 if you're married filing jointly) you lose some of the exemption amount.

STEP 3: INCOME

Total up your earned and unearned income.

Earned income includes your salary and any income from self-employment, sick pay, strike benefits, unemployment benefits, and some company perks such as a company car.

Unearned income includes dividends and interest (unless from tax-deferred retirement plans), capital gains (profits made on investments that are not tax sheltered), last year's state and local tax refunds, money withdrawn from retirement plans, and prizes and awards (such as lottery winnings).

Among items that are not taxed are child support payments, gifts, and some scholarships and fellowships.

STEP 4: DEDUCTIONS

Claim a standard or itemized deduction. In 1998, a standard deduction—taken by roughly three-quarters of all taxpayers—is $4,250 for single filers; $7,100 if you are married and filing jointly. (If you are blind or sixty-five or older, the amount is higher.) Itemize your deductions only if they add up to more than that.

Itemized deductions that you might be able to take include mortgage interest, medical expenses, charitable donations including noncash items such as clothing (*Cash for Your Used Clothing* by William R. Lewis lists values endorsed by the IRS), employee expenses not reimbursed by your employer, tax preparation, and investment fees. If your income is high (usually over $121,200 if you are married), your itemized deductions get phased out as your income increases.

STEP 5: ADJUSTMENTS

Adjustments are deductions that can be deducted directly from your income. Among these are alimony you pay and many self-employment expenses.

STEP 6: TAXES

Figure out the taxes due by subtracting adjustments from total income to get your Adjusted Gross Income (AGI). (In 1998, if your AGI was $124,500 or more if you are single, or $186,800 or more if you're married filing jointly, your ability to take exemptions and itemized deductions begins to be limited.)

Then subtract itemized deductions from your AGI to determine your taxable income. Finally, subtract the amount you already paid—those funds that were withheld from your paycheck or any quarterly tax payments you made. If you are owed a refund, you can take it now or apply it to next year's taxes.

SURVEYING THE DAMAGE

This is the bottom line: do you owe, or do you get a refund?

If you owe taxes, pay them by April 15 to avoid penalties. If you don't have enough money to cover your tax bill, do not attempt to hide income in order to lower your taxes. If you get caught, which is likely because employers report your income directly to the IRS, you will face stiff penalties. Pay as much as you can, and then contact the IRS to request a payment plan. They will charge you interest, but that is a far more economical option than paying late fees.

☞ **Wake-up Call:** Did you get your federal tax refund last year? Every year, thousands of taxpayers never receive their checks because they moved and the check did not get forwarded, or there was some other mix-up with the Postal Service. If you think you are owed a refund, contact the IRS (see the Appendix for more information).

If you are getting a refund, it means that you have given the government a tax-free loan of your money for the past year. Don't apply your refund to next year's taxes. Instead, increase your exemptions so you have less money withheld, then have that money automatically deposited into a savings account—or better yet, into a tax-sheltered retirement plan.

Doing one's own taxes is not for everyone. About half of Americans use professional help. Here are some reasons why you might go to a professional tax preparer:

- you have used help in the past (have never done it on your own)
- you don't fully understand how to do it yourself and don't know what forms to use
- you own your own business or have substantial self-employment income
- you own, or have bought or sold, investment real estate or limited partnerships this year
- you bought, sold, or refinanced your house this year
- you retired this year and are taking retirement distributions for the first time.

If you decide to do your own taxes, you can get help from a number of sources, including software programs and tax preparation books (there are many good ones on the market) and the IRS Help Line at 1-800-TAX-1040. The IRS has set up more than ten thousand VITA (Volunteer Income Tax Assistance) sites around the country staffed with trained volunteers who offer free assistance. Some national income tax preparation services will review your tax return for free. Call around if you want to try this strategy.

If you use money management software such as Quicken or Microsoft Money throughout the year, you can purchase coordinated tax software that takes your data and allows you to do your taxes in a few hours. You may even be able to deduct a portion of the cost of your home computer if you use it primarily to research investments and maintain your investment portfolio.

If you are able to pay for professional help, your options include individual tax preparers and tax preparation firms. You can choose between CFPs; financial planners who specialize in taxes; enrolled agents who take special exams and can represent you to the IRS); CPAs; and tax attorneys. Check on their credentials by asking to see copies of licenses, designations, and state registration board telephone numbers.

One advantage of professional help is that a tax preparer will stand behind her work and represent you before the IRS if you are audited. The IRS does not guarantee that the advice you get over the phone or that your VITA-prepared tax return is correct.

☞ **Wake-up Call:** There may be deductions you have missed. If you itemize deductions, I recommend you have your return reviewed by a tax professional.

■ Should You File Your Tax Returns Electronically? ■

The IRS is making a major initiative to get taxpayers to file their returns electronically. Last year, almost twenty million Americans filed individual tax returns by computer, which is both the way of the future and the way in which the IRS would like the future to proceed. Your tax preparer may also suggest it. You can even file electronically with most of the tax software available.

Instead of mailing your return to the IRS, you can transmit it electronically to the government's computers. You will still have a paper tax return in your hands as a copy, but the original is the one that is electronically sent.

The advantages to this method are that there is less of a chance for an IRS error in computing your return, and if you are getting a refund, it will arrive earlier (usually about three weeks before standard refunds). Plus, you know your return has been received because you get a confirmation from the IRS, and you avoid those long lines at the post office on April 15!

The primary disadvantage is cost. Tax preparation services sometimes charge up to $50, and individual preparers charge whatever they want to file electronically. Some will do it for free, however. Make sure to ask ahead of time what the charge will be.

There is also a new service called TeleFile, which allows you to file your return with a touch-tone telephone. This is only for simple returns for people with standard deductions and no dependents. Unfortunately, if you were not one of the twenty-six million taxpayers who qualified, based on their income and the simplicity of their return, and who therefore received a TeleFile tax package in the mail, you cannot use the service.

You can obtain forms and other information from the IRS (see the Appendix for more information).

■ Choosing a Tax Preparer ■

If you decide to get help with your tax return and your return is fairly uncomplicated, you might consider going to one of the big national tax preparation services, such as H & R Block, Jackson Hewitt, or a well-respected local regional firm. You can find them by consulting your local Yellow Pages and their average charge is usually not much more than $100 for a relatively simple return.

If your situation is more complicated—perhaps you run your own business or you just received a large inheritance—a certified public accountant (CPA) might be your best bet. If you get audited, having a CPA is advantageous because he can represent you before the IRS. A generally less expensive option is an "enrolled agent"—someone who has either five years' experience with the IRS or has passed a comprehensive exam. Many financial planners and accounting and bookkeeping services also offer tax assistance and preparation. Always ask about their credentials and experience, and make sure what they tell you checks out. If they tell you they earned a particular degree, for instance, check with the school. Ask for references and call them.

Once you feel comfortable with your choice, try to meet with him before tax time rolls around so you can take advantage of any tax-saving strategies he suggests as early as possible.

■ What if You Can't Get Your Act Together by April 15? ■

Lives are so hectic these days that we barely have time to catch up on sleep, much less do something as unpleasant as our taxes. It is only natural to put them off. So April 14 rolls around, and you haven't even gotten started. What are your options? The first piece of good news is that you can get an automatic extension until August 15 just by filing federal form 4868 with no reason needed. If you do this, you are certainly not alone, because in 1998 about 6.5 million Americans asked for additional time to file their tax returns. You even can get an extension until October 15. But don't use that as an excuse to avoid getting the work done—it hangs over your head, and the longer you put it off the worse it is—I know this from experience! If you have extreme circumstances, such as a house fire where your records were destroyed, the IRS will work with you to come up with a reasonable time schedule for filing your returns. You will also need to know which state tax forms need to be filed for extensions, and you must do those as well. You can get those forms by calling your state's Department of Revenue.

▪ Financial Planning: Consulting with a Professional ▪

Do you need a planner? That's a question only you can answer, but in most cases the answer is probably yes. You can consult with a planner just once and then implement his or her advice on your own. Or—and this is the method I prefer—consult with a planner once or twice a year so that you can monitor whether you are meeting your goals and make adjustments as needed.

If you have no specific goals, that's reason enough to consult a planner. She can help you set goals and figure out how to meet them. She can also help you determine how much insurance you need and even do some estate planning, if you have children or other dependents. You may want to seek out a planner for either onetime or ongoing help if you are starting your own business, are confused about changes in tax laws, or if in general you feel your finances are out of control.

Most important, perhaps, is that a planner can help motivate you to take action. Planners' clients tend to save 10 percent of their annual income, a percentage that is double the national average. The sooner you make small changes, such as increase your monthly savings rate by $100, the more impact they will have in helping you reach the goals that really matter to you. A plan will show you where you will be in ten or fifteen years if you make—or do not make—financial changes in your life.

▪ Alphabet Soup ▪

Be cautious when selecting a planner because the term "financial planner" is not regulated, so anyone can claim to be one. You can get a list of the planners in your area simply by looking in the Yellow Pages (the worst way to find a financial planner) or calling The Institute of Certified Financial Planners, The National Association of Personal Financial Advisers, or the Personal Financial Specialists division of the American Institute of Certified Public Accountants (call your local CPA society for a referral). See the Appendix for ways to contact these organizations.

The first thing to do is to look for credentials, usually listed after the person's name. Designations indicate that the planner has passed a series of examinations, has met experience requirements, and has not run afoul of the strict laws of the Securities and Exchange Commission, the federal watchdog of the securities and investment industries. CFP means Certified Financial Planner and is the most common and important designation because all the required training is specifically related to personal finance. CFPs have to pass six exams, then a comprehensive exam, and have a certain number of years of experience in the financial planning field. Other designations you might look for are CPAs (Certified Public Accountants) who have gone through rigorous additional training in personal finance and have earned the letters PFS, meaning Personal Financial Specialist. ChFC stands for Chartered Financial Consultant, which is also focused on financial planning, and CLU means Chartered Life Underwriter (the courses are geared more toward insurance, but the person may have good financial planning experience). If a financial planner is an attorney, that is also a plus. I have three designations, CFP, ChFC, and CLU, but I think one, especially if it is CFP, is sufficient. Ask your prospective planner to explain to you what her designation (or designations) means. Now do you see why I call all of these designations "Alphabet Soup"?

A disturbing trend is the sudden proliferation of new designations that do not have such rigorous requirements, but allow people to put letters after their names. Many of these new designations have been created by for-profit organizations as a way to make money from the booming financial planning and investment management fields. A journalist from a major daily national financial publication called me recently to ask me what a certain set of letters after the name of one of his sources meant. I told him I had absolutely no idea but would check it out. A couple of phone calls later I found out that this designation—which looks as if it has as much of the authority and experience as the ones I have listed above and usually take a few years to earn—was granted after paying a fee, studying about sixty hours, and then taking an exam long-distance. This is a trend that is only going to continue in the future. So don't just be lulled by letters after someone's name; find out what—if anything—they really mean.

Once you are satisfied that the planner you are considering has the necessary training, ask "How do you get paid if I work with you?" There are three ways that planners can be paid: commission only; fee plus commission; and fee only.

A *commission-only planner* does not charge you for a financial plan, but gets compensated for her time by receiving commissions if you buy products such as mutual funds or life insurance from her.

A *fee-plus-commission planner*, who sometimes calls himself "fee-based," which implies that he does not sell any products (because "fee-based" used to mean "fee-only"), might charge you a relatively low fee for a financial plan (this can range from $200 to $5,000 if you are extremely wealthy and have major tax and estate issues), and then also gets paid if you purchase financial products. He may even refund your fee if you buy products. A fee-plus-commission planner will typically charge you less for a plan than if you choose the following type of planner.

A *fee-only planner* does not sell any products at all and is only compensated by the fees you pay her.

Your financial planner needs to be paid for the time she spends with you, so there is nothing wrong with using a planner who sells products. You just need to know how that planner is being compensated. So ask for a statement in writing that explains exactly how your planner will be paid. Also ask to see your planner's ADV, or advisory brochure that she has filed with the SEC if she manages over $25 million in assets. Otherwise, ask to see her state Securities Commission filing. This will tell you about your planner's credentials, experience, past jobs, and method of compensation.

☞ **Wake-up Call:** Unfortunately, when you ask about payment, you may not always get a straight answer. The Consumer Federation of America (CFA) recently conducted a random survey by calling financial planning firms in the Yellow Pages in a major metropolitan area and asking how they were compensated. The majority of answers were "fee only." The CFA caller then asked that sales material be sent, including the ADV.

When the CFA reviewed the material, it turned out that the majority of firms had misrepresented over the phone how they were compensated. They were not fee only; they or a related company that they own sold products that they recommended to clients. Write the Consumer Federation of America (see the Appendix for the address) to request its brochure *How to Choose a Financial Planner*.

Right now I am working with a client who was told several years ago by his first "financial planner" that she was a fee-only planner and sold no products. After paying $2,000 for a financial plan, the only advice he got was to buy two insurance policies, which he dutifully purchased. By the time Jonathan caught on that she was earning commissions from these policies, which were wrong for him anyway because they were expensive whole life policies and he only needed term insurance, she had earned something like $10,000 in "financial planning" fees and policy commissions.

If a planner has a designation, it usually means that he has had at least three years of direct financial planning experience. Still, it's important to ask how long the planner has been in financial planning, and how much of her time is spent doing full-fledged financial planning (cash flow, college saving, retirement, and estate planning, etc.), as opposed to spending her time focusing on one aspect such as investments or insurance. You want someone who is willing to look at the *big picture*, including setting goals, saving, insurance, and retirement planning, in addition to investment advice.

There also needs to be some chemistry between your planner and you. Inquire about the types of clients the planner works with. If you have $50,000 or less to invest, you don't want to select a planner who specializes in estate planning for clients who have at least $500,000 to invest. You need to feel comfortable with your planner because you will be revealing intimate details about your financial and personal life to this person. You also need to have some trust in the person, so if you can get a recommendation from someone you respect, consider that a mark in the plus column as you search for the right planner for you.

✔ Settling Down Checklist

Signs that you are financially alert:
__ I am keeping a running list of reasons why I deserve a raise, and backing them up with documentation.
__ I have found a financial planner to begin working with.
__ I have signed up for my 401(k).
__ I have an up-to-date will.
__ I have signed a living will, a health-care directive, and a durable power of attorney.
__ I have named guardians for my children.
__ I've carefully considered the pros and cons of renting vs. buying a home.
__ I have adequate homeowners' or renters' insurance.
__ I started a college fund for all my children age one and older.
__ I've started to teach my children good money habits.
__ I've started files for my tax documents, and I update them monthly.
__ When I have an important decision to make with financial implications, I "run the numbers" first so I don't make a decision based purely on emotions.

4

Building Up

_____

When I answered my telephone one Monday evening a few years ago, a very deep male voice identified itself as "State Trooper Johnson" of a state 300 miles from my home. I had driven through that state the previous weekend, and the first two words that came into my mind were "speed trap." In my defense, it had been one of those holiday weekends when everyone was going well over the speed limit, and if you didn't keep up with traffic you found yourself the subject of a cacophony of horns and the victim of some rather rude hand gestures.

I fully expected to hear that I was going to be slapped with a $300 ticket if I chose not to drive back three hundred miles and appear in court, but State Trooper Johnson was calling for another reason. It seems I had left an old briefcase with some personal papers and my address book in a telephone booth at one of the interstate rest stops. Some kind soul had turned it in and this state trooper had tracked me down four states away. He even offered to have it shipped to me so that I did not have to drive back and pick it up. I was overwhelmed at his generosity and asked what I could do in return. He said to me, "Ma'am, we are not allowed to accept gifts of any kind, but I appreciate your offer. I will say that when your briefcase was turned in yesterday I recognized your name from *The Today Show* and when I went home this sparked a conversation with my wife about our own financial situation. We really need help, and we would even be willing to drive 300 miles to Boston if you would take us on as paying clients. That's how desperate we are for financial guidance."

I suggested that it made more sense for me to refer him to a planner in his area, but that we could spend a few minutes talking on the phone about his situation. I thought I could give him some suggestions that could get him off on the right foot. What he said to me after that encapsulated exactly what financial planning is all about, and shows just how many issues come into play when it comes to building up assets.

"I'm a lifer," he said. "I have been a state trooper for twenty years, my dad was one, and I will be one until I hope to take early retirement at age fifty-five. Our union pension is not very good, and my wife and I realize that there is no way we can live on it. We have recently had twins and could really use a bigger house, and we would like to start the kids in parochial school in kindergarten. But it seems that we are just making it paycheck to paycheck, partly because my wife and I are so exhausted all the time that we are not paying enough attention to our spending.

"When I found out we were having twins, I started trying to become educated about where we should be investing the money we have been able to save—about $20,000 that is sitting in a money-market account right now—by subscribing to a couple of those monthly financial magazines and also watching the financial channels on cable TV. I have a list of mutual funds that look good, but I am just not sure. A friend of mind keeps trying to sell me an annuity because he says I have to save more for retirement and I am not eligible for any other plans because of my union pension. But my wife works part-time, so it seems to me she could do something, and my brother-in-law tells me that's not true, that I can open an IRA, so I am completely confused.

"I also know I need more life insurance and we think we might start having to send money to Jan's mother because her father just died and she doesn't have much to live on except Social Security. So as you can see, our situation is a mess and we don't know where to turn. I am sure you must have been frantic about where your briefcase was but Jan and I decided that we are actually lucky you lost it because now we have found you."

I will repeat to you what I said to State Trooper Johnson that day, and it was not just to flatter him. I told him that the issues he had were exactly like those of everybody else, but he should consider himself particularly fortunate. That's because, in addition to experiencing the joy of having twins, he had also had perhaps guaranteed himself and his wife the ability of meeting their financial goals. They had managed to overcome that psychological state of *temporal myopia*, which, as I talked about in Chapter 1, "Beginnings," means denial about the future.

Not everyone has cashed in on the stock market boom. A recent study showed that over half of baby boomers are so overwhelmed by the vast array of investment choices that they do not know what to do. They suffer from information overload from television financial channels, the Internet, financial magazines and newspapers, and the result is that many of them do nothing—and their money just sits in a money market account earning as little as 3 percent. Even with the market drops, this is not a good strategy. Here's why: Instead of building up your assets, they will likely stay about the same or even lose money if they only keep up with (or, worse yet, fall behind) the pace of inflation.

Building up your assets is a five-step process, and let's use the Johnsons' example by way of illustration:

1. **Goal setting**—consciously choosing which goals to pursue, depending on whether they are "Building Up" or "Using Up" goals (saving for retirement, education, a bigger house)
2. **Power saving**—spending as little as possible by making major and minor sacrifices today in order to reach your goals for the future (overcoming their exhaustion from work and small children to try to cut their budget so they can meet those goals)
3. **Intelligent investing**—learning about investing and then *doing it* (subscribing to financial magazines, watching financial news shows—and then gaining the confidence to make the actual purchases)
4. **Tax-sheltered investing**—using tax-advantaged investments such as annuities that are available in addition to your retirement plans (in the Johnsons' case, should they buy an annuity?)
5. **Protecting your assets against loss** with insurance and recognizing other financial obligations that may get in the way (having enough life and disability insurance, caring for aging parents)

I think that State Trooper Johnson hit the nail on the head when he added, "I know what I'm supposed to do in general terms. Spend less, save more, invest better. But how am I supposed to know how to do that? Sometimes it feels as if I am in Las Vegas making bets about whether I'm going to be able to live the life I want, but one bad roll of the dice and I have lost the game. The worst part is it is not a game—because I will have to live with the consequences every day."

At least Mr. Johnson is aware of the problem and is trying to do something about it. All too many of us have failed to "wake up" and recognize the importance of building up our assets. As the above charts show, the younger you wake up, the better, thanks to the wonder of compound interest. So the next time you are confronted with a choice between hitting the outlets during your vacation so you can "save" 40 percent on $1,000 worth of clothes, or funding an IRA, I hope you will think twice before you (like most of us) go for the clothes.

STEP 1: GOAL SETTING

You can build up for any particular goal or any number of goals, but let me be up-front about my biases. Based on all my years of financial planning experience, the most important goal is retirement, regardless of your age—but especially if you are in your thirties, forties, or fifties. If you are a baby boomer like me (born between 1944 and 1960), it's likely that having enough money at retirement is your biggest fear when you think about aging. Yet it's just as likely that you have not yet begun to increase your savings rate. Only about one-half of the seventy-eight million boomers in the United States are putting away enough money to live the retirement life they envision. And as I mentioned in Chapter 2, surveys show that boomers have less realistic expectations than 20-year-olds about the support they will receive from Social Security, Medicare, and other government programs.

What will happen to my peers who expect to be taken care of financially by the government? They will probably not wake up until it is too late to do much about it, and then spend their retirement years in a much less comfortable style than they had ever imagined.

Take a look at the chart below and see how long you are likely to live based on your age. Chances are you have a good long life ahead of you, and if you're married, one spouse will often outlive the other by many years. This should help motivate you to save as much as you can now—during your "Building Up" years—so you can support yourself in the manner you desire once you retire.

Life Expectancy Table

Use this table to calculate the average life expectancy of a person your age. Does your estate plan take into consideration your remaining life expectancy? A good plan will serve you and your heirs.

Completed Age	Expectancy of Life U.S. Life Table; 1988	Completed Age	Expectancy of Life U.S. Life Table; 1988
0	74.9	27	49.7
1	74.7	28	48.8
2	73.8	29	47.8
3	72.8	30	46.9
4	71.8	31	45.9
5	70.8	32	45.0
6	69.9	33	44.1
7	68.9	34	43.1
8	67.9	35	42.2
9	66.9	36	41.3
10	65.9	37	40.4
11	64.9	38	39.4
12	64.0	39	38.5
13	63.0	40	37.6
14	62.0	41	36.7
15	61.0	42	35.8
16	60.0	43	34.9
17	59.1	44	33.9
18	58.2	45	33.0
19	57.2	46	32.1
20	57.2	47	31.3
21	56.3	48	30.4
22	55.3	49	29.5
23	54.4	50	28.6
24	52.5	51	27.8
25	51.6	52	26.9
26	50.6	53	26.1

continued on next page

Life Expectancy Table (cont.)

Completed Age	Expectancy of Life U.S. Life Table; 1988	Completed Age	Expectancy of Life U.S. Life Table; 1988
54	25.3	82	6.7
55	24.4	83	6.3
56	23.6	84	6.0
57	22.8	85	5.61
58	22.0	86	5.29
59	21.3	87	4.99
60	20.5	88	4.70
61	19.8	89	4.43
62	19.0	90	4.17
63	18.3	91	3.93
64	17.6	92	3.71
65	16.9	93	3.51
66	16.2	94	3.34
67	15.6	95	3.19
68	14.9	96	3.05
69	14.2	97	2.93
70	13.6	98	2.82
71	13.0	99	2.73
72	12.4	100	2.64
73	11.8	101	2.57
74	11.2	102	2.50
75	10.7	103	2.44
76	10.1	104	2.38
77	9.6	105	2.33
78	9.0	106	2.33
79	8.5	107	2.29
80	8.1	108	2.24
81	7.1	109	2.20

■ Play the Goal Game ■

Mr. Johnson was right when he said that financial planning is not a game you want to lose. What's at stake is your material comfort and your chance to make your dreams come true. In addition to having an enjoyable retirement, most of us would like to own a home, put our kids through college, drive a nice car, take vacations, and have a decent lifestyle in the meantime. Believe it or not, all that is attainable, but it takes self-discipline and financial know-how.

Self-discipline is required to *power save*, which means investing every penny you can in retirement plans and then spending as little as possible. To help inspire you to power save, you need to calculate how spending money now will affect you in the long term. That's why I have included the "Play the Goal Game" chart, which shows you if you use a dollar today, how much less you will have in the future for other goals, especially retirement.

There are really two categories of goals: "Using Up" goals and "Building Up" goals. The first—"Using Up goals"—are those that cost money and won't get you any money in return (in other words, you cannot sell them in the future or sell them without buying an equivalent item). Among these are experiential goals such as vacations and cooking classes, material goals that you'll never sell, such as collectibles or antiques, or ones that you'll always replace with newer or larger versions of the same item, like TVs or stereo systems. They may be very worthwhile goals, well worth their cost. But from a financial standpoint, they have a huge drawback: The money you spend on these goals can never be used toward goals that are more important, such as retirement or college.

If you look at the Goal Game chart, you will see how taking $10,000 out of your Building Up fund—the money you are setting aside for college or retirement—at different stages in your life will affect how much money you have at retirement. The results are staggering—and they may make you think again about spending the extra cash on those new car options, an expensive vacation, special camps and adventures for your children, or a vacation home (if you have no plans to ever sell it and use the money for retirement or college).

The second category—"Building Up Goals"—consists of those goals that require money, and that you are investing *for*, such as retirement or college. It also includes those goals for which you assume that you will get something back, and if you're lucky, more than what you paid. The

Play the Goal Game

Building Up		Using Up	
$1000 invested once with a 10% return		$1000 spent	
Year	Amount You Would Have	Amount Could Have Had	Amount You Have*
1	$1,100	$1,100	$0
2	$1,210	$1,210	$0
3	$1,331	$1,331	$0
4	$1,464	$1,464	$0
5	$1,611	$1,611	$0
6	$1,772	$1,772	$0
7	$1,949	$1,949	$0
8	$2,144	$2,144	$0
9	$2,358	$2,358	$0
10	$2,594	$2,594	$0

*Assumes you never sell the asset or replace it with another nonliquid one (e.g., trade in your car).

classic example of this type of goal is a more expensive home than you have now. The old rule of thumb was to keep buying more and more expensive houses throughout your life because they would be a good investment. But they are *only* a good investment if you plan to sell that last "more expensive" house you are in at some point during your lifetime. Otherwise—unless you decide to get a reverse mortgage (see page 312), which will eventually result in your losing ownership of the house—you will be living in a house that may have a lot of home equity, but you will not have access to it.

■ Now You *Really* Need a Planner ■

Now that you have committed to "Building Up," a good financial planner can help you sort through and set priorities within your goals. In addition to figuring out how much you need to meet your most important goals, you may often need help when other financial issues arise, such as how to handle unexpected expenses or a sudden loss of income or even an unanticipated windfall.

Until you retire, your whole life can be classified as a "Building Up" phase, so over the years it is crucial that you continue to reset and revisit your goals. In fact, it is smart to revisit your goals every few years because they can change as your circumstances change—and they can change suddenly, or over time. My recently widowed client is no longer interested in buying that second home in Montana so that her husband can fly-fish to his heart's content. Now, it is much more important for her to be in as close proximity to her children as possible. You may suddenly find yourself responsible for taking care of your elderly parents, and I will give you some ideas about how to manage that later in this chapter. And life changes and even catastrophes can happen to any one of us at any time—drastically altering our dreams and wishes for the future, and therefore, how much we need to save and how well we need to invest. If you are married, your goals may be markedly different from those of your spouse, and a financial planner can help you reach common ground.

THE BIG GOALS

■ Retirement ■

Some long-time clients of mine, Evan and Mary Ellen, had a particularly difficult time with the "Building Up" process. They had a handsome joint income, but they had trouble getting motivated to save—because they, like many of their forty-something peers, hadn't thought about what would happen when the paychecks stopped coming in. My diagnosis: a common strain of temporal myopia.

Before our last meeting, I wracked my brain trying to figure out how to drive home to them that they needed to "wake up" and take control of their money. The issue for them was learning to *power save*—making smaller sacrifices today so that they could reach their more important future goals. Finally, I decided to ask them to give me a list of the reasons why they did not make attempts to build up their assets. It seemed like the most powerful way to get my point across would be to walk through each item on the list with them and gently point out instances in which their reasoning was faulty. Retirement was their number one priority, so we focused on that. They came up with a litany of reasons, some of them stated defensively. Their first reason may sound familiar to you; it certainly is one I hear day after day:

My parents seem to be doing just fine in retirement, and I am making so much more than they ever did. I figure that I will be just fine, too.

So, I took out a piece of paper and made two columns with a line down the middle. On one side I listed all of the income sources their parents have now and on the other side I listed all of the resources Evan and Mary Ellen would have at retirement. Their parents' list was twice as long as my clients'. Evan's father received a monthly pension plan of about $1,000 for life from his company, his mother would receive a reduced benefit of about $650 monthly if she out-lived him, and their combined Social Security income was about $1,500 a month. In addition, they had been extremely frugal and had built up IRA accounts and an investment portfolio that, in total, were generating about $30,000 a year in dividends and capital gains without even eating into any of their capital.

Mary Ellen's parents were even better off because her father had owned a company and structured a retirement plan that paid him a monthly benefit of $5,000, with Mary Ellen's mother receiving two-thirds of that amount if her husband predeceased her. Their joint monthly Social Security benefit was $1,800. They also had IRAs paying $500 a month, and monthly investment earnings of $750. Both sets of parents had Medicare and Medigap insurance that provided coverage for virtually all of their medical needs except nursing home care.

Then we moved to the right side of the paper, which listed the income sources that Evan and Mary Ellen would have if they retired today. Neither one of them had a pension plan, so I wrote down "$0" next to the word "pension." I then wrote down their Social Security income based on their current estimated annual benefit at retirement of about $20,000 (which would be much less today, so I made it three fourths of that amount, or $15,000). I put a question mark next to it, because it is virtually certain that there will be major changes in Social Security by the time baby boomers retire. On the next line I wrote their investment income. Based on their accumulated assets of $50,000, I wrote $250 a month—assuming a 10 percent return for the long-term, with 4 percent reinvested to keep up with inflation. (The good thing was that they actually had saved more than most baby boomers, because the average boomer has only $1,300 in his lifetime savings account.)

So Evan and Mary Ellen, who are currently living on about $200,000 a year (or almost $17,000 a month) before taxes, would have about $18,000 in retirement income—or $1,500 a month. And this does not take into account the fact that they have two children they would like to send to private colleges in the interim. After working with this couple for five years, I had *finally* figured out a way to make them "wake up" to the fact that they needed to drastically change the way they were living if they wanted to reach their retirement goals. They left the office with a totally different perspective on their futures and a new vision of what they needed to do to get where they wanted. They realized—one of the prerequisites of the "Waking Up" process outlined in "Beginnings" (Chapter 1)—that by choosing to have their wealth now, they would be living on very limited means in the future. In fact, before they left, we hammered out a new financial plan:

They each agreed to contribute the maximum amount to their 401(k) plans at work. Evan, whose small consulting business on the side had supplied them with "fun money" for trips, decided to set up a Keogh plan where he would invest his profits. They also made a commitment to keep track of their expenses for two months, and made an appointment to meet with me two months later to go over what they discovered. Because they had trouble turning down their kids' requests for toys and clothing, the final part of the plan was to keep track of what they spent on their children, and to make a note of each time they said "yes" and each time they said "no"—with a goal of saying "no" at least 50 percent of the time.

Take a few minutes to fill in the chart below, similar to the one I drew up for Evan and Mary Ellen. What would your income be if you retired today, based on your current financial resources?

It is understandable to avoid thinking about saving for retirement because the numbers are so big. But you have to start! Let's look at some other reasons that people avoid planning for retirement:

"I've gotten this far in life without much planning, so I'm sure I will manage to get by at retirement."

Before you start beating yourself up because you might see a bit of yourself in Mary Ellen and Evan, let us look at some economic realities. The bottom 60 percent of the workforce is making less money per hour in real dollars than they did twenty-five years ago, and real family incomes are far below 1973 levels even though so many women have entered the workforce. So it is harder to save, and with lower savings people have less money to invest. In 1975, Americans were saving almost 9 percent of their disposable savings, and in the mid-1990s that number has dropped by more than half to just over 4 percent. And twenty-five years ago, workers were usually covered by pension plans that were fully funded by their employers—today, *we* must take on

Will Evan and Mary Ellen Be as Well Off as Their Parents?

Monthly figures, in today's dollars:

Retirement Income Source	Evan's Parents	Mary Ellen's Parents	Evan and Mary Ellen
Pension	$1,000	$5,000	$0
Social Security	$1,500	$1,800	$1,250*
401(k) Plan	$0	$0	$0
IRA Distributions	$1,000	$500	$0
Non-Tax-Sheltered Investments	$1,500	$750	$250
Other Retirement Income	$0	$0	$0
Medicare/Medigap	Have	Have	Unknown
Total Monthly Income	$5,000	$8,050	$1,500

*Estimated. Amount is three fourths of their estimated retirement benefit they would receive at sixty-five.

some (or all) of that responsibility ourselves through contributions to our 401(k) plans.

But as Mary Ellen and Evan's example shows, it can be very difficult to get by when your retirement income is far less than your current paycheck if you have not saved enough to make up the difference. If you find yourself in that position, you also may have difficulty getting any loan other than a reverse mortgage, which will eventually mean that you will lose ownership of your house. Basically the bottom line is this: What will the loss of your paycheck do to your income? If you are working, chances are you can get a loan. Nobody is going to loan you money to retire on.

"I know I am going to be getting an inheritance someday, and that should take care of my retirement."

Your parents may well be in excellent financial shape now, thanks in part to being members of that lucky postwar generation of unparalleled affluence. They also were probably very frugal (and still are), logging

Who Saves and Who Doesn't

Gross Annual Income	Savings Rate
$20,000–$29,999	−11.8%
$30,000–$39,999	−3.3%
$40,000–$49,999	+7.4%
$50,000–$69,999	+8.5%
Over $70,000	+27.2%

SOURCE: Bureau of Labor Statistics, 1995

the highest savings rate in U.S. history. As a result, even middle-income people may have built up estates of $1 million or more due to their investments, real estate holdings, and pension plans. But you need to be aware that inflation, increases in longevity, cutbacks in Medicare and Social Security, and the rising cost of long-term medical care can eat away at the value of your inheritance, which you may not get until you reach or are near retirement yourself. I will talk about the financial implications of taking care of one's parents later in this chapter, but I tell my clients not to count on an inheritance no matter how much they expect to inherit. In 1998, the average yearly nursing home bill was $46,000, and costs are escalating rapidly. That would eat up an inheritance pretty quickly.

"I haven't done much for retirement. It's just too late to try."

"Too late" is just an excuse to keep spending, or more often, an expression of a feeling of powerlessness. It is better to have something when you reach retirement than nothing at all. If you don't save anything, you won't have anyone to blame but yourself. In the meantime you have daily opportunities to cut your spending so that you will have more money in the long term.

"It's too soon to start thinking about retirement."

It's never too soon to think about retirement—and with the new tax laws, you can "save for retirement" but use the money in the meantime for other things. Often, people defer putting money into their retirement plans because they want to save for a new house or for college or for their children. But there are tangible tax benefits that you get now, be-

The Power of Investing

If you invested $1,000, look below to find out how much you would have, at varying rates of return, after a certain number of years.

Years	8%	10%	12%
0	$1,000	$1,000	$1,000
1	1,080	1,100	1,120
2	1,166	1,210	1,254
3	1,260	1,331	1,405
4	1,360	1,464	1,574
5	1,469	1,611	1,762
6	1,587	1,772	1,974
7	1,714	1,949	2,211
8	1,851	2,144	2,476
9	1,999	2,358	2,773
10	2,159	2,594	3,106

If you are a certain age and you invest $1,000, look below to find out how much you'll have at 65, at varying rates of return.

Age	8%	10%	12%
25	$21,725	$45,259	$93,051
35	10,063	17,449	29,959
45	4,661	6,727	9,646
55	2,159	2,594	3,106

cause you may be able to deduct the contributions, and all of the income and appreciation grows tax free until you take it out. In fact, with many plans, even if you end up withdrawing money from your retirement fund for a new house, college, or medical expenses, there is no penalty. (See Chapter 3, "Settling Down," page 120 for rules about withdrawing funds from different types of retirement plans.) Even if you do have to pay the 10 percent penalty, you still may be better off contributing to a retirement plan because of the tax breaks you received during the years the money was in the plan. Depending on how well your investments do in your retirement plan, you can break even in as early as five or so years, even factoring in the 10 percent penalty.

For example, if Tara and Randy contributed $10,000 to Randy's 401(k) at work, and earned 10 percent for ten years until their son, Andrew, was ready for college, they would have saved $25,910 (before taxes). The 10 percent penalty for early withdrawal before age fifty-nine and one-half would have been waived because the money was being spent on higher education.

In the meantime, you will be less inclined to use that money for other things because of the penalty and the fact that *it is not in your hands or in your checking account.* I have found with my clients that in most cases they end up having more money *even after paying the 10 percent penalty for early withdrawal* than if they had saved the money outside of a tax-exempt retirement plan.

■ The Classic Goal-Setting Quandary: ■ Which Comes First, College or Retirement?

This is the double whammy of parenthood. You need almost $700,000 saved up by age sixty-five if you want to retire today on a modest yearly income of $40,000. Meanwhile, the nation's most exclusive colleges cost more than $25,000 a year in 1998 and you don't want to deprive your kids of the opportunity to attend, if you think it's important. (On page 150, there is a chart estimating college costs for the next twenty years.)

It is little wonder that the two most frequently asked questions of financial planners are:

Which goal is more important?

How can I possibly save for both?

Somehow parents in the past accomplished this dual feat, yet today it seems hard enough to accomplish just one of the two. If you are worried that you are doing something fundamentally wrong that your parents did right, the answers I give to the above questions may help you feel better.

First, remember that Americans enjoyed an unprecedented period of prosperity between the early 1950s and the early 1970s, when real income (purchasing power) increased dramatically. Second, substantial percentages of employees (almost 75 percent) had pension plans entirely funded by their companies into which they paid nothing but from which they received monthly income for life. In addition, in real dollars, college costs have increased hugely: The cost of our post-high school education was much lower than our children's will be (and we or our parents may have even gone to college for free through the GI Bill). Also, many parents had children earlier in life, which meant they got college payments out of the way earlier and thus had more time to save for retirement later on.

To the question "What's more important, college or retirement?" my answer is simple: *Save for retirement first.* I know that most people would consider it selfish to protect their own assets at the expense of sending their children to college. You may have an understandably romantic (and parental) notion that college comes first and that you are willing to have a lower standard of living at retirement in order to give your children that high-priced four-year private school education. But just how romantic is it if you spend most of your money on your children's tuition bills and then, a few years into retirement, you run out of savings and are forced to turn to your children for help? Many adults in their forties and fifties are now finding themselves a part of the "sandwich" generation, trying to raise their children and provide some financial support to their own parents at the same time. They often say that their own expensive college diplomas hanging on the wall were not worth it, and that they would have preferred to go to a less expensive school so their parents had more money now. They feel a combination of guilt and resentment. You don't want to encourage your children to make the same mistakes.

The best thing to do for your family is for *you* to stay financially strong. So retirement comes first. It may feel selfish, but that's the best strategy for your entire family. Take the long view and envision yourself at age seventy-five. Will you be resentful that you have to live frugally while you see your children spending more than you think they should? Will you feel that your children are not grateful enough for your sacrifices?

Will You Have Enough Money for Retirement?

Part One: Total Assets You Need

	Your current living expenses	A.
Less	Expected annual reductions in living expenses	B.
Equals	Anticipated annual living expenses	C.
Times	8	× 0.8
Equals	Annual living expenses at retirement	D.
Less	Approximate annual Social Security benefits (monthly benefit multiplied by 12)	E.
Less	Approximate annual pension* and other income (part-time job earnings, etc.)	F.
Equals	Additional income you will need to provide with assets	G.
Times	16	× 16
Equals	**Assets you must have to provide the additional income needed**	H.

Part Two: Assets You Have

	Bank accounts	
Plus	Investments	
Plus	Retirement plans*	
Plus	House equity (if you plan to sell at retirement); equals house value minus mortgage	
Plus	Other assets you are willing to sell for cash at retirement	
Equals	**Your total existing investment assets**	I.

*Include either your annual income benefit in line F, or the lump-sum value of your plan in Part Two, but not both.

continued on next page

Will You Have Enough Money for Retirement? (cont.)

Part Three: Figuring Your Shortfall or Surplus

	Assets you must provide (see above)	H.
Less	Your existing investment assets	I.
Equals	Your asset shortfall (if I is less than H); or	J.
Equals	Your asset surplus (if I is more than H)	J.

Chart for Readers to Estimate Their Retirement Income if They Retired Today

Retirement Income Source	You Would Have:
Pension	$
Social Security	$
401(k) Plan	$
IRA Distributions	$
Non-tax-sheltered Investments	$
Other Retirement Income	$
Medicare/Medigap (do you have it?)	Yes/No
Total Yearly/Monthly Income	$

It's a different world today. Protect your own financial strength, because that's the way to ensure that you'll live an independent retirement without being a burden to a future generation.

■ Moving Up: Other Goals ■

Saving for a comfortable retirement is important, but we don't want to sacrifice all of life's other pleasures along the way. Moving into a bigger house or a more expensive neighborhood is a very common financial goal at this stage of life. And if you do plan to sell your house, there is some good news: You will be able to keep more of the profits than in past years. Thanks to the Tax Reform Act of 1997, profits from the first $500,000 for married couples ($250,000 for singles) of capital gain on your principal or vacation residence is tax free, and you may use that tax relief every two years—before that, it was a one-time exemption of only $125,000, and you had to be at least fifty-five to qualify. So if you plan to sell your home at retirement, you already have saved yourself some taxes.

But taxes should not be your only consideration. Here are some questions to ask before you decide to sell your existing home and purchase a more expensive one:

1. Am I going to have to use up assets out of my Building Up fund to buy this new house?
2. Will my new house appreciate faster than my current house? No one can predict the future, but make your best guess.
3. Am I planning to sell this house at retirement so that I can move to a less expensive one and free up some home equity to add to my Building Up fund?
4. Is now the right time to sell?
5. Who will sell the house for me and is it worth a commission to sell? In a recent year, approximately 600,000 homes (15 percent of total sales) were sold by owner, without a broker. If you sold your house for $200,000 without a broker, you would save approximately 6 percent, or $12,000 in fees.
6. What are my answers to the questions posed in the Settling Down chapter about buying a home? (See Chapter 3, page 113.)

A few years ago, Jesse and Camille, a couple in their midforties, came to see me because they had been fighting for six months over whether or not to "buy up." She said they should, he said they shouldn't. It turned out that in order to sell their house and purchase a more expensive one, they would have had to take on a much higher mortgage. Jesse was very concerned about his job stability, which he had been reluctant to discuss with Camille for fear of upsetting her. (In the United States, 28 percent of spouses do not even know how much the other spouse makes, so his behavior is not surprising.) Buying the larger home would also require taking money out of their nest egg—about $30,000, and the house Camille had in mind was the one she wanted to live in forever—meaning that the money they took out of their Building Up fund would be gone for good. When we looked at the Goal Game Chart, we saw that taking compound interest into account they would have about *$325,000 less* at retirement. They agreed to stay put until Jesse's job situation was more certain, and Camille began to seriously rethink the idea of buying a more expensive house. We also agreed that in a few months we could look at the issue again. Later, the couple decided to refinance their current mortgage, which was relatively high, and stay in their current home.

■ Selling Your House ■

There are two reasons why people sell their homes—because they choose to, or because they have to for financial or job-related reasons. Either way, selling your house is a financial act that is laden with emotion. After all, whether you are moving to a new section of the country or even just across town, it means a change in your life. If you are choosing to sell, you may think, "Do I really want to leave my home, where so much happened?" Even if you are anxious to move, it's not uncommon to have mixed feelings when you face such a major change.

That's why it's very important to get some dispassionate advice as you prepare to sell your house—even if you think you might sell it on your own. Before you settle on a price, gather as much information as you can about the local market—your town, neighborhood, and street. Start by inviting at least two brokers you trust, or who have been recommended by other satisfied customers, to tour your house and give you a recommendation on the asking price. In addition, you may want to hire an appraiser to value the house—this may cost several hundred dollars, but because he will not receive any commission from the sale of the house, he may be your most objective source from which to determine your home's value. In addition, be sure to look up the recent sales prices of homes like yours in a similar location in your town or city.

Resist the temptation to price your house too high just because you love it. If it's overpriced, your house may stay on the market longer than the average home in your market, which will make prospective buyers think there is something wrong with the house before they even see it.

Another warning: Don't price your house simply by adding the price you paid for it plus all of the money you've spent on remodeling it over the years. You've also probably spent a sizable sum on maintenance! Some improvements do increase the value of your property, however. The best return for your remodeling dollar comes from improvements made to kitchens and baths—often you'll recoup 90 percent or more. Other improvements popular with prospective buyers are adding a family room, a bathroom, a sun room, a master bedroom, replacing siding, and converting an attic to a bedroom. Landscaping or a pool does not generally increase a home's value, so don't do either one for purely investment purposes. A pool can even decrease your home's value if the prospective buyer wants to have it filled in to create a yard or garden.

Once you settle on a price, your next step is to decide whether to sell through a broker or to sell your home on your own. Selling by owner is a good way to save money if you have the time to show your house and enough detachment to negotiate directly with a buyer without the screen of an intermediary. If you choose this route, make sure you line up an attorney when it comes time to draw up a final sales contract.

If you decide to go with a broker, find out at the outset what he charges—it's typically 5 to 6 percent of the selling price. If competition is strong among brokers in your area, you may find some who are willing to negotiate the fee. It certainly doesn't hurt to ask. And even if the broker you choose does not offer to give you a break on the fee, he may change his mind if you come very close to reaching an agreement with a buyer but remain a few thousand dollars apart. Sometimes the broker will cut his fee in order to bring the two sides together and seal the deal.

☞ **Wake-up Call:** Seemingly minor things can make a big difference. To prepare for showings to prospective buyers, clear the clutter, wash the windows, and make minor repairs. If your inside or outside paint is peeling, consider repainting, but stick with neutral tones.

In terms of evaluating prospective buyers, the larger down payment they can put down and the higher their income, the better. The buyer you choose should ideally be preapproved by a bank, and it also is generally better to sell your home to someone who is not currently trying to sell a house of his own.

■ Capital Gains Taxes ■

Congratulations! You've sold your house and made a profit. Now, you may wonder, what do I owe Uncle Sam for my good fortune? The great news is that recent tax law changes, in the form of the Taxpayer Relief Act of 1997, have given sellers a significant tax shelter. You will not be taxed on your capital gains—the difference between what you paid for your house and what you sold it for—up to $250,000 (double that for joint filers). To take advantage of the tax relief, the house must have been your principal residence for at least two of the five years prior to the sale.

What happens if your profits exceed the tax-free limits? You'll still get a break from the Taxpayer Relief Act, but how much of a break depends on your tax bracket. If your income tax bracket is above 15 percent, you'll have to pay a 20 percent rate on profits that exceed the exclusion limit. If your income tax bracket is 15 percent, you'll have to pay 10 percent. In the past the rates were 28 percent and 15 percent, respectively.

And what happens if you sell your house at a loss? The Taxpayer Relief Act did nothing to improve that situation. Losses weren't deductible before the law was passed, and they still aren't.

■ An Alternative: Stay Put and Refinance ■

When interest rates are low and expected to stay that way, you should consider refinancing your home—you can use the extra money to contribute to your Building Up fund. With the Asian financial crisis that started in 1998, people began moving money away from Asia and back to the United States. This meant that treasury bills' interest rates were the lowest they'd been in the last thirty-five to forty years. That was good news for homeowners because mortgage rates came down as well and, depending on the economy, they may stay down for quite a while. For example, in June 1998, the average thirty-year fixed rate mortgage was 6.8 percent and the lowest was 6.4 percent. The average one-year adjustable mortgage rate was 5.7 percent and the lowest was 4.4 percent. For those of us who remember the 18 percent mortgage rates of the 1970s, these numbers are staggering. If they ever come your way, they should not be passed up.

There used to be a hard and fast rule that if your new mortgage rate was 3 percent less than your current mortgage rate, you should refinance. But since that rule was calculated, your mortgaging options have changed drastically. Now you can get a mortgage with no points down, or no closing costs, or with as many as 3 points and an annual rate that can vary for years to come. So if current rates are even 1 percent lower than the rate you are paying on your mortgage, you may be able to save thousands of dollars of interest over the life of your mortgage if you stay in your house that long. Even if you move, in the meantime your mortgage payments will be less, so you will have more cash at your disposal (but you must also take closing costs into account). Perhaps you can invest this extra money in a tax-sheltered retirement plan. Or, if you have credit card debt, the extra cash flow can help you pay off that debt faster, which should be another top priority.

If you have other debts at a higher interest rate, such as credit cards or a home equity debt, you may be able to refinance them all into a first mortgage at a new lower rate. If the interest on the debts is nondeductible (such as credit cards), you get the added benefit of switching them to a deductible loan.

☞ **Wake-up Call:** A recent study of people who refinanced their homes in order to pay off credit card debt showed that a substantial percentage had once again run up their credit cards to the limit within eighteen months of refinancing. In other words, all they did was use up home equity to pay off credit card debt—*not* change their spending behavior. Do not refinance to pay off your credit card debt until you make a commitment to stop using those cards and stay within a budget!

If you can refinance at a lower rate, you may be able to take a new mortgage that is larger than the one you have now without increasing your monthly payment. The advantage to doing this is that if you finance more than the amount you owe on your house, you get the difference in cash. This cash can be used for much-needed home repairs—such as replacing your roof or repainting your house—that you cannot finance out of your current cash flow. You can even use the cash to pay college tuition for your children.

Refinancing doesn't make sense for everybody. But if you think it might make sense for you, check first with your current lender. That bank may give you a break on loan processing costs, particularly if you've already refinanced once, because it may already have many of the documents that are needed.

Compare closing costs carefully, and only deal with a mortgage lender who will give you a side-by-side comparison of different mortgage options, including a number of points, a no-closing-cost option, and fifteen-year vs. thirty-year mortgages. If you think you may be moving in the next few years, make sure you determine the break-even point if you refinance—in other words, how many months that must elapse before you start profiting from going through the refinancing process.

Stay away from any loan programs advertised aggressively on TV that feature famous pitchmen. These lenders typically allow you to borrow more than the value of your house, which is not smart, and the interest rates are incredibly high—up to 25 percent. That is why it is important to work with an established mortgage lender or a mortgage broker who will check for the best rates for you from a variety of different sources.

■ Should You Pay Down Your Mortgage? ■

This is another common goal, but it doesn't always make financial sense. In fact, I recommend against it in the vast majority of cases—most often, it is a Using Up goal.

A few months ago I sat down with a couple who were struggling with credit card debt. "We fight about who *has* to open the mail because neither one of us wants to see our credit card balances," the husband said. When I asked about the interest rates, I found that they were ranging between 15 and 21 percent for about five thousand dollars of credit card debt. Yet, this couple was making an extra mortgage payment of $100 a month on an 8 percent mortgage "because it feels good." Their situation was obvious—that $100 needed to be directed to paying down their credit card debt, which was non-tax-deductible.

It is true that sending in an extra principal payment each month with your mortgage payment can save you thousands of dollars of interest over the long term, and it feels good in the meantime. But when this question comes up over and over again with clients, I almost never recommend that they pay their mortgage down except in extreme circumstances. Why?

You lose flexibility. Unless you are absolutely sure that you are going to have enough money for retirement (and very few people can say that), you need that extra money to live on. If you pay down your mortgage, you are locking up your money in your house, and the only way to get at it may be to take a reverse mortgage. Of course, you could sell your house and move to a smaller one or to an apartment or a life-care community, but many people are attached to the homes they live in. However, I have seen far too many people retire with a debt-free house they don't want to leave and only enough investment money to live on for four or five years.

Paying down your mortgage is a bad investment. If you have a mortgage at 7 or 8 percent, over time you could invest those extra principal payments and potentially earn a higher rate if you invest in diversified stock mutual funds. In addition, when you make those extra principal payments, you are losing one of the last great tax deductions available, home mortgage interest.

If you have enough money on hand to make extra principal payments, pay off your credit card debt and other debt that has nondeductible interest. Even if you have a credit card at 6 percent and a mortgage at 8 percent, you are better off paying off the credit card because you can deduct the mortgage interest paid.

Put the money instead in your retirement plan, which is tax-sheltered, or just invest it.

■ Buying a Vacation Home ■

The same rules apply here as with any other goal. If you plan to purchase a vacation home and not sell it during your lifetime, it goes into

Building Up/Using Up Goals

Building Up Goals	Using Up Goals
Retirement	Digital TV
College	New car
Classic car to restore & sell	

the Using Up category and takes away from your Building Up fund. If, however, you plan to sell your main house at retirement and move to this vacation home (which many people do), or you plan to sell the vacation house at some point in order to free up the home equity to put back into your building up fund, a vacation home is a Building Up goal that may be a good investment.

STEP 2: POWER SAVING

Once you have determined which of your goals you most want to pursue, you are probably more motivated to save than you were when you didn't have a clear picture of the future. Ironically, many of us spend just as much money (or more) on unnecessary daily items during the year than we do pursuing our dreams, so you can probably step up your savings significantly by closely examining your day-to-day spending habits.

Elaine and Kathy are a perfect case in point. They really wanted to take a trip to Europe two years after they met, and estimated that it would cost $3,000. They looked at the Goal Game Chart and decided it was worth it because the trip was essentially the vacation they had never been able to take. Elaine had been in law school when she and Kathy committed to each other, and until Elaine graduated, every penny of Kathy's income had gone to help her pay for school. So we decided to look at their budget and see if there was a way they could "power save" in order to meet that goal.

Believe it or not, together we were able to cut enough fat from their budget to make it possible for them to be on that plane to Europe in less than a year. For instance, they stopped buying coffee outside of home or work, limited themselves to one nice dinner out a month, and used coupons to save money at the grocery store. They also put a halt to their habit of going to the mall on a recreational basis (where they spent money on items they didn't need), decided not to buy any new camping or biking equipment, and threw out every catalog that came into their house because they also had a tendency to order gadgets that they never used.

Unfortunately, it had gotten harder and harder to maintain self-control in the spending category—and every dollar you spend is a dollar you could have saved. Of course, credit cards have long been a problem, but now we also have shopping networks on television and ads plastering the Internet, using sophisticated sales hype and technology to get you to part with your hard-earned dollars. You remember the old saying "and if you believe that, I can sell you the Brooklyn Bridge"? Well, QVC attempted to do just that in its adopt-a-highway project—and succeeded *too* well! They gave people the opportunity to "buy" a section of the Brooklyn Bridge for $25,000—the money would be used to repair and maintain "their" section of the bridge. QVC advertised the project on its network, and was so flooded with buyers that it decided to take the offer off the air in order to set a higher price. Financial planners are beginning to see more and more "television shopping addicts" than ever before and, unfortunately, they can be just as addicted as gamblers. If you avoid watching those networks altogether, you won't find yourself with a garage full of merchandise you will never use.

Now imagine that you had spent $25,000 on a section of the Brooklyn Bridge. Look at the age nearest yours on the Goal Game Chart and multiply that by 2.5. That's how much less you would have in your nest egg at retirement.

Whatever your savings goals are, the easiest way to save is to make it automatic. Contribute as much as you can up to the limit in retirement plans, and have it deducted from your paycheck. If you can afford to save more than that, have automatic payments taken out of your paycheck or checking account and deposited into a mutual fund account (we will discuss this later in the chapter).

If you are having trouble finding money to save, think about how you might trim your budget, even just a little. Here are some easy ways to save $5 a week:

- Bring your lunch to work once during the week, instead of eating out
- Wash your car instead of taking it to the car wash—and if you get your kids to help out, it can be family time together—what child can resist the urge to squirt a hose at her parent?
- Rent a video for free from the library instead of paying to get one from the video store (especially the kind you take out, don't watch for three days, and then pay late fees when you return it)
- Skip a couple of desserts—you will save calories as well as money, so your waistline will thank you as well as your pocketbook
- When friends call suggesting that you get together for dinner, instead of meeting at a restaurant, why not meet at someone's house and make it a pot luck meal?

■ How Can You Save if You Are ■
Having Trouble Making Ends Meet?

These days the truth is that a lot of people are having trouble saving for the future because they are having trouble paying for the present. If you fall into that trap, here are some very practical tips to help you downsize your budget on a larger scale without seriously compromising your lifestyle. Doing so will make it easier to sleep at night, knowing that you have more money in the bank and less on your credit cards.

Do Something Yourself That You Pay Someone Else to Do

One of the easiest ways to downsize your budget is to do a job yourself that you are currently paying someone else to do. That may sound like it would just take more time, which is also probably in short supply. But, in this fast-paced society it can give you what you need most—time for yourself.

I got this idea from a client who was complaining that he was spending $500 a summer to have his lawn mowed. In the next breath he said he never had any time to himself, now that he had small children. I suggested that he stop thinking of lawn mowing as a chore and instead think of it as an opportunity to have time completely on his own with no interruptions. He agreed to cancel the lawn service and mow the lawn himself, as long as a family rule was established that no one could interrupt him during that time. At our next meeting, he and his wife agreed that it was a great success. The children understood that they couldn't be involved in "dad's mowing time," and he was also setting a good example about doing manual labor himself. They saved $500 and began to look for other ways to "carve out personal time" and save money at the same time.

Even if there is a job you hate to do—and I confess that mine is certain types of housework—figure out what it will take to make the job bearable. For me, it is blasting rock music and singing while I am working, although my voice is so bad that I have to make sure that everyone else is out of the house!

What job are you paying someone else to do that you can take over? Think of it as your "special time"—as an opportunity rather than a chore.

Reduce Your Food Bill and Improve Your Life and Your Eating Habits at the Same Time

Some of us remember when Sunday dinner was a ritual family gathering; you missed it on pain of death. Today, with extracurricular activities, blended families, and longer work hours, family meal times have all but disappeared. But whether you live by yourself, with a partner, with or without children, you can create a new family tradition: a home-cooked meal at the same time every week.

Forty percent of our food budget goes to restaurants and fast food. But if you are like me, you prefer a home-cooked meal. Look at your own and the family's schedule and create a sacred family cooking time of a few hours on the weekend, preferably the same time every weekend. Together you can share the work of cooking a meal and then sit down together to eat it. If the weekend doesn't work, pick a weekday evening. If you are single, pair up with a neighbor or friend.

(If you can whip up meals for more than one night during your family cooking time, so much the better.) Everybody gets together in the kitchen, and jobs are given out according to age and skills. Together you create the week's meals and catch up on each other's lives at the same time. Each week, you decide on the next week's menu so the shopping can be done in advance.

Even if you use one of the food-delivery shopping services now available, you are bound to save money and you may have created the *only* real family time of the week. You have created a new family tradition even if you can't sit down to dinner together every night (or even two or three times a week). I have found that even teenagers love this idea (although they might not admit it); let them pick the music, if that's what it takes to get them involved. But start now—the younger your kids are when you get them involved in this tradition, the better your chance of success.

Cut Back on Gifts: It's the Thought That Counts

Gifts are one way to spend money without improving your lifestyle one bit. If you can cut down on your gift-giving by talking about the issue frankly with your friends and family, most people will be receptive to the idea.

I'm always amazed when I look at clients' budgets and see that their eight-year-old is expected to bring a $15 gift to fifteen parties a year. That's almost $250 a year, and many parents are carrying credit card debt to buy these gifts! Of course, when your own child has a party he gets fifteen $15 gifts back. But is that really necessary? By setting limits, you are teaching your children good lessons early on.

If your children are at the age where they are attending birthday parties, talk to the parents and see if you can all agree on a dollar limit for gifts. You could even write the limit on invitations.

When it comes to talking with your family about gift-giving, I suggest you handle the topic as gracefully as possible, perhaps presenting it with another relative who you know agrees with you. If you have a large extended family, for instance, many people choose to draw names for gifts at holidays. Let's face it: How many of us really want that sweater our aunt picked out for us, or that belt from our brother that we wouldn't be caught dead wearing? And our relatives probably don't want our gifts either. So it's all wasted money!

I know this from a friend's experience. She and her sisters keep passing around the same hideous earrings as a joke every Christmas. Some relative bought them for the oldest when she graduated from medical school. The sisters know who has them now, but never know who will get them next. It's hysterical, but the sad part is that they probably cost close to $100.

Shop at Discount Stores, Especially for Larger Items

Don't be sucked into buying something just because you see it at a discount store. On the other hand, if you are shopping for an item you need, you can save big bucks on certain items. For example, in 1994 there was an 11 percent increase in the number of off-price or speciality discount stores in the United States. By 1996, that number had risen to 35 percent, and women were spending 8 percent less on clothes than they had four years earlier, indicating that they were taking advantage of the lower-priced stores. Good things to buy discounted include electronic equipment, designer consignment clothing for yourself and "penny-a-pound" used clothing for your teenagers. Many discount clothing warehouses are open only on weekends.

☞ **Wake-up Call:** *Check the fees you are paying for banking, especially checking and ATM fees. A 1997 report by the U.S. Public Interest Research Group (US-PIRG) showed that customers pay 15 percent more to keep a regular checking account at a big bank than a small bank. So check out your local community bank and credit union if you are eligible for one. Compare all service fees, including ATM fees, checking fees, bank teller usage fees, etc.*

Rethink Your Vacation Plans

We are changing the way we take vacations. Today's trend is to take more vacations, but to make them shorter. The number of pleasure trips taken by Americans has increased 42 percent during the past decade, and at the same time, the average number of nights per vacation has slipped from six to four. Although these minivacations mean less time off from work, they tend to be more expensive when you factor in the more frequent airline flights to and from your destination.

Before you make major vacation plans, look at the Goal Game Chart to decide whether the cost is worth it. (*Parade* magazine interviewed people about whether they would prefer an extra week off or a 10 percent pay increase, and 42 percent said they would take the time off over the extra money. And it didn't matter what income bracket the participants were in.) I'm not suggesting you cut back on your time off, but simply that you reconsider how much you need to spend to enjoy that free time. How about touring the sights in your nearest big city or resort town? I am embarrassed to say that I've lived in Boston for twenty years and have never walked the Freedom Trail. But I'm sure many of us have not explored much of what is literally in our own backyards. And plan ahead if you have frequent flyer points—frequent flyer tickets are often difficult to get on short notice.

Set an Office Limit on Parties and Gifts

Especially if you work in a close-knit office, it seems that every week someone has a birthday, job anniversary, wedding, baby, or is moving on. Everyone is expected to chip in for a gift and maybe even go out to lunch. Even one lunch can blow your weekly budget right there. See if you can set some ground rules with your colleagues—I bet they have the same concerns that you do. One client of mine, Sophie, was spending about $30 a week on these kinds of events, which was expected as part of the corporate culture. As a result, she could not even put any money in her 401(k) even though the company matched her contribution. Talk about a nightmare situation! Sophie brought up this problem with her superior, who wrote a memo with guidelines about reasonable occasions and amounts, suggesting when gifts or lunch (not both) might be appropriate.

Her department had a meeting, and everyone in the office had the opportunity to chip in their thoughts and ideas. The solution they came up with was to bring pot lunches from home (which made the boss happy, because the entire department didn't disappear for two hours at noon) and set a strict budget limit on gifts. If someone didn't want to contribute money to a gift, he or she could make something or, of course, bow out altogether. Needless to say, Sophie was a heroine with her co-workers, who had the same financial pressures and concerns as she did.

STEP 3: INTELLIGENT INVESTING

Although I live right outside of Boston, my town has a population of only 20,000 so it very much has a small town feel. Having spent plenty of time on the sidelines of soccer fields, watching play practices, and volunteering for various kids' activities, it seems as if I know everyone in town. One morning a year or so ago, I sat next to an acquaintance on the commuter train, a high-powered banker named Erica whom I had previously just known as "Justin's mom." She apologized for not carrying on a conversation, but pulled out a dog-eared small notebook and began to furiously look through the *Wall Street Journal* to see how her investments had done the day before.

I was curious for two reasons. First, she is a banker and would have access to this information at her fingertips, via computer, the moment she got to her office. Second, I thought that as a banker, she would understand that following her investments on a day-to-day basis brought nothing but misery—that constant buying and selling get you nowhere.

But she was so obsessed with her investment portfolio that she could not even wait to get to the office. And on this particular day, the word "misery" applied in spades. It seemed that her portfolio had gone down, and from the expression on her face you would have thought that her dog had died. It was clear that her entire day was ruined. I tried to make her feel better by telling her I was sure she had time for her investments to go back up before she had to sell them (I knew that her kids were at least four years away from college) and what she had to say next astonished me. "Oh, I am not investing this money for any particular reason. I just want it to grow. I don't plan to ever use it."

I spent the rest of the day thinking how sad it was that her entire day was ruined because some money she'd never planned to touch had gone down a little in value, and how this scenario must be repeated over and over for her day after day—experiencing good days when her portfolio went up, and bad days when it went down.

It also amazed me that, as a banker, she had missed one of the cardinal rules of investing: Investing is not a goal in and of itself. It is a means to an end—your goals. Investing, which is central to any successful financial plan, means making your money grow so that you can use it in the future.

☞ **Wake-up Call:** Today's stock price doesn't matter. It is only when you actually sell that price makes a difference. Stop worrying about what the Dow Jones Industrial Average did yesterday! You may not own any of the thirty stocks that make up the average, so your investments may not have gone down even if the average did.

The biggest obstacle to investing is *finding the money to invest.* I just gave you a number of ideas to help you "power save," but in working with my own clients, I find that people often feel that they should get out of debt *before* they begin to invest. And since almost half of all households carry credit card debt, they never start investing. People who don't pay attention to their spending rarely find the money to invest, because they fritter away sums that could be set aside and invested for the future. In my speeches, I make jokes about the "Savings Police." I ask if anyone in the audience has ever heard of them, and of course no one has. But then I ask if they have ever heard of creditors' collectors coming to knock on your door to get a bill paid. Of course, everyone has heard of that. That is my point exactly: No one is ever going to come knocking at your door to make you invest. You have to do it on your own—so you have to save at the same time you are getting out of debt.

You don't have to save a lot to have it add up. How would you like to have $5,000 in 10 years? All you have to do is save $5 a week. To save almost $22,000 in twenty years, keep saving that $5 a week. If you can manage to save $20 a week, you will have close to $100,000 in 20 years. This assumes that you invest in a tax-sheltered retirement plan and get a 12 percent return.

■ What Kind of Return Can You Expect? ■

Let me share a story with you that illustrates the classic issue of unrealistic investor expectations. This is a real 1990s story, because during this decade the stock market has performed at historic levels. A couple was referred to me by their therapist because they were fighting so much about investing the therapist felt professional financial guidance was necessary. One spouse was making all of the financial and investment decisions; the other spouse, who had virtually no input into the day-to-

Investing $5 a Week

Years	5%	Return 10%	12%
5	$1,597	$1,685	$1,779
10	$3,979	$4,461	$5,017
15	$7,530	$9,036	$10,914
20	$12,828	$16,575	$21,651
25	$20,728	$28,999	$41,202
30	$32,509	$49,472	$76,801
35	$50,080	$83,211	$141,623
40	$76,285	$138,811	$259,654
45	$115,366	$230,435	$474,572
50	$173,649	$381,426	$865,908

Investing $10 a Week

Years	8%	Return 10%	12%
5	$3,194	$3,369	$3,357
10	$7,957	$8,921	$10,034
15	$15,061	$18,071	$21,827
20	$25,655	$33,149	$43,302
25	$41,455	$57,997	$82,404
30	$65,019	$98,944	$153,603
35	$100,160	$166,423	$283,246
40	$152,570	$277,622	$519,308
45	$230,731	$460,871	$949,144
50	$347,299	$762,852	$1,731,815

Investing $20 a Week

Years	8%	Return 10%	12%
5	$6,388	$6,738	$7,114
10	$15,914	$17,843	$20,068
15	$30,122	$36,142	$43,655
20	$51,310	$66,299	$86,604
25	$82,910	$115,994	$164,807
30	$130,037	$197,889	$307,205
35	$200,321	$332,845	$566,492
40	$305,140	$555,244	$1,038,616
45	$461,463	$921,741	$1,898,288
50	$694,598	$1,525,703	$3,463,631

day management of the finances, much less the selection of investments, was complaining bitterly because they had "only got an average of a 20 percent return for the last couple of years, and I know people who have gotten over a 25 percent return investing in the S & P 500." The nonparticipating spouse wanted to take overall control, but the one who had managed their money for so many years was unwilling to abdicate complete responsibility to someone with so little knowledge of investment strategy.

When I looked at their portfolio, it was clear why it had returned 20 percent, which is still an excellent return. A fair portion of their investments were in fixed income investments, which are less risky than stocks and therefore do not tend to do as well as the stock market over the long-term. But the real issue here was unrealistic expectations. In the mid-1990s, with the unprecedented run-up in the Standard & Poor's 500 (it tripled in seven years), there was not even one 10 percent "correction" or drop until September 1998.

Money has been pouring into the stock market in no small part because people expected such high returns. In fact, in 1997, 28 percent of all household wealth was tied up in stocks, and as of May 1997, 90 percent of all mutual fund assets had been invested since 1990. This market boom means new investors, inexperienced investors, investors

How Have Different Investments Performed?

Average annual returns for each decade.

	1920s	1930s	1940s	1950s	1960s	1970s	1980s	1990s	Long-term Average
Small Company Stocks	–4.5%	1.4%	20.7%	16.9%	15.5%	11.5%	15.8%	16.5%	12.7%
Blue Chip Stocks	19.2%	0.0%	9.2%	19.4%	7.8%	5.9%	17.5%	16.6%	11.0%
Long-term Corporate Bonds	5.2%	6.9%	2.7%	1.0%	1.7%	6.2%	13.0%	10.2%	5.7%
Long-term Gov't. Bonds	5.0%	4.9%	3.2%	–0.1%	1.4%	5.5%	12.6%	10.7%	5.2%
Inter-Term Government	4.2%	4.6%	1.8%	1.3%	3.5%	7.0%	11.9%	8.0%	5.3%
U.S. Treasury Bills	3.7%	0.6%	0.4%	1.9%	3.9%	6.3%	8.9%	5.0%	3.8%
Inflation	–1.0%	–2.0%	5.4%	2.2%	2.5%	7.4%	5.1%	3.1%	3.1%

SOURCE: Ibbotson Associates (12/31/97 figures)

with unrealistic expectations. Stock market mania has taken over. But keep in mind that in 1979 a *Business Week* cover story was entitled "The Death of Equities" and the Dow Jones Industrial Average actually fell 45 percent from 1973 to 1974. Stocks have not always been the best performers.

Since the end of World War II, the Dow Jones Industrial Average has dropped at least 20 percent over ten times. And throughout the twentieth century, the market has dropped 10 percent about every eighteen months on average. True to form, the market dropped about 12 percent between July and September, 1998.

Let's see how different kinds of investments have performed over the long run.

Large company stocks returned on average about 11 percent, and small company stocks averaged just under 13 percent. That is a lot less than 30 percent, so a 20 percent return on a portfolio that includes fixed income investments with lower returns is in fact an excellent track record.

■ Intelligent Investing ■

When you think about investing, especially for the first time, managing your own expectations is key. It would be great if the stock market would generate a consistently high return, but you can't count on that. Intelligent investing is a three-step process:

1. determining how much *risk* you can afford to take;
2. learning the *basics* about the different types of investments and the ways you can own them;
3. choosing an *investment strategy* that takes into account your risk tolerance, your goals, and when you need access to your money.

STEP 1: RISK

Risk is a big issue in investing, yet because of the spectacular returns of the 1990s, many people have thrown their money into the stock market without fully realizing that they can lose most or all of it. Too many people walk through my door with investments that are entirely inappropriate for them because they don't understand the risk involved.

☞ **Wake-up Call:** You could lose all the money you have tied up in investments. There are different kinds of risks, but the two big ones to keep in mind when planning your investment strategy are *investment risk* and *inflation risk*. With investment risk, you are taking the chance that whatever you put your money into will lose value. With inflation risk, there is a chance that the rate of return on your money won't keep up with inflation, so you lose purchasing power. The quandary is that the more guarantees you get on an investment (the fewer risks you take), the lower your rate of return is likely to be—and the greater your money's risk of succumbing to inflation.

You *do* need to take as much risk as you possibly can, because the greater the risk, the greater the potential reward. But you shouldn't take on any risk without first determining that it is a risk you can afford to take, both financially and psychologically. The more educated you become, the more "smart" risk you will feel comfortable taking. And most of us need to invest with maximum returns to make up for lost time, so it's time to get educated! By the time you finish this chapter, and use the reference charts to design your own individual strategy and choose your own individual investments, you will feel comfortable handling the level of risk that is necessary for you to reach your goals.

STEP 2: THE BASICS

Once you realize that it is important to take some calculated risks so you can reach your goals, you have a framework in which you can learn about different investments. Believe it or not, the basic types of investments are easy to explain. I have used the analogy of a lemonade stand for years; I have even been told by a number of investment experts that it is the simplest way of explaining stocks and bonds they have ever heard. So even if you consider yourself a sophisticated investor, you might find this new explanation to be of interest.

Most people invest their money in two basic kinds of investments— *fixed income* and *equities* (also called *stocks*).

First, let's look at *fixed income investments*. Fixed income investments include checking and savings accounts, money-market accounts, corporate bonds, government bonds, intermediate-term government bonds, certificates of deposits, U.S. Treasury bills, and others. Suppose you decide you want to build a lemonade stand and need to buy the grocery items for making lemonade. But you do not have enough money, so you have to borrow it. The kid up the street offers to lend you $5, provided you pay him the $5 back, plus $1 in interest, a month later. He has just bought a fixed income investment! In essence, he is now a bond holder. He gets his money back plus interest, which is what you are obligated to pay him. Regardless of how well or poorly your lemonade stand does, you still owe the money because he does not own any part of your business venture.

Because fixed income investments offer guarantees to the investor, they are considered low risk. A bond holder gets his money back plus a guaranteed rate of interest at the end of the loan period. If the kid up the street wanted to sell his fixed income investment in the lemonade stand to a neighbor, there would be no incentive for the neighbor to pay more than the kid invested—the amount of the loan plus interest—because that's all he'll get when the loan period is up. The price of the bond isn't affected by how much lemonade you sell or have left over.

Now let's look at the second basic type of investment: *equities* or *stocks*. Continuing with the lemonade stand analogy, you and the kid up the street agree to pool your money and buy the equipment and grocery items you need to get the stand up and running. You each own a share of the business, which is usually based on what percentage of the total you put into it. If the stand does well, you split the profits according to your percentage of ownership; if it does poorly, you lose money on the same basis. The point is that each of you has an ownership stake, and that there are no guarantees that you will get your money back if business is bad. On the other hand, if business is great, you could each make a bundle.

In the business world, business "incorporate" (become corporations) and issue stock. The price of a stock fluctuates because there are no guarantees that your chosen business will make money and the stock will increase in value. Instead, stock prices are based on various perceptions in the marketplace. And these perceptions are based on a host of things that can include anything from the price of lemons to the expected performance of the lemonade stand to the underlying strength of the neighborhood economy where the stand is set up. If you decided to sell your share of the business to a neighbor, perhaps you could convince a buyer to pay more for it than you did, based on their beliefs that the business will return greater profits.

Many people think that a third type of investment is a *mutual fund*. Actually, to use the same analogy, a mutual fund is just a way to buy and hold lots of different lemonade stands (stocks), or loans to lemonade stands (fixed income), or both. A mutual fund is like a big basket that holds different investments, and there are all kinds of different mutual funds, as the chart shows. When you buy a mutual fund, you rely on an investment manager and his staff to research the kinds of investments their fund is legally chartered to hold, and to then pick the stocks to buy and sell. An advantage of investing in a fund is that you own a variety of stocks or bonds, so that you don't get hammered if one investment takes a dive. You also don't have to depend on yourself to pick a successful investment: instead, trained market researchers do it for you.

The chart "Is This Mutual Fund Right for You?" shows the variety of mutual funds available today as well as their goals, investments, and degrees of risk and return. As you can see, there is a mutual fund for every investor and every degree of risk (and you should have mutual funds in each category to reduce your own degrees of risk as well—I will give you a blueprint for doing this later).

In recent years, public interest in mutual funds has grown in leaps and bounds. Six and a half million households have become first-time mutual fund holders in just three years (1994–1996), and there has been a veritable explosion in the number of mutual funds offered. In fact, there are now about 10,000 funds to choose from, and more than 15 percent of those have been opened since January 1997.

So how do you get educated about which mutual funds to buy? Fortunately, the Securities and Exchange Commission mutual fund regulations now allow mutual fund companies to give prospective purchasers three-page summaries of their prospectuses (the real ones are often dozens of pages long and completely full of legalese). A prospectus is a description of the investments in the fund, all fees and charges, past investment performance, the fund's objective, the investment management team, et cetera. It is important to examine all of these before you invest your hard-earned money!

There are also a number of mutual fund rating services that you can consult in your local library or on the Internet, such as Morningstar, which operates on a star system. It's kind of like going to the movies: the higher the number of stars, the better the fund has performed in the past relative to funds with similar objectives and investments. Of course, as the prospectus always states, past performance is no guarantee of future performance, but the longer the period of success, the better.

Most mutual funds require minimum investments (sometimes of $2,000 or more), but many will reduce those requirements if you commit to monthly direct transfers to your mutual fund account from your checking or savings account. Some minimums are waived entirely if you are saving in an IRA or other retirement plan account. If you can't find a fund that waives the minimum, simply accumulate your weekly or monthly savings in a savings account until you have enough to make that minimum investment in a mutual fund.

All funds are not created equal when it comes to charges. *No load* mutual funds do not charge any sales fees. A *load fund* charges a sales fee when you buy or sell it (it can be up to 8.5% of the initial investment or the price when you sell it, but sales fees are usually much less), some charge you every year, and so on. Some also charge extra annual marketing fees, called 12b-1 fees. And some funds have different classes that charge different fees! It can be very confusing.

All funds charge management fees, however. The chart "Is This Mutual Fund Right for You?" explains the various charges you may end up paying.

STEP 3: STRATEGY

Once you know your risk tolerance, and you understand the different types of investments, it is time to develop your investment strategy. That is a lot easier said than done! In mid-1998, when the stock market started to drop precipitously and then values continued to fluctuate all over the place, the financial media repeatedly advised the average investor to "just keep on with your investment strategy; that is the best blueprint for the long-term." I admit that I was even guilty of this myself in one particular segment of a national news program.

The next day I got a call at my office from a man who lived in another part of the country. With complete exasperation in his voice, Eduardo said to me, "I am sick and tired of you so-called experts telling me to 'stay the course' with my investment strategy. What happens if I never had a strategy to begin with? I'll bet that most of the people who watched you yesterday bought investments over the last few years exactly the way I did. I bought what looked good at the time or what you folks in the financial media told me was the latest high mutual fund or stock and sold the ones you told me to sell. It seems to me that it is too late for an investment strategy—my stocks are losing money left and right and I don't know whether to sell them or not."

Unfortunately, Eduardo practiced the same investment strategy that so many of us do, because we don't know a better way and we all are bombarded on all sides by advice about investments to buy and sell. I call it the "grocery store investment strategy." It is just like going to the grocery store when you are hungry and have no shopping list—you are just picking items off the shelf that look good. You have no idea of how many days of meals you are buying for (how long your investment time horizon is), how many people you are feeding (your goals), what the menu is (the investment options you have researched and selected), who has special dietary restrictions (how much risk you can take), and how prices compare (past performance, transaction costs such as commissions and fees, and possibilities for future performance).

In addition to getting you better returns over the long term, if you have an investment strategy, you can weather lots of ups and downs in your investment portfolio without developing an ulcer or making a foolish investment decision and selling something just because it has gone down in value. You know that you have a plan, and you know that the smartest thing to do is to stick to it and not worry about looking at the financial pages from day to day.

THE "WAKE-UP" INVESTMENT STRATEGY

My "Wake-up" Investment Strategy has four components—asset allocation, diversification, the use of index mutual funds as the cornerstone of your portfolio, and dollar cost averaging. The investment management firm I was with in the late 1980s first exposed me to asset allocation and index funds, at a time when neither strategy was widely used. When I saw the results, I became a convert and I use it in my own practice in investing money for my own clients.

Asset Allocation
The first component of my "Wake-up" Investment Strategy is asset allocation. With asset allocation, you invest your money in different types of investments—fixed income, United States stocks, and international stocks. International stocks are becoming more and more important as the U.S. share of the total global economy shrinks, so you should have at least some of your money there. With the financial crisis in Asia and other international spots in the latter half of this decade, you may be surprised to hear me make this recommendation. Some of the most sophisticated investors I know, however, are buying up investments from that part of the world. The principle of asset allocation is that certain kinds of

Is This Mutual Fund Right for You?

Type of Mutual Fund	Typical Investments	Goals of Fund Manager	Risk and Returns
Money Market Fund	Money Markets	Income	Low
Bond Fund	Government and/or Corporate Bonds	High Income; Little or No Growth	Low to Moderate
Balanced Fund	Stocks and Bonds	Moderate Income; Moderate Growth	Moderate
Equity Income Fund	Income Stocks	High Income; Moderate Growth	Moderate
Asset Allocation Fund	Cash, Bonds, and Stocks	Some Income; Moderate Growth	Moderate
Growth and Income Fund	Income Stocks, Growth Stocks	Some Income; Higher Growth	Moderate to High
Growth Fund	High Growth Stocks	High Growth; Low Income	High
Small Company Fund	Stocks Smaller than S&P 500s	High Growth, Low Income	Higher to Highest
Aggressive Growth Funds	High Growth Stocks, Riskier Strategies	Very High Growth; Low Income	Highest
Sector and Other Specialty Funds	Stocks from a Narrow Industry (Technology, Health Care, Precious Metals)	Very High Growth; Probably Low Income	Highest
Global Fund	Stocks from US & International Companies	High Growth; Low Income	Moderate to High
Foreign Funds	Stocks from Other Countries	High Growth; Low Income	Highest
European Funds	Stocks from Companies in Continental Europe and the U.K.	High Growth; Low Income	Highest

continued on next page

Is This Mutual Fund Right for You? (cont.)

Type of Mutual Fund	Typical Investments	Goals of Fund Manager	Risk and Returns
Pacific Region Funds	Stocks from Companies in Pacific Rim, Including Japan	High Growth; Low Income	Highest
Emerging Markets	Stocks from Companies in Developing Countries	High Growth; Low Income	Extremely High

SOURCE: Warner A. Henderson, Aequitas Investment Advisors

investments will do well at any particular time while other kinds will not do as well. So you protect yourself by spreading your money among a whole range of investments. That way, you are likely to do much better over the long term than if you bet all your money on one or two kinds.

Studies have shown that asset allocation accounts for well over 90 percent of how well your investment portfolio will do over time. The kind of investments you have (large company stocks, money-market accounts, etc.) are much more important than trying to figure out when is the best time to buy or sell an investment (called "market timing") or to pick XYZ stock or ABC stock (called "individual asset selection"). In fact, *together,* market timing and individual asset selection account for only about 7 or 8 percent of how well your portfolio is going to do over time. Boston Market is a great example. The company went public in the mid-1990s, and at one point the stock was at $40. It then dropped to a low of $2, and the company filed for bankruptcy. If you bought at $40 to make a profit and had to sell at $2, you were a victim of market timing. And by selecting Boston Market to start with, you were picking one particular stock, which is individual asset selection. I am not picking on Boston Market; it is one of my favorite restaurants. It is, however, an unfortunate illustration of why asset allocation works and these other methods don't. Picking a particular stock and trying to figure out when is the best time to buy and sell it just don't work as well as asset allocation does.

How Much Are You Paying for Your Mutual Fund?

All mutual funds charge a management fee (which includes investment research, administrative costs, etc.). "No-load" funds charge management fees only. "Load" funds charge additional fees (commissions, etc.) on top of management fees.

The rates of return you see quoted don't take front-end loads* or back-end loads† into consideration. But the same "load" mutual fund can even have different classes, each class with different charges!

For XYZ mutual fund:

Mutual Fund Class	Type of Fees
Class A	Front-end load and no extra annual management fees
Class B	Back-end load and no extra annual management fees
Class C	Extra annual management fees but no front-end or back-end loads
Class D	Level annual load and extra management fees

*Front-end load: fees incurred when you buy the fund.
†Back-end load: fees incurred when you sell the fund.

Whether you are a novice investor or a sophisticated wheeler-dealer—and no matter how long you have been investing—the most important thing to do is to develop a long-term strategy based on asset allocation. My "Wake-up" Investment Strategy chart, based on asset allocation, gives you my recommendations for how much of your money should be invested in which types of investments, depending on how long you have before retirement. (Refer back to "How Have Different Investments Performed?" to give you an idea of the kinds of returns you might expect over time.) And remember that "return" includes dividends and interest as well as appreciation (increase in value) of the investment itself. Just because a stock only paid you a 1 percent dividend, that does not mean that you only got a 1 percent return. It may have gone up 20 percent in value, so your total return for the year would be 21 percent.

As you can see from my investment strategy, the longer you have before retirement, the more risk you can afford to take (and remember, using the four components of my investment strategy will reduce your own investment risk as much as possible). Look at your own portfolio as a whole and see where you have your money invested now. It is probably not invested according to these percentages, so you will want to make changes slowly over time to bring it in line with my recommendations, but you should always feel free to do your own research and revise my percentages according to your comfort level.

Diversification

The second component of my investment strategy is the use of diversification. That is another fancy way of saying "don't put all of your eggs in one basket."

As you may suspect, I am a great fan of using mutual funds to give yourself the diversification you need. To get adequate diversification using stocks as a portion of your portfolio, you need at least twenty individual stocks. Since the cheapest way to buy stocks is in blocks of one hundred shares at a time, it is easy to see that many of us cannot achieve diversification just by buying individual stocks. And who knows which stock to buy? It is hard enough for the investment experts to predict this, much less the lay person who doesn't spend his or her entire working day researching with the most up-to-date computerized analytical tools.

Here is where you can use mutual funds to reduce your risk. First of all, the mutual funds you buy may each have dozens of holdings, so you end up owning lots and lots of stocks, bonds, etc. Second, you can use my "Is This Mutual Fund Right for You?" chart to choose a mutual fund in each asset allocation category that matches your risk. For example, under "small company stocks," you could have a small company fund and/or an aggressive growth fund. Both use "small cap" stocks, but the aggressive growth fund is riskier than the small company fund.

Since I have brought up the term "cap," let me explain it to you, because once you start investing, you see this term everywhere. "Cap" refers to "capitalization," which basically describes how large the company is. Stocks and stock mutual funds are described in this fashion, and there are small, medium and large "cap" companies. My chart "Caps" explains capitalization and what the size is for each of these categories. If you don't know this already, you should not feel ashamed. An investment specialist with ten years of experience recently confided in me that

The Wake-up Investment Strategy, Using Asset Allocation

Percentages are the portion of your money that should be in each type of investment. For example, if you have twenty or more years until your retirement, you should have 25 percent of your money in small company stock.

Type of Investment	Years Until Retirement					
	0	1–5	6–10	11–15	16–20	20+
Stocks						
Small company stocks	8%	10%	14%	17%	20%	25%
International stocks	7%	10%	13%	16%	20%	20%
Large company stocks	45%	45%	43%	42%	40%	40%
Fixed Income						
Bonds, CDs, etc.	30%	25%	20%	15%	10%	5%
Money market/checking account	10%	10%	10%	10%	10%	10%

Note: This assumes all of your money is to be used for retirement. If you have other goals that will be funded in the next ten years, more of your money should be put in fixed income than the percentages shown here. This also assumes that you have a diversified portfolio with mutual funds or at least twenty individual investments.

he had only figured out what "cap" really meant after about five years on the job. And different investment experts may use different valuations, but the ones I have included on my chart are standard definitions.

Index Funds

The third component of my investment strategy is the use of index funds. An index is a way to measure how a particular part of the investment market is doing. For example, the Standard & Poors 500 is an index, and so is the Dow Jones Industrial Average. The number of indices has skyrocketed in the last decade—as of July 1998 Morningstar's Principia software for professional investment managers listed 101 indices measuring everything from a tiny part of the bond market to 6,500 stocks! More and more people are finding that a great way to invest is in index funds.

Index funds are exactly what they say they are—the assets in the fund are exactly the same as what makes up that particular index. The beauty of index funds is that the index mutual fund is buying *exactly* what is in the index, so no expensive research teams are required. And when you realize that most "actively managed" (where there is an investment manager and research team trying to beat the index) diversified U.S. stock funds have been outperformed by the S&P 500 stock index over the last few years, you see the beauty of indexing.

When I work with novice investors, I always recommend that they

Caps

"Cap" is short for "capitalization," and, in this context, is another name for "company." Stocks are constantly referred to as "small cap," "medium cap," or "large cap." There are differences and risks for each. The smaller the company, usually the riskier it is. Market capitalization is the value of the company.

Capitalization = (current price per share) × (number of shares outstanding)

Company Size	Market Capitalization
Small cap	under $1 billion
Medium cap	$1 to $5 billion
Large cap	$5 billion and over

put at least some of their money in an S&P 500 Index fund. This is to get them "hooked" on investing, because they can open up the business section of the newspaper every day and see on the first page how well their funds did—most papers put index returns at the top of the headlines in a box. You can also hear the results every night on the evening news, and usually while driving home from work.

There are so many indices these days that it is smart to know what is in each of them, so if you decide to invest in index funds you need to have some good information at your fingertips. My chart on the next page describes the most well-known index funds and what is in them.

Dollar Cost Averaging

The last component of my investment strategy is dollar cost averaging. Basically, this means that you should not put all your money into the stock market at once, nor should you take it out all at once. If you do this, you risk buying high and selling low—buying when prices are at a peak and then selling when they are at a low. The best way to invest over time (or to de-invest) is to mentally divide up the money that you plan to invest in the stock market and invest it every month or every quarter for a year or eighteen months. Investment studies have shown, over and over again, that this is the least risky way of investing in the stock market, and the way to get the highest returns.

Thinking back to my acquaintance who tracked how well her portfolio was doing in her dog-eared notebook every day, you may be wondering how often you should look at your own portfolio. You should look at your portfolio every three to six months or so, and make changes every six months or a year as needed to make sure that your assets are invested according to the percentages of my "Wake Up" Investment Strategy (some investments will do better than others, so your percentages will be off at the end of any time period). In addition to getting a better return on your investments, you'll also sleep better at night because you won't be obsessed with what is happening on a day-to-day basis in the market in general and with your investments in particular. And you won't be tempted to buy or sell due to market timing or how well one particular investment is doing.

Whether you are a new investor or have been investing for thirty years, I recommend a long-term investment strategy. Even if you are about to retire, you are likely to live twenty or more years, and if you put all your money in fixed income investments their value is going to be beat out by inflation. It is very tempting to do this, and many retirees do

What's in a Stock Index Fund?

Index Fund	Types of Investments
Dow Jones Industrial Average	■ 30 stocks ■ largest, most established companies ■ represent a range of industries
Standard & Poor's 500	■ large firms ■ 400 industrial, 40 financial, 40 utilities, 20 transportation
Russell 2000	■ 2000 smallest US companies in the Russell 3000 (which is made up of the 3000 largest American stocks), based on total market capitalization ■ represents about 98% of US investable equity market
Morgan Stanley: MSCI-EAFA	■ Europe, Australasia, the Far East ■ 1000 stocks traded on stock exchanges around the world
Morgan Stanley Emerging Markets	■ 700 stocks from 23 developing countries
NASDAQ Composite	■ disproportionately tech-heavy ■ mostly smaller companies, but does include big companies like Microsoft

move their money to CDs as soon as they get that last paycheck, but it is a big mistake. Remember that the longer you have to invest, the more risk you can take. But my investment strategy of asset allocation, diversification, using index funds, and dollar cost averaging reduces your risk to the lowest possible minimum.

■ The Mechanics of Investing ■

Because I work with money all day, I sometimes forget just how complicated investing can be, especially for the new investor. A client pointed this out to me when, in response to my follow-up call from our meeting, she admitted that although she knew exactly what I had recommended she invest in, she did not know the mechanics of opening an account. If you are buying investments through a company retirement plan, the process is easy—you simply go to your employee benefits manager (or whoever is in charge) and sign up. But what if you are buying investments on your own, either for an Individual Retirement Account (IRA), other retirement plan for yourself such as a Keogh, or a regular account? If you are just buying CDs, money market accounts, etc. you can do that at your local bank. You simply open the appropriate type of account, be it IRA, regular (nonretirement plan), etc. But when you are buying investments such as bonds, stocks, and mutual funds, you need to use a *brokerage firm,* which is an investment firm that is overseen by the Securities and Exchange Commission (SEC). To open an account at any kind of brokerage firm, you complete an application and send a check along with instructions on how to invest the money. After that, you can usually buy and sell your investments over the phone.

When your parents bought stocks or bonds, they really had only one option and that was to deal with a *retail stockbroker.* These days you have so many options it is mind-boggling. A retail stockbroker is a person who works for a retail stock brokerage firm and who specializes in "trading" (buying and selling) investments for individual clients and giving them advice about which stocks, bonds, and mutual funds to buy and sell. These days, retail stockbrokers have also branched out to offer some other financial planning services, insurance products, and more. A retail stockbroker is usually paid on a commission basis, for the trades that he makes for you. The advantage is that you get individualized attention; the disadvantage is that you will probably pay higher fees and commissions for that attention than if you take the do-it-yourself approach.

If you feel confident making your own investment decisions, you can use a *discount brokerage firm,* such as Charles Schwab, Jack White, Waterhouse Securities, or others. In general, you do not have your own personal stockbroker but you call the firm and instruct to buy or sell as you see fit. There are even Internet discount brokerage firms. The disadvantage is that you will not be given any personalized advice; the advantage is that the commissions are usually substantially less than with a retail brokerage firm. Some people also prefer not to deal with a salesperson, especially if they have a hard time saying no. Some stockbrokers can be very aggressive, although most are very professional.

Both retail and discount brokerage firms now allow access to virtually all of their services via the Internet. In fact, there are now even specialized Internet brokerage firms that allow you to do your own trading online at rock-bottom prices. To remain competitive in such an environment where the consumer has so many options, all brokerage firms give their clients access to extensive research information on the vast array of stocks, bonds, and mutual funds available.

Another investment option is to use a professional *money management firm,* which usually charges you a fee based on the amount of assets it is managing for you. Many money management firms have minimum required investment account amounts such as $100,000 or much higher (many are $500,000 or more). If you have a sizable portfolio, a professional money management firm probably makes sense for you. Many people like money management firms because they can give overall responsibility for their money management to an institution and not have to worry about making decisions on their own or based on the recommendation of a stockbroker.

A final word is in order, and that is about investing in your own company's stock. Company stock is usually offered as an investment option in the company retirement plan, and company stock makes up on average about 25 percent of an individual's investments in his corporate retirement plan. This is not an investment strategy I recommend. Why? Your current income and future financial security are already tied up in your company, so why invest your retirement plan money in it as well? If the company does poorly, the stock value may not only drop but you may lose your job as well—a real double whammy. You need to diversify by buying other investments in your company retirement plan. Unfortunately, many companies try to pressure their employees into buying company stock by making it an issue of "employee loyalty." This is illegal, and if it happens to you, you should resist the pressure—in fact, the more pressure you get, the more concerned you should be about the company.

Although investing in company stock in or out of your retirement plan is usually not a good idea, there actually is one scenario where it makes sense. To keep valuable workers, companies often give them stock options which allow them to buy a certain number of shares of stock at a certain price, starting at a certain date. Right now six million American workers have stock options, and that number is likely to grow. All you have to do is look at the many Microsoft millionaires to see how valuable stock options can be.

The idea is that the company gives you the right to buy company stock at a relatively low price at a certain date. If you are fortunate, by the time that you can "exercise the option" (buy the stock) it will have gone up in value by a substantial margin. There are all kinds of tax implications involved, and you'll need to talk to a professional financial adviser who has experience with stock options before you make any decisions. But they can be a very valuable way to increase your net worth.

STEP 4: TAX-ADVANTAGED INVESTING

Tax planning around investing is a simple matter for most investors. The biggest break you'll get is by investing the maximum in your retirement plans at work and also in an IRA you set up on your own if you are eligible.

If you are fully funding all of the retirement plans available to you, another type of investment with tax advantages is an annuity. Cora and Edward personify many of the clients I have seen over the years—they have a great fear of outliving their money as well as the desire to take advantage of every tax shelter available. If you are like them, annuities may be worth considering.

There are a variety of annuities available that can be tailored to your particular needs. An annuity is like a "tax wrapper" that protects the assets in it until you open the wrapper. And they are becoming more and more popular; as of early 1998, $1 trillion in assets were sitting in fixed and variable annuities. That's a lot of money being tax sheltered (no earnings or appreciation in the annuity is taxed until you start to take the money out, and only part is taxed with each withdrawal). Annuities also guarantee to pay you an income for as long as you live—even if you have spent every other dime you have. The insurance company that issues the annuity guarantees a monthly or quarterly payment to you (and perhaps your spouse if you have selected a joint and survivor payout option) even if the money you invested in the annuity as well as its earnings ran out long ago.

There are two types of annuities, based on how the money is invested, and within those types you can choose when you want payments to start. A *fixed annuity* pays a guaranteed minimum interest rate (and usually an interest rate a point or two above that), adjusted on a regular basis, such as quarterly or annually. If you want guarantees, this is the annuity for you, but you run the risk of having the return barely outpace inflation.

An alternative is a *variable annuity*, which is actually a "tax wrapper" for a variety of mutual funds from which you have to choose. With a variable annuity, *you* are responsible for making the investment decisions, and the worst thing you can do (which I see all the time) is buy a variable annuity and then put all the money in a money-market or guaranteed income account. The reason this is a problem is that annuities generally have high annual fees, and after you subtract those expenses you actually may be getting a negative rate of return.

My recommendation is almost always a variable annuity with your investments primarily in the stock mutual funds available, as long as you understand that you are taking some stock market risk. This way you are likely to get a higher return overall than with a fixed annuity.

When you choose a fixed or variable annuity, you must decide whether you want a deferred or immediate annuity. A *deferred annuity* means that you are putting money in now (either a lump sum or payments over time) without taking any money out. An *immediate annuity* means that you are putting in a lump sum and planning to start taking out regular payments now.

Right now, in your Building Up years, it makes sense for you to buy a deferred annuity. But you should not be investing in annuities until you have fully funded all of the other retirement plans available to you. It is also best to avoid the commission-based annuity products and buy directly from insurance companies and discount brokerage firms—more and more are offering these "no-load" products. The reason is that the commission must be paid out of the annual expenses charged to the annuity, and the average expense is 1.25 percent and can sometimes exceed 3 percent. With a "no-load" annuity, however, you may be able to get that annual expense down to as low as .5 percent.

STEP 5: PROTECTING YOUR ASSETS AGAINST LOSS

LIFE INSURANCE

This is the section no one likes to read, the topic no one likes to discuss at my client meetings—and it's easy to see why. As Connie said to me, "I came for financial planning because I want to think about living, not dying. But I'm divorced, and I need to plan for my kids if I die." No one likes to contemplate his own death. But if you think of life insurance as a way to ease the financial pain inflicted on your loved ones in the event that you die prematurely, perhaps that will stop you from skipping over the next few pages. Certainly those who love and depend on you will appreciate your courage and foresight if they ever have to face the prospect of living without you, especially when it comes to your children, because this decision literally determines their future.

The purpose of life insurance is to guarantee that the people you currently support can continue to enjoy the same lifestyle after your death. In fact, it is an amazing financial product. How else can you make sure that your loved ones will have enough money after you die, even if you only have $500 in the bank at the time?

Most people need life insurance. The only exception is if you are single with no dependents, and your parents or other relatives didn't give you money for college or a down payment on a house that you'd like to repay, and you also have enough assets to cover the cost of your funeral. Even then, you might want to consider taking out a policy and naming your favorite relative or charity as the beneficiary (or at least name him, her, or it as the beneficiary on your policy at work). Today, I sometimes see singles buying insurance to cover the costs of college for their nieces and nephews. As Jane said, "I figure I'll want to—and need to—help out when my three nephews go to college, and I want to make sure the money will be there, even if I'm not." At the time when you are building up your assets for the future, it is reassuring to know that with a life insurance policy, you can provide for your dependents so they can meet their financial goals, even in the event of your death.

Once you reach midlife, the reality of your mortality begins to show in the actuarial tables (and you have perhaps experienced the death of someone close to you). If you are twenty-five, your odds of dying in the next twenty years are one in forty-one. If you are thirty-five, the odds are one in fifteen. But the time you reach forty-five, the odds are one in six. Life insurance should be used to generate the cash needed to cover your financial responsibilities after your death. But it can also accomplish some things that you may have wanted to do in life but couldn't afford—such as paying off a big debt (for instance, your mortgage) or funding a good cause.

■ How Will the Money Be Used? ■

Dying is expensive! The cost of a funeral, even a simple one, can easily run $10,000 or more, not counting travel expenses for your loved ones. Other costs may include medical expenses not covered by insurance; the legal and administrative costs associated with settling your estate; and estate taxes (although very few estates actually owe estate taxes; see Chapter 6, "Happy Endings," page 331 for more information).

If you don't want your family to have to keep paying your mortgage if they retain ownership of your house, you may want to get enough coverage to pay it off so they don't have to worry about it—or at least give them the option to do so. Mortgage payoffs are particularly important if your mortgage exceeds the market value of your home (this happens when real estate values drop). In that case, if your spouse or other beneficiary sells the home, he may even have to add some of his own cash on top of the sales proceeds to pay off the mortgage bill. But avoid "mortgage" insurance that will pay off your mortgage if one of the mortgage holders dies. These policies are offered by lenders and are usually overpriced—just get regular life insurance instead. And don't confuse them with the private mortgage insurance (PMI) you may have had to buy if your down payment was less than 20 percent. PMI is protection for the lender in case you default on your loan, NOT life insurance.

You may also want enough coverage to pay for educational goals (for your children, or for your spouse to return to school to develop a new career) and for life's little "extras" like being able to continue going to the same beach house for vacations every summer. When we looked at one couple's insurance situation, Phyllis said, "I've wanted to go back to school to become a physical therapist ever since I fell and broke my ankle five years ago. But with the three kids, I'm pretty much a full-time, stay-at-home mom. On the other hand, if Jack were to die, I'd need a profession. Being able to go to school for physical therapy would give me a marketable skill, and also would allow me to pursue something I'm interested in."

On top of these goals, add enough for an emergency fund of at least

Do You Need More Life Insurance?

Lump Sum Need

			Example
	Funeral expenses	A.	$5,000
Plus	Final expenses (medical, etc.)	B.	$5,000
Plus	Estate taxes (vary by state of residence and size of estate)	C.	$0
Plus	Current mortgage balance (optional)	D.	$135,000
Plus	Current balance of other debts (optional)	E.	$10,000
Plus	College fund	F.	$50,000
Plus	Special need (any amount you want your family to have after your death)	G.	$5,000
Equals:	**Total Lump Sum Need**	**H.**	**$210,000**

Living Expense Need

			Example
	Your current living expenses	I.	$35,000
Times:	0.8		× 0.8
Equals:	Family living expenses after your death	J.	$28,000
Less:	Spouse's take-home pay/other income	K.	$10,000
Less:	Social Security survivor's annual benefit (multiply monthly benefit by 12)	L.	$11,100

continued on next page

Do You Need More Life Insurance? (cont.)

Living Expense Need (cont.)

				Example
Equals:	Additional annual living expense need	M.		$6,900
Times:	Number of years needed		× _____	15
Equals:	**Total Living Expense Shortfall**	N.		**$103,500**
Total assets you need (H + N)		O.		$313,500
Current insurance death benefits		P.		$55,000
Current investment assets		Q.		$25,000
Total assets you have (P + Q)		R.		**$80,000**
Total:		S.		$393,500
Your Additional Insurance Needs (O − R)				

$25,000 for your heirs because the rest of your money may be tied up for months—or even years—in the estate settlement process. Meanwhile, the bills will continue to mount. One of the beauties of life insurance is that as long as you name a person, not your estate, as beneficiary, the death benefit is usually paid to that person right away—you don't have to wait for your estate to go through the probate process (which we will discuss in Chapter 6).

■ **How Much Do You Need?** ■

A classic rule of thumb is that you need life insurance equal to five times your salary, but in twenty-five years as a financial planner, I've never seen anyone who has needed that exact amount. Putting an exact number on how much life insurance you need requires some careful figuring, but it is worth being as accurate as possible. Otherwise you may spend too much on unnecessary premiums, or too little. Your beneficiaries will never complain that you had too much insurance, but if you don't have enough, you could deprive your beneficiaries of the financial security you intended to provide.

Among the factors you should consider are:

- the kind of lifestyle you want to provide for your family
- your nonworking spouse or partner, who wouldn't have an income if you died
- the cost of child care if your nonworking spouse or partner returned to work
- your working spouse or partner, who may need to "retire" to raise your children
- any debts that you want paid off (such as mortgage, car loan, or credit card)
- college expenses, if you have children
- special needs, such as a handicapped child or a child who will never be self-supporting
- your parents, who may eventually become financially dependent on you
- anyone else who currently depends on your income or might in the future
- a relative or nonrelative for whom you would like to provide additional income
- any special bequests to charities

In addition, if you are childless now, but think you might have children in the future, you might want to buy an inexpensive life insurance policy now that guarantees you the right to purchase additional insurance at future dates, regardless of your health. (You usually have at least five specific dates—typically three years apart—at which you can buy more coverage.) Waiting until you have children to purchase a policy can be a mistake if between now and then you develop a health problem that makes insurance very expensive or even makes you uninsurable.

One myth is that the rich don't need life insurance. There are sophisticated policies designed for the super rich that pay their huge estate taxes. If your taxable estate currently approaches $700,000 and you're single, or $1.4 million if you are married (in which case you should have already done estate planning to minimize your estate taxes), you will need enough liquid assets (converted to cash) to pay estate taxes, which the IRS will want paid within nine months. (You can get more details on estate taxes in Chapter 6.) If you don't have enough, you should consider investing in a life insurance policy to cover these costs.

Another reason to buy a life insurance policy is to leave money to a charity. Would you like to set up a scholarship fund in your name for your alma mater? Do you want to fund a community outreach program for your church or synagogue? Is there a nonprofit group you'd like to assist? You can do this by naming the charity as the owner and beneficiary, with your paying the annual premiums. You get to support a good cause, and as long as the charity is the owner of the policy, you can deduct the premiums as charitable contributions on your annual income taxes.

■ Divorced or Single? ■

If you fall into either one of these categories, you have special insurance needs. If you have financial obligations toward your ex-spouse and/or children, your divorce agreement may stipulate that you have to carry a policy worth a certain amount to cover your obligations if you die. Even if it is not required by your decree, if you don't have the assets to cover college costs or to leave an inheritance to your children, you should buy insurance.

Single people are often told they don't need insurance, or that the small policy that comes with their work benefits is enough. In many cases, that's correct. If you lead a simple life with no mortgage or "significant other" to provide for, a life insurance policy may be an unnecessary expense. Certain circumstances may cause you to reconsider, for instance:

- if you have a mortgage that is more than the value of your house (based on the current market value of similar houses in your area) so that extra cash would be needed to pay it off if the house were sold
- if a relative has co-signed your mortgage; having it paid off immediately at your death means he does not have to keep making monthly payments until your home is sold
- you have a friend or relative to whom you want to leave money
- you have bought a house with your live-in partner and you have an agreement that each person's share of the mortgage is to be paid off at death
- your parents are already (or will be) depending on you for financial support
- you want to leave money to a charity or other nonprofit organization

■ Capital Needs Analysis ■

Completing a "Capital Needs Analysis" is the most accurate way to determine your life insurance needs. This can be done by the expert from whom you purchase your policy (I recommend either a fee-only financial planner who can arrange for you to buy a commission-free policy, or an insurance sales agent whom you trust).

■ Term Versus Permanent Insurance ■

Once you figure out how much coverage you need, you face the question of what kind of policy is right for you—*term, permanent,* or a combination of both?

First, let's run through the basic definitions:

Term life policies offer death benefits only so if you die your beneficiaries get paid, but you get no money back when you cancel the policy if you live. If the only way you can afford all the insurance you need is to buy term, *do it*. The amount you get is more important than the length of the policy.

Permanent life policies offer death benefits and a "savings account" (also called "cash value" or "account value") so if you live you usually get at least some money back, and if you keep paying the premium long enough, often much more than the amount you spent on premiums. You can get this money back either by cashing in the policy or by borrowing against it.

As you might expect, permanent life insurance premiums are the more expensive of the two because some of the money is put into a savings program. The longer the policy has been in force (in existence), the higher its cash value. More money has been paid in, and the cash value earns interest, dividends, or both.

Here's the $64,000 question that has had insurance experts arguing for years: Is it better to pay higher permanent insurance premiums in the early years, or choose a less expensive term policy and invest the premium money you saved in other types of investments (such as certificates of deposit, mutual funds or stocks) where the return may be higher than what the insurer is offering?

Some advisors suggest that you should buy term and invest the difference. But if you keep a permanent life policy long enough, a permanent policy is a better investment because the increase in its cash value is free from taxes until you cash it in. "Long enough" varies, depending on your age, health, insurance company, the type of policy chosen, interest and dividend rates, and more. There isn't a simple answer, because we can't predict the future—how fast a policy's cash value will grow or how your insurance needs may change.

One key variable is how long you expect to keep the policy. If your answer is less than ten years, term should be your clear choice. If you plan to hold onto a policy for more than twenty years, you should consider permanent life. The big gray area is if your time horizon falls somewhere in between. That's usually when you need an expert to run a term-vs.-permanent analysis for you.

■ Term Insurance ■

For most people, term insurance is the way to go. It is the least expensive option for taking care of your beneficiaries' financial needs. It's easy to understand and relatively simple to purchase. You can buy policies that stop after ten or twenty years, or that can even be continued until age 100. You can select a policy with annual premium increases (called "annual renewal term") or that stays fixed for a certain number of years (usually ten or twenty). The ten- or twenty-year term insurance may be cheaper in the long run.

Most term policies offer both a "current payment schedule" and a "maximum" rate for each year because they reserve the right to increase premiums if company costs increase. With others, the issue is your health. At certain "reentry" ages you may have to prove your good health in order to keep the lower premium. I avoid reentry policies because they mean my client has to be reexamined by a health professional at each reentry period, and if he is not healthy enough, he is stuck with a very high premium to keep the policy in force. This happened to Duncan, who (of course) never expected to develop heart trouble, and ended up with premiums that almost doubled when he was reexamined five years after buying his term policy.

The good news is that if you realize you will need the coverage for a much longer period of time than you originally thought (for example, if the policy you bought for a college fund in five years will now be needed for estate taxes, which is a lifetime need because your stock options have now become so valuable), most term policies are convertible to permanent ones without evidence of good health.

■ Permanent Life ■

Permanent life is an option worth considering if you plan to hold onto your policy for twenty years or more and if, after socking away as much savings as you can in tax-free retirement plans and other tax-advantaged investments such as annuities (see "Step 4: Tax-Advantaged Investing"), you are looking for other ways to build up some savings.

It is a much more complicated product to buy, however, because most policies have guaranteed and nonguaranteed portions, and it should never be bought for investment purposes alone, because of the high annual expense fees and life insurance costs. There are three main types of permanent insurance:

Whole Life
This type of coverage has a guaranteed annual premium, and there are minimum guaranteed cash values and death benefits. Most whole life policies these days are "participating," meaning that they earn dividends that can be used to increase the policy's cash value and/or death benefits, decrease its premiums, or be refunded in cash. If you are a conservative investor and have trouble saving, whole life insurance can make sense for you.

Universal Life

If you need premium flexibility, especially in the early years of the policy, you should consider universal life. Universal life, developed in the 1970s when industry regulations were loosened so that insurance products could be more competitive with other financial products, is more flexible than whole life. The premiums can vary from year to year and sometimes can even be skipped. It carries maximum guaranteed premiums and minimum guaranteed cash values and death benefits. Instead of dividends, universal life policies earn interest at the "credited interest rate" determined each year by the company.

Variable Life

If you consider yourself a knowledgeable and risk-accepting investor, check out variable life insurance, which has the fewest number of guarantees and therefore offers the greatest potential for cash value increases. There are required guaranteed annual premiums and a guaranteed minimum death benefit. There is no guaranteed cash value, however, and *you* have to select the investments for your policy. You get to choose from a variety of mutual fund accounts ranging from money market to aggressive growth funds, and the cash value amount you get depends on the funds you choose.

☞ **Wake-up Call:** Life insurance should never be purchased solely as an investment. After all, some of your premiums will be used to pay for death benefit coverage (mortality costs) and to cover other expenses (sometimes including large commissions that, in total, exceed 100 percent of the first year's premiums). Nor should life insurance be purchased on children as a way to save for college. It is often marketed this way, but if you do this, you must pay all those unnecessary extra expenses such as term insurance costs for insuring your child, *and* you need to make sure that you (and your spouse or partner) first have all the coverage you need on yourselves.

Some advice if you are considering permanent insurance:

■ Find an Agent You Trust ■

Buying permanent insurance is so complicated that it is usually wise to consult an expert. In fact, I think it makes sense to decide *who* you want to help you make this decision before deciding exactly what you want to buy. (This is not as necessary for term insurance, which has a guaranteed premium for a guaranteed period of time, so you can more easily "compare apples to apples.")

You can consult a fee-only planner (who will not earn a commission on the sale). Other possibilities are an insurance agent whom you trust, and who sells a variety of products.

■ Avoid Churning ■

Some unscrupulous insurance agents urge their clients to replace their policies unnecessarily as a way of drumming up additional commissions. If you are advised to replace a policy you bought in the past, get a second opinion from a fee-only planner or another expert who doesn't stand to benefit from the extra commission. Ask the agent advising replacement to give you a completed copy of the Society of Financial Service Professionals (formerly known as The American Society of CLU & ChFC) Replacement Questionnaire.

■ Avoid the Illustration Trap ■

Recently, I got a call from a friend who was in absolute despair. She said she'd been trying to buy $300,000 worth of permanent life insurance and was going crazy. She had two agents, each with four illustrations, and the stack of paper was over six inches tall. She was more confused than when she'd started—and had spent thirty hours on the project!

A life insurance policy illustration is a set of projections prepared by the actuarial department of the insurance company. It shows how your policy may perform over your lifetime, including financial projections for each year, typically to your 100th birthday and sometimes beyond.

The problem is that these documents can run ten pages with 1,000 or more numbers, most of them not guaranteed. Reputable agents will tell you to forget the nonguaranteed numbers and simply look at the guaranteed premiums, cash value, and death benefits. But if your agent tries to sell you a product based on a company's "current interest rate" and "current dividend rate," walk away. If you read the fine print, you will discover that most of these rates are only guaranteed for three to twelve months. The financial strength of an insurance company is much more important.

■ Check Out Your Insurance Company's Rating ■

Before you settle on a permanent life insurance policy, check out the company's financial ratings. Insurance ratings are letter grades assigned to insurers based on the financial strength of the company. Don't panic—insurance companies are very well-regulated by state insurance departments, and after the debacle of a few insurance companies getting into financial trouble in the last ten years, the rules are stricter than ever. Even so, it's smart to go with a company with a top strength rating.

The top rating agencies use letter grades to rate insurance companies ranging from A to C, but each company has its own version. (See chart below.) The general rule of thumb: Buy a policy from a company that is rated by at least three of the five rating services and has one of the top three ratings by at least two of those services. You want to be certain that when you or your heirs deserve a payout, you'll get the entire amount you deserve.

■ Disability Insurance ■

It is hard for me to be dispassionate about disability insurance because of my own personal experiences. After all, I spent five years bedridden when I was only in my twenties, unable to work, after spending several years on a career "fast track." If it can happen to me, it can happen to you. And it can happen: You have a 20 percent chance of being disabled for five or more years before you reach age sixty-five. It's not a cheering thought, but it is less frightening if you have some protection in place.

What is *long-term disability insurance?* It guarantees you an income in the event that you cannot work for an extended period because of a serious illness or accident. How much do you need? I advise getting a policy that will guarantee as much income as you can get, and that will provide payments until you reach age sixty-five, if that option is available. Insurance companies normally won't sell you a policy that, combined with any coverage you have at work, will exceed 60 percent of your income. That's because you would be getting just as much money while disabled as you would if you were working—companies call this a "disincentive to work."

Even though you obviously will have fewer work-related expenses, like clothes and office supplies, you probably will have more than enough new expenses related to your condition—you may have to pay someone

Insurance Ratings Services: How They Rate the Financial Strength of Insurance Companies

A.M. Best	Duff & Phelps	Moody's	Standard & Poor's	Weiss
A++	AAA	Aaa	AAA	A+
A+	AA+	Aa1	AA+	A
A	AA	Aa2	AA	A−
A−	AA−	Aa3	AA−	B+
B++	A+	A1	A+	B
B+	A	A2	A	B−
B	A−	A3	A−	C+
B−	BBB+	Baa1	BBB+	C
C++	BBB	Baa2	BBB	C−
C+	BBB−	Baa3	BBB−	D+
C	BB+	Ba1	BB+	D
C−	BB	Ba2	BB	D−
D	BB−	Ba3	BB−	E+
E	B+	B1	B+	E
F	B	B2	B	E−
	B−	B3	B−	F
	CCC	Caa1	CCC	
	DD	Caa2	CC	
		Caa3	R	
		Ca		
		C		

Note: For each rating service, the higher the ranking (AAA for Duff & Phelps vs. AA+ for A.M. Best, for example), the better. However, each ratings service has different criteria, so the third-highest ranking from one service is not equivalent to the third-highest ranking from another (for example, an A from A.M. Best and AA− from Duff & Phelps are not necessarily equal).

to come in and help you with household chores, for instance—to make up the difference. The advantage of any disability income from policies on which you pay the premiums is that the benefits are income-tax free.

When you buy an individual policy, try to buy one in which the definition of total disability is "own occupation" rather than "any occupation." That way you will be covered if you cannot continue in your own line of work. Otherwise, you have to prove that you cannot do any job that matches your skills and education.

The policy also should be "guaranteed renewable and noncancelable," so that the insurance company must continue to insure you even if you develop a health problem and the company discovers it.

Usually you can choose between policies that will begin payments a week after you are declared disabled by the company (through physical exams and a doctor's diagnosis), or that will not begin payments until six months after diagnosis. If you have a sufficient emergency fund in place and you want to lower your monthly premiums, choose as long a waiting period as possible: I usually recommend ninety days.

If you have worked enough quarters (usually forty) to qualify for Social Security disability benefits, use the chart below to estimate your benefits in the event that you become disabled. But don't count on Social Security for your primary source of disability income—it's very hard to get. In fact, over 80 percent of applications are turned down the first time around. If it comes through, consider it a nice bonus (if there is any "bonus" to being disabled).

AN OBSTACLE TO BUILDING UP: ELDER CARE

Right now you are focused on building up, but the biggest threat to your ability to do so is the fact that you may become responsible for the financial and physical care of your elderly parents. In fact, in 1997 40 percent of people whose parents were still living said that they already supported them financially or that they expected to—this is up from 22 percent in 1994.

Recently a client called me in a state of physical and emotional exhaustion. She was trying to raise her own children while caring for her mother in her own home, and there was simply not enough money to go around. The crisis came when she and her husband were doing their annual budget and they realized they had to make a choice between summer overnight camp for their son and the home health care they

Social Security Disability Benefits

To find your monthly benefit, select the age and family situation nearest yours and move right until you reach the column for the salary nearest yours.

Your Age	Your Family	$20,000	$30,000	Your Earnings the Year Before Disability $40,000	$50,000	$59,000 or more
25	You	$793	$1,065	$1,200	$1,328	$1,410
	You, your spouse, and one child*	$1,189	$1,598	$1,800	$1,992	$2,114
35	You	$793	$1,065	$1,201	$1,328	$1,391
	You, your spouse, and one child*	$1,189	$1,598	$1,800	$1,992	$2,008
45	You	$793	$1,065	$1,195	$1,291	$1,329
	You, your spouse, and one child*	$1,189	$1,598	$1,794	$1,937	$1,993
55	You	$793	$1,060	$1,160	$1,225	$1,251
	You, your spouse, and one child*	$1,189	$1,589	$1,740	$1,837	$1,876

*The maximum family benefit.

Note: These figures assume you become disabled in 1995; your earnings over the years have remained steady, and you have earned enough credits to qualify for Social Security. They are calculated in today's dollars.

Source: Social Security and author's estimates, based on previous years.

desperately needed to relieve them from some of the burden of caring for her mother. Lest you think that burden is small, the average caregiver of an elderly individual spends eighteen hours a week at the task. Add that to the results of the National Alliance for Care Giving survey showing that 40 percent of those who care for elderly family members have children under eighteen living at home, and at least two-thirds of the caregivers have jobs out of the home as well, and you can see just how painful it is to be a member of the "sandwich generation." It is even harder if your parent lives some distance from you, which is a situation that twenty-five million Americans face now and that number is expected to grow. See the Appendix for resources for families with aging parents.

What is the answer? In order to plan properly for your own building up strategy, you must have that painful conversation with your parents about what will happen to them if and when they are no longer able to care for themselves. One hopes that they have Medicare, Medigap, and long-term insurance, all of which will help with the burden. But this problem needs to be approached as a family, with all siblings of all generations present. It is worth a plane ticket to have a family meeting to discuss this painful issue of what is going to happen if and when something happens to your parents.

You want to have a game plan in place before Mama falls and breaks her hip, moves from hospital to rehab, and then can no longer live by herself. And if one sibling is doing the lion's share of the caregiving, the other siblings should be paying him or her a monthly salary as well as contributing their share of expenses. Nothing drives a family apart faster and creates more animosity than when one sibling feels that he has been taken advantage of by the others, especially when that sibling is struggling to raise his own family as well.

The possibility of having to care for your parents should cause you to "wake up" to how important it is to build up your assets now so that when your time comes you do not become a burden to your own children. They will thank you for it and will perhaps do the same thoughtful planning with their own children in mind. No matter what your income, that is a rich legacy to leave behind.

5

Fresh Starts

As I start to write this chapter, I'm on the third floor of my old house in Massachusetts, working away in my home office and looking out over the town green. Contemplating all the fresh starts that can happen in one's life, I find myself reviewing my own situation. At this point in my life, if the plans I made at age twenty had held true, I would be celebrating my twenty-fifth wedding anniversary with my college sweetheart. Armed with a Ph.D. from Harvard, I would be comfortably assured of lifetime employment at a good university thanks to tenure, and would be supplementing my teaching income with consulting and writing. My medical insurance plan would be comprehensive because I would be part of large university group. My children would both be attending top colleges, perhaps with part of their tuition paid, thanks to my professorship. Finally, we would have amassed quite a large fund for retirement and could be coasting from here on out because we would have miraculously escaped any major life crises.

It sounds like a great life, but it didn't work out that way, and as I think back on it I'm not sure I would have wanted it to. The personal, spiritual, and professional growth I have experienced over the last twenty-five years might not have occurred if my life had been on Easy Street, if there had been no "fresh starts," each an opportunity to wake up and face the future anew.

Here's what happened to me: As I said earlier in the book, I was bedridden for five years in my twenties with two small children. I never made it to Harvard, and changed my career path back to financial planning (which was the only job I knew how to do). Just like half of all marriages, mine ended in divorce and I found myself a single parent. In 1991, I finally took the plunge and started my own business. One child is at an excellent college, and the other began world travel virtually the day he graduated from high school so that he could amass experience and become a writer. I am fortunate to be part of a small insurance plan, which certainly saved the day when I was in an auto accident in 1993 that almost sank my business. As you can see, I know from personal experience that it may be necessary to make a fresh start at just about any stage of your life.

Remember those sitcoms of the 1950s? Dad went to work at the same job every day, Mom stayed home and cooked and cleaned, and family problems were always small enough to be cleared up in thirty minutes. The parents never fought or got divorced even if they were miserable (which they never were on TV), and nobody ever quit his job, got fired, or changed careers. All I can say is, thank God times have changed. Now we can reinvent ourselves and our lives at any age—we can start over at forty, fifty, sixty, and beyond. I know a seventy-year-old woman who just got her college degree and a downsized (read: "fired") manager who is now running a multimillion dollar business. (His fury at being let go after so many years at the company provided the energy he needed to start a new business and prove he could succeed.) And women who chose to stay home and raise children are now entering the workforce at a higher level than ever before—many by packaging all of the skills they acquired and used while running a household (which is a minibusiness in and of itself).

So don't be surprised if you find yourself revisiting one of the activities of your youth: going to school, dating, launching a career. You may be a woman starting a business after twenty years at home raising your kids. Or a midlevel manager who was downsized and now is pursuing the work he always dreamed of. Or a widow or widower who's making it on your own for the very first time. So many things can happen that require you to pick yourself up and start all over again. Some of these events are in your control, but many are not. Successful "Fresh Starts" depend on your facing your future head-on, even when you would rather escape to some far-off island to forget all your problems.

Fresh starts often are precipitated by a traumatic event—such as a divorce or layoff. Others, like starting your own business, require the courage to take a major risk. But these life changes always seem to bring forth the best in people, who are now forced to rely on their own inner strength. In fact, I have never had a client who was not able to rise to the occasion, even the widow who met with me once a month because my office was her only "safe place to cry." Once she finished grieving, she was able to move forward. She now is remarried to a man who adores her, and they recently purchased a home together.

"When one door is shut, another opens," is the way Miguel de Cervantes put it, and he is right. Once you get through the hardest part—the part when you feel as if you don't have any control over what will happen to you—you'll begin to see new ways in which you can resume control of at least some parts of your life. And each time you take control of one piece, you gain the strength to go on and master the next task, no matter how difficult. That's when you'll feel like a new person—perhaps ten years younger—and certainly a thousand times stronger. Even if it was initiated by a painful setback, a fresh start is a stage in your life with enormous potential for both personal *and* financial growth.

NEW CAREER

One of my clients was a math professor who was denied tenure at two universities. Tired of the academic pressures in a shrinking market, he decided to apply his computer skills to a totally different field—Internet programming. Since he took the plunge two years ago, he has switched jobs four times, increasing his salary with each change. His wife, a painter, has started studying for a degree in art therapy—a new way to use her skills, earn a living, and enhance her own painting as well. They devoted a good deal of time doing research into the future job market before they settled on their new occupations—both in growing fields where they could use their skills and feel personally fulfilled.

As job security has disappeared over the years, and the markets for various skills have shriveled while others have blossomed, it has become increasingly common for people to switch jobs and careers multiple times during their work lives. For men especially, the time spent at one job has been steadily shrinking. In 1996, the average thirty-five to forty-four-year-old man had been at the same job for six years, down from more than seven years in 1983. The numbers shrank from thirteen years to ten years for men between the ages of forty-five and fifty-four.

For older men (ages fifty-five to sixty-four), the drop was even more dramatic—from over fifteen years to ten and a half years, according to the Employee Research Institute. (Women's tenure at the same jobs at the same ages was even less.)

Having a high paying job is no protection from being downsized. A recent study by the search firm Challenger, Gray & Christmas found that 60 percent of the people who are looking for jobs were laid off from posts that paid at least $60,000, compared to 28 percent in 1987. Fortunately, long periods of unemployment are not frowned upon as much as in the past. So if you have been out of work for more than a few months, perhaps you can take some solace in this finding from a recent survey: Most top executives feel that senior managers could be unemployed up to eleven months without having their careers suffer. The current rule of thumb that executive recruiters use is that it takes one month for every $10,000 of salary to get a job equivalent to the one you have left.

Many women face an even more daunting challenge: returning to the workplace after years at home. In 1997, 240,000 women ages fifty-five to sixty-nine took a job in 1997 after not having worked for twenty years, and there is no good data on how many looked but failed to find employment. Women without current job experience need special help, in part, because they lack computer skills, which are essential today. The good news if you are in this situation is that there are ways to package your life experience so that it is attractive to potential employers. One of the most important first steps is to become computer literate in a variety of software packages that are used in businesses, such as word processing, databases, and spreadsheets. I had a client a few years ago who was "computer-phobic" and absolutely refused even to put her hands on a keyboard, even though she typed about ninety words a minute on an electric typewriter. After six months of job hunting without success, she finally broke down and started taking computer classes at night at her local community college. The result? Three months later she had a job that paid $10,000 more than the one from which she had been "let go" because she was unwilling to adapt to its new technologies!

When women enter the workforce after a period of time at home, they often devalue their charitable activities. One friend who describes herself as "just a housewife" trying to enter the job market after eighteen years at home neglected to include in her résumé that she chaired a charitable fund-raising social event, virtually a full-time job, and raised over $500,000 in donations. Her nonpaid job required more business acumen, sales, organization, and management than running many small businesses. We were able to re-word her c.v. to include this achievement, and she soon had a job as an executive assistant to the senior vice president of a corporate communications firm. This job allowed her to capitalize on her social contacts, which turned out to be a fast track to an executive position.

■ Growth Industries ■

Enhancing your job prospects often means applying your skills and passions to a new field entirely. If you love teaching, for instance, instead of pursuing a job at the university level (where competition for jobs is fierce and tenure is being phased out), perhaps you should consider a career as a secondary or elementary school teacher, both growth areas.

Government sources have projected growth through the year 2005 in service jobs, retailing, health, and education. Some of the better-paying positions you might consider are registered nurses, clerical managers, and systems analysts. Information technology and the Internet are also definite growth industries. Perhaps not surprisingly, as our financial lives become more complicated, financial planning has become one of the fastest-growing professions. In fact, it is one of the most popular midcareer changes around. Other positions for which there is a growing need are: personal aides, home health aides, computer engineers, physical therapists, occupational therapy assistants, residential counselors, human service workers, and corrections officers.

Don't dismiss the possibility of returning to school. Jobs that require masters' degrees are expected to grow 28 percent between 1994 and 2005. Fortunately, the old days of stigmatizing students who went to school at night or only part-time are gone, and many excellent colleges now grant credit for "life experience"—work or travel, so you may find that a master's or professional degree is much easier to obtain than you ever thought possible. There even are programs where you only have to attend class one night a week, or every other weekend. If you are changing careers, and you need more education, you owe it to yourself to check out the programs in your area. And don't assume that you cannot pay for them: Often, financial aid and student loans are available—and not just for twenty-year-olds.

■ Financial Implications of Changing Jobs ■

Sometimes you are so unhappy with your job that you want to move to another company just to have a chance to start over. Other times, you will consider a job change because it is a promotion to a better company and a better position. In either case, before you make the leap, spend some time evaluating the many financial implications of changing jobs. Is it worth it from a financial point of view? The rule of thumb is that unless your *total compensation package* is 30 percent higher than your current job, it is really a lateral move and you should think carefully before leaving—especially if you have good financial benefits at your current job and are happy there.

One client, who was making $80,000 at a Fortune 500 company where he had been for five years, was offered $90,000 at a smaller but established firm with a 30 percent bonus potential, if he met sales targets. It sounded great—$120,000. But after he took a good look at the sales plan and his territory, and called some colleagues who told him they thought the target was unrealistic, he started to think twice. Then he looked into the medical plan at the new employer, which was important because his son had asthma. It would require him to switch doctors; pay higher premiums, deductibles, and co-payments; and do without a prescription plan, which he had at his current job. These were big issues because his son went to the doctor frequently and took medication daily. In addition, if he stayed where he was, in two years he would be fully vested in his employer's contributions to his 401(k) plan, which totaled over $20,000. In the end, he figured he was better off staying where he was, especially since he wasn't unhappy there.

So, just as important as evaluating your new salary and bonus potential is comparing the benefits of your current job vs. the new one. We've talked about health care. But how does vacation time compare? How about disability insurance? Everyone needs it, and it is expensive to buy on your own, so the company you work for needs to have a group policy that will cover you. Have you considered the reimbursement plan for child-care, or health-care expenses, if those are relevant? And, most important, how do the two companies' retirement plans compare?

I consider a company retirement plan so crucial that I advise you to think very carefully before switching to a company that does not have one. Otherwise, your only other option is to put $2,000 a year into an IRA, which, as we've discussed in previous chapters, is not going to give you enough money at retirement. If you have a pension plan where your employer is putting all the money in for you, that is free money as long as you stay with the company until you are vested (after a certain period of employment, the money is yours). The same holds true if you have a 401(k) plan and your employer is matching your contributions.

The biggest mistake that people make is that they forget or don't know that they have to stay at the company for a period of time before their employer's contributions become theirs. There are two methods of vesting: either you get nothing until you've been employed for five years and after that all of the employer money is yours; or a percentage of the money belongs to you after three years and it's all yours after seven years.

☞ **Wake-up Call:** I have actually seen cases where people have left companies two or three months before their five-year anniversaries and forfeited all of their employer's contributions to their retirement plans. Find out the date you will be vested *before* you give notice, and stay on past that date, if at all possible!

■ Should You Roll Over Your 401(k)? ■

A friend of mine left her job and called me for advice about how to handle her 401(k). It was run by an insurance company affiliate, which meant high sales and management fees were deducted and she didn't have many investment options. When we looked at the performance of the funds in the plan, not one was in the top quartile for its category. She was not eligible for the new 401(k) at her firm for the first year of employment, and heard they were switching plan administrators (which meant that company stock and mutual fund offerings could change). So she decided to open an account at a discount brokerage firm and invest her retirement money in index funds, because she felt most comfortable with a fund that mirrored the performance of the entire market, instead of betting on how well individual managers would perform. The whole process took about an hour.

When you leave a job where you had a 401(k) you have several options to consider. You may leave it where it is or roll it over. A rollover simply means that you are moving your retirement account money from one retirement plan to another. You can roll your existing 401(k), 403(b), or a defined contribution retirement plan into a new IRA you set up yourself, called an IRA rollover. Or, you can put the money into the retirement plan at your new job, or simply leave the money where it currently is—in the plan at your old job. Once you leave a job, you can usually roll over your 401(k) at any point.

In my opinion, this is a no-brainer, and the reason has to do with investment choices. Your old 401(k) has limited investment options. Your new retirement plan at your new company will have limited investment options as well, and who knows how long you will stay there? And all of those investment options may change as companies change their plans. If you roll your existing retirement plan into an IRA, you will have a whole universe of investments from which to choose.

Often people avoid rolling over their money because they think it is hard to do, but actually it is very easy. I recommend you pick a discount brokerage firm such as Fidelity, Schwab, Jack White, or some other firm (I am not recommending one over the other). Call their office or go there and ask for IRA rollover forms, complete them, and return them to the brokerage firm—and the brokerage firm will take care of the transfer for you!

If you take money out yourself (that is, have the check made out to you), you have sixty days to put the money in a new retirement plan to avoid a 10 percent penalty and income taxes for that year. If you decide to take the money out and keep it for yourself permanently, you will have to pay ordinary income taxes on that money as well as a 10 percent penalty. If you spend it, you will have just lost a big chunk of your savings for retirement or other goals!

By the way, if you tell your current company to have your retirement plan check made out directly to you, it is required by law to withhold 20 percent for income taxes. You could get that money back when you file your tax return, depending on whether you owe taxes, but you will have lost the use of that money in the meantime. So make sure that your retirement plan assets are directly transferred from your current company plan to your new retirement plan.

Wake-up Call: A 1 percent higher brokerage fee means 1 percent less of an annual return on your investment. When you leave a company, especially if you are part of a large layoff or you have a high-profile position, you will be inundated with brokers and financial planners wanting to invest your money. Check their fees carefully.

■ Health Insurance ■

Once you land a new job, unless you are covered by a spouse's plan, you should sign up for the plan offered by your new employer as soon as you can. Unfortunately, many plans don't cover new employees until they have been at the company for six months or even a year. If you sign up during the initial enrollment period, many companies do not require you to prove you're in good health. But the new policy may have pre-existing limitations, so that any condition for which you have recently sought medical insurance may not be covered for the first three years. That means you may want to continue your previous insurance through a federally mandated program called COBRA (Consolidated Omnibus Budget Reconciliation Act.) COBRA requires your old employer, whether you are laid off or quit, to offer health coverage for at least up to 18 months after you leave, as long as you pay the premium yourself. These premiums can be expensive, but it is better than having no insurance at all.

STARTING A BUSINESS

Hanging out your own shingle can be one of the quickest ways to get reemployed after being laid off, or to enter a brand-new field of your own choosing. It also can be both the most terrifying and most exhilarating experience of your life. My decision to open my own firm came at my sister's kitchen table in California in 1991. We were talking about the direction my life was taking professionally and personally. My sister trains entrepreneurs in management skills and works with large corporations to help them adapt to changing corporate culture. I will never forget the words she used to push me forward: "I know it's scary, but you have to have confidence in yourself. Look at what you've been able to accomplish, even under such adverse circumstances. That shows you have the drive, guts, organizational skills, and entrepreneurial spirit necessary to succeed. You're almost forty. If you don't do it now, you never will." That was some of the best advice I ever received in my life.

Many people start their own businesses as an ego trip, but most do it to try out an entrepreneurial idea, to recover from being downsized, to escape frustration at their places of employment, to gain flexibility in their lives, or to expand their growth potential, which may be limited by a glass ceiling or other circumstances. It is also a great idea to start a business on the side so that you can put more money in a retirement plan (such as a Keogh) and continue to have a small business to run at retirement, as my father, a mechanical engineer, does at age seventy-nine.

The problem is that while you may have a great idea, its implementation can be expensive. According to the American Marketing Association, over 250,000 individuals who start a business lose money every year and many of them lose over $50,000 before they ever have a prod-uct to offer customers. That should be a sobering statistic, but it should not dampen your dreams if you take the right steps.

If you've long had the goal of becoming your own boss, you're not alone. More than half the workforce feels the same way (70 percent for workers between the ages of twenty-one and thirty-two). Last year about five million Americans took the plunge and started their own business, some with partners and some without. And women were the most active entrepreneurs, starting businesses at twice the rate of men. In fact, women-owned businesses employ 35 percent more people in the United States than the Fortune 500 companies do worldwide.

When you first think about going into business for yourself, you are usually overcome with excitement and anticipation. Then reality sets in, and you need to figure out what it is you are going to sell—yourself or a product. Obviously, it is easier to start a business selling services than products, because you do not have to invest in a lot of inventory or in having products made. This means you need much less working capital, which is very hard for a new company to get. So let's focus first on ser-vices you can offer.

Starting a new business involves much of the same advice I offered in the section on changing careers (see page 252), because you *are* changing careers in a way. Even if you are doing the same thing you did as a salaried employee, now you are an entrepreneur with no one else sign-ing your paycheck. Think about what you are good at or love doing—make this a brainstorming session—and not just about what you are doing now. For example, Samantha, the former comptroller of a For-tune 500 company, tripled her income by starting a business providing exquisite wedding flowers to extremely wealthy clientele in the Boston area. She has always been an avid gardener and, deep down, loved dig-ging her fingers in the dirt more than running numbers on the computer.

There are numerous creative ways to capitalize on your special area of proficiency, whether it's a hobby or your long-time profession. The most obvious one is to become a consultant, because you can start with very little overhead and probably no employees, other than yourself. That way, you get paid to teach others how to do what you already have mastered, or to provide special skills.

Many writers and designers who earned their stripes writing and de-signing for newspapers or magazines, for instance, go into business for themselves. My friend Jackson, a writer, makes a good living teaching adult education classes at the two major adult-ed centers in the Boston area, as well as running weekly writers' groups in her home. She also provides consulting in how to get published, a service every would-be writer needs.

Brendan, an M.D. I know, grew tired of providing patient care and left a hospital staff job to set up a consulting firm catering to HMOs that were taking over hospitals. Caitlin was a veterinary assistant who was fed up with earning barely more than minimum wage after ten years of experience. She started a pet sitting and "doggie play group" service and has more requests than she can handle. Also, because of her background, she is available to take pets to the vet for checkups and to perform certain specialized functions, such as giving shots to diabetic pets when their owners are out of town. Michael left a twenty-five-year position as the director of admissions at an exclusive boys' school to become an education consultant, helping parents and students pick the right colleges and maximize the students' chances of admission.

If you have the talent, writing a book or regular magazine or newspaper column can solidify your credentials in a particular area. This rarely pays much, but it can be an excellent way to publicize your expertise. And if you can't write a word, you can always hire a freelance writer to do so for you. If you think you have an idea that might be marketable to a magazine or book publisher who specializes in reaching your audience, approach him with a well-written, concise proposal outlining your credentials, the proposed content, and the potential audience.

Self-publishing is another option worth considering, and the cost is less than it once was. What once required a professional design firm to accomplish can now be done on your home computer. You can start your own newsletter or put together a book (or even a booklet) and circulate it via the Internet, E-mail, or mail. Another option is to market your publication directly to corporations or organizations. If you specialize in children's nutrition, for instance, you might target schools, day-care centers, and children's hospitals.

A great self-promotion success story is that of the Dave Matthews Band. In 1991, the members of this little-known band played fraternity houses on the East Coast, but they encouraged the audience to tape their shows and circulate them to friends. They then self-published a tape that was not even sold in stores, but they distributed 130,000 copies by word of mouth alone. The rest is history. A major label signed them, their next two albums sold five million copies each, and the CD they released in 1998 sold almost 500,000 copies the first week alone. Of course, very few of us have their musical skills, but their story does show how taking risks, having confidence in yourself, and knowing your product or service is worthwhile can pay off in the not so long run.

■ The Pros and the Cons ■

Certainly, the freedom of running your own business, one that prospers based entirely on your own effort, sounds appealing. But to give yourself the best chance of succeeding, you must start out on a firm financial footing. If you don't have enough savings to sustain yourself until you can make a profit, you should consider launching your business while you still have a steady paycheck coming in. Sound tough? You won't be alone. Moonlighters account for up to a quarter of all new businesses launches. Starting a business on the side is a great way to get your feet wet and see if you have the stomach for the nights and weekends your new business will require. I had one client who was determined to start a business in carpentry, but he quit after six months. As Jeff said, "I realized that my children are too young for me to do this now. Maybe later. I just couldn't stand skipping so many soccer matches and family dinners, and the kids really missed having me around."

Before you quit your day job, I strongly recommend seeing an industrial psychologist, who can perform a series of personality tests with you to determine where your career strengths lie, and whether you're a "big picture" person or a "detail" person. It's also important to figure into the equation the pressures you may have as a business owner that you probably escaped as a salaried employee. Maybe you'd rather not manage client relationships, or forgo your own paycheck to pay your suppliers. Lots of people like to leave their work at the office, but that is not possible when you run your own business. One survey found that 20 percent of small business owners take their cellular phones with them on vacation and one-third check their answering machines regularly. Nearly half say the won't enjoy their vacation as much as nonbusiness owners, and a quarter don't take any vacations at all.

■ Deciding What Form Your Business Will Take ■

You may have had a business idea in the back of your mind for years, or it may be that you and a colleague at work or a good friend have been talking about going out on your own. Before you do so, you need good legal and accounting advice to help figure out the right legal form your business should take. If you are a sole proprietor, you own the business yourself and its profit or loss is reflected on your personal tax return. Legally, if you die, your business dies. In a partnership, each partner owns a share (usually equal to the amount of investment each makes) but it also is dissolved if one of the partners dies. Your other option is a corporation, which is considered a separate legal entity by the IRS. A corporation continues whether the owner dies or not. I am focusing on death for the purposes of differentiation, but the right form for you depends upon your projected income, current situation, and type of business. Don't make this decision on your own; the legal and accounting fees you pay for professional advice will be well worth it in the long run. Especially if you have co-owners, you want to make sure that you are getting your appropriate share of income and equity in the business.

■ Create a Business Plan ■

There is a standard phrase among business consultants and business owners—"businesses don't plan to fail, they fail to plan." When you realize that 70 percent of companies closed by the end of their fifth year in business, you see how important a business plan is. In fact, no one should start a business without a plan in place because it serves two important functions: It gives you a blueprint to follow for the year ahead, and if you are looking for any capital (outside investors) there is no way you are going to get any money without one.

If you haven't got a clue how to make a plan because you've never done one before, you can get low-cost consulting help from the Small Business Administration Consulting and Education Programs. The SBA offers an enormous amount of written material and support, and there may even be an SBA Small Business Development Center in your area that offers classes and helps you think through the process (the joys and pitfalls) of starting a business. The SBA also has the Service Corps of Retired Executives who can help you develop and review business plans at little or no cost. You can also be assigned a retired executive who is an expert in your field to consult with you on an ongoing basis.

Books such as *The McGraw-Hill Guide to Writing a High-Impact Business Plan* can be great resources. This one also offers a free diskette with a model business plan and financial spreadsheets you can use. The American Marketing Association also publishes *The AMA Complete Guide to Strategic Planning for Small Business*, and offers a free membership kit. For a $149 annual membership fee, the Independent Business Alliance gives home-based businesses and small firms access to affordable insurance and other financial services. See the Appendix for these and other resources.

☞ **Wake-up Call:** It's unrealistic to think that you can get venture capital when you're first starting a business, because most venture capital firms want to invest in larger businesses—those with several million dollars in sales and a need to raise a million dollars or more for expansion. Plus, there is a price to pay for receiving backing from a venture capital firm: you usually lose control of your company and you probably will end up with a minority interest.

■ Make Sure You Can Survive Until You Are Profitable ■

Sarah, a high-powered television reporter I have worked with in the past, consulted me a few months ago about her plans to leave her solid network-affiliated on-air job for a start-up company that wanted to develop educational programs for nonprofit organizations. She would be half-owner of the new company, and her long-time producer would be the other partner. Sarah is fortunate, because her husband is a real estate developer and makes enough money to cover all of the family financial obligations, even if Sarah doesn't make a penny for the next five years. Unfortunately, most of us are not in that situation—we depend upon our current paychecks, and there has got to be some other money coming in to cover the bills as well as to pay for the start-up cost of a new business.

New realtors are told to put aside a year's worth of income before they enter the field, which pays solely by commission. Actually, that is a general rule of thumb for anyone who is moving into a commission-based business. If you are entering a business in which you have no experience, or where you are facing stiff competition, you may need to have at least eighteen months of office and personal expenses socked away before you make the leap to self-employment. It's no good starting a business if you can't sustain it until the red ink starts flowing in. Most new businesses don't survive past two years. Despite a strong economy in 1997, business failures reached 17 percent.

☞ **Wake-up Call:** Tired of not being paid on time? Here are some tips: Always ask for a retainer up front of 25–50 percent of your estimated project fees with the balance payable on a regular or monthly basis. Have a contract drawn up and make sure that interest is due if your bills are not paid within fifteen days. I have found from experience that charging interest on bills makes them come in much faster. Another solution is to offer a 5 percent discount for any bill paid within ten days. That also can get big results.

Get help before trouble starts, because it's much easier to raise funds then. Here is where a business plan is key, especially if you are looking for outside funding from a bank or a Small Business Administration loan. You always need to have a backup line of credit. But you must ask yourself how much you are willing to lose. *The Wall Street Journal* reported in its annual survey that about 33 percent of entrepreneurs with nineteen or fewer employees said they used credit cards as one of their financing options, which is up from about 17 percent in 1993. Another option is a home equity line of credit—but ask yourself, "Am I willing to bet my house on the success of my business?" Those are the exact words that one client, Tim, told me he wished he had asked himself before he took out a home equity line of credit. If you decide to do so, apply for the loan while you are still employed at a regular job so you can show a regular paycheck.

Also, make sure that all of your owners are putting in their proportional shares. I know of a contractor who carried the financial obligations of his partner during his partner's difficult divorce, and the contractor ended up losing his own house during the 1980s depression.

For more advice on starting your own business, I recommend Terri Lonier's *Working Solo* (New York: John Wiley & Sons, Inc., May 1998) and *The Small Business Money Guide: How to Get It, Use It, Keep It* by Terri Lonier and Lisa M. Aldisert (New York: John Wiley & Sons, Inc., 1999)

■ Protect Yourself and Your Partners ■

You may feel invincible when you gather the courage to start your own business, but the reality is that you are just as prone to unexpected accidents or illness as when you were a lowly employee. When you run your own shop, you must protect against the possibility of your death or disability, and that of your partners or co-owners as well. This requires putting the proper insurance and buy-sell agreements in place.

First, you'll need *disability office overhead insurance,* which will pay your office bills for up to eighteen months if you become disabled and are unable to work. This will pay your employees and suppliers, and will keep your business going until you're able to return. Disability office overhead insurance has saved countless businesses from going under.

A *buy-sell agreement* is a legal document that requires your other owners to buy your interest if you die or become disabled, and sometimes when you retire, too. This guarantees that all of the hard work and capital you have put in the business will come back to your family if you are no longer around, or you become disabled and your paycheck is no longer coming in. There are different kinds of buy-sell agreements, but they should be funded by disability and life insurance so that the money is guaranteed if something happens to you.

If you plan on handing your business down to one or more of your children, make sure you prepare a *transition plan.* Nearly 70 percent of family businesses don't survive past the first generation because of an inadequate transition plan. I see one successful business owner virtually every week, and every week he says to me, "I need to call you to talk about passing the business on to my kids." We have been having this conversation for five years, and he has never called. I warned him that unless he made appropriate arrangements, the very successful antique business he had built up was going to become virtually worthless (except to the IRS, which will happily assess its value at death) unless he made plans now about how he was going to pass it on to his two children who were working in the business. Currently, there is no succession plan stating who will take over when he retires—which could mean a huge fight in the offing. In fact, 40 percent of family firms are sold to new owners because the next generation cannot agree on who will take control of the business, how the children who aren't part of the business will be compensated financially, and where that money will come from. Another common reason that family businesses fail to stay "in the family" is that the owners stay in charge too long and never give the next generation a chance to learn the business by running things under their supervision.

■ The Thrills and Chills of Working from Home ■

Imagine yourself sauntering up the stairs after breakfast—still in your pajamas, coffee mug in hand—to your home office with a peaceful view of the garden. Sounds like the ideal work space, doesn't it? Now get a dose of reality: Imagine yourself getting an early morning call from a key client at the same time you are trying to get the kids off to school. One is desperately trying to find his homework, while the other one looks feverish. Or your most talkative neighbor shows up when you are trying to finish a report for a client. Suddenly, fielding professional telephone calls and turning out high-quality work seems more difficult than when you could work uninterrupted in your downtown office.

Working from home has all kinds of advantages (flexibility, no commuting costs, expandable lunch hours) and disadvantages (loneliness, domestic work as a distraction to professional work, and you must supply your own equipment) compared with commuting to an office. Make sure the pros outweigh the cons before you convert your guest bedroom into your permanent work space. For one thing, you'll need certain character traits and skills. To help you figure out if you could handle it, consider the following questions:

1. Can you stand working all by yourself?
2. Do you have sufficient self-discipline to avoid flipping on the TV every time you walk past it, and then look up and see that three hours have gone by?
3. Are you organized?
4. Do you have separate work space available in your home (which you can create using folding screens purchased for as little as $100)? Is the work space quiet?
5. What about telephone lines? Can you afford to install and maintain a separate business line?
6. Do you have sufficient equipment—computer, fax machine, copying machine, etc? Can you afford to purchase it if you don't?
7. Does your spouse understand that you need to set aside time that's devoted just to work, not domestic chores (this is one of the most common complaints I hear from male and female friends of mine who work at home)?
8. Do you have adequate child care? (It does not look very professional to be on a conference call when your four-year-old is crying in the background because his older sister accidentally whacked him with a Frisbee.)

These are just a few of the issues you should think through before deciding whether working from home is suitable for you. I know this from personal experience because I have had a home office as well as an office in downtown Boston. If you have a home office, think about whether your callers will be able to hear background noise from your children, dog, stereo, etc.

■ Health Insurance ■

No one in today's world can afford to go without medical insurance, so if you are not covered by your spouse's plan, medical premiums need to be included in your new business budget. You'll be working hard to build up your new business, and medical insurance is your safeguard against spending your hard-won profits on medical expenses.

I gave you some tips on health insurance in the section on changing careers, but it is particularly important that self-employed persons look for group insurance. Believe it or not, there's group insurance available even for a "group" of one. If you can't get coverage through your own business, consider plans offered through organizations affiliated with your line of work. If you can't get insurance because of chronic illness or ongoing expenses due to an accident, call your state representative or your state Department of Insurance, because you may qualify for a special state program. Even if you can't get coverage for yourself, you may be able to obtain coverage at a low cost for your children.

Another option to consider is extending your insurance from your former job, if it's still in effect, via COBRA. (See page 258, earlier in this chapter, for more detail.)

■ Can You Take a Home Office Deduction? ■

Can you write off the new 27-inch TV? How about your new deck?

New IRS rules, effective this year, have made it somewhat easier to qualify for a home office deduction. But that doesn't mean that the areas of your home or equipment that you buy that have nothing to do with your business can be applied against your taxes.

You qualify if:

- your home office is your main place of business and you use it exclusively and regularly for business
- you meet with customers or patients at your home office, even if you do a little bit of business outside of the office
- you provide day-care on a regular basis (not just for children but for the elderly or disabled) even though you might use that space (such as a living room) for your own use after business hours

■ you store business items such as product samples or inventory in your home—but they must be kept in a separate storage area

Even if you do most of your work elsewhere, as a consultant or house painter, for example, you can deduct your home office as long as that area is used exclusively for business purposes.

A home office deduction means that you can deduct a portion of your rent or mortgage, home insurance, real estate taxes, utilities, and other costs of home ownership. The portion you can deduct is equal to the portion of the house that you devote to your business activities. If you use one room in a four room apartment for business, for instance, your deduction is 25 percent of those expenses.

☞ **Wake-up Call:** A home office deduction is a red flag to the IRS. It is one of the first places the IRS will look when evaluating returns for an audit. Many CPAs recommend against claiming a home office deduction, because the amount of taxes you'll save isn't worth the cost and hassle of defending yourself if you are audited. So if you don't save much money by claiming a home office deduction, it may not be worth it to claim one. Here is where competent accounting advice can really make a difference in your life—there is nothing worse than an unnecessary audit that involves a home office deduction. Calculate your taxes assuming you take the home office deduction and then assuming that you don't. See how much money you save by claiming your home office, and then decide whether it is worth risking an audit.

■ Women's Business ■

I have already touched on the impact that the extraordinary explosion in women's business has had on the economy, but I want to spend a few minutes more on it to encourage women to "take the plunge" and try their hands at starting their own businesses. Currently, women own one-third of all firms in the United States—about eight million total. And by the year 2000, 40 percent of businesses are expected to be owned by women. That is quite a block of power! And, I hope, a motivator. Dunn & Bradstreet has reported that women-owned businesses have the same credit worthiness and have equal or better staying power than businesses owned by men. Yet because many of these businesses are small, only about 1 percent of the $6 billion invested in firms by venture capital companies goes to businesses owned by women. According to the National Foundation for Women, from 1992 through 1996, the number of women using credit cards to finance their businesses has almost halved (52 to 23 percent), while the number who use their own business earnings to finance operations and expansion has doubled, to about 72 percent.

So don't let the fact that you are female hold you back anymore. All you have to do is look around you to see role model after role model, such as Bobbi Brown, Eileen Fisher, and Martha Stewart. There are local chapters of professional businesswomen's organizations in your area, and in all my media-related travels around the country, I have heard only positive and generous things about what women are willing to do for each other in terms of business. You have no doubt heard of the "old boys' network"; several women's organizations, such as Catalyst in New York City, are trying to create the "old girls' network."

DIVORCE

It must have been about fifteen years ago that a colleague of mine told me that he and his wife were divorcing. He said that the divorce was perfectly amicable, however, and that they were even going to write a book about how to go through the divorce process and remain best friends. (This was not the first time I had heard the "write a friendly divorce book" idea.) Of course, I heard regularly from him about the progress of this "friendly divorce."

The first battle was over custody. Although it was unusual at the time, Eric wanted custody of the children. Mary also wanted custody because she only worked part-time and spent her daily life working around her children's schedules and spending time with them.

The second battle was over assets. This couple who had been best friends was suddenly obsessed with the idea that one might be hiding assets from the other.

Alimony was next in the skirmish that became a war. Mary had given up a promising career to work part-time in order to devote herself to the children. Eric had just joined a small start-up company and had stock options that could potentially multiply both his income and his net worth. So, deciding what was fair to both depended on very speculative circumstances. Child support couldn't be decided until they knew who would have custody of the children.

Eric and Mary lived in an expensive house, and they both agreed (for once) that whoever had custody should keep the house in order to minimize the divorce's impact on the children. But Mary's parents had given them a substantial down payment, and Mary wanted it back if she were to move out.

Fortunately, each already owned a life insurance policy on the other's life, which could help pay for college and other costs if one parent died. This was great, since each was paying the premium on the other's life insurance policy, so they could be sure that the policy remained in force. But Mary remained worried about being dropped from Eric's medical insurance plan if he decided not to pay the premium or to take her off his policy altogether.

Obviously, no "friendly divorce" book was ever going to be written out of this experience. The saddest part was the impact on the children who suffered through every battle their parents had. The second saddest part was that, when it was all over, their legal fees exceeded $100,000.

But there are ways you can protect yourself on all of these fronts, and try to make your divorce a fresh start even if it feels like a fresh wound at the moment. The point is, whether you initiate or are devastated by it (and usually you *are* devastated, regardless of who initiated it), in most cases divorce will alter your financial situation in very profound ways. That is why it is so important to know your financial options and to have a game plan when you are facing one of the most emotionally difficult fresh starts of your life.

One thing you can do to lessen the financial impact is to try to achieve some kind of cooperative relationship between your soon-to-be-ex-spouse and yourself. So many couples make their money situations worse because they spend a great deal on lawyers to fight what are essentially emotional battles—just as Eric and Mary did, at great emotional and financial cost. Instead of dragging out a divorce—and adding to the divorce attorneys' fees—use that money to put your lives back together after the divorce. If you each use your resources to pay for your children's education or to start your new life with more financial security, the anger you feel for each other will be minimized. Remember, there was a time when you felt so much passion for each other that you wanted to spend the rest of your lives together. Now that things have changed, if you can at least cooperate when working out the financial terms, the emotional battles won't eat up whatever financial resources you may have to divide up.

You should *never* go through the divorce process without legal advice. It is also important to seek the counsel of an accountant and a financial planner who can calculate the monetary impact of each choice.

For example, if you have lots of equity in your house and you are offered that in return for relieving your ex-spouse from any child support, is that a good financial decision? It could be, especially if you suspect that getting a monthly child support check from your ex-spouse is going to require one fight after another—with frequent court orders as enforcement—which will take an enormous emotional toll on both you and your children. If it's not a good plan for you, armed with the numbers and the proper advisers, you will be in a position to make a more equitable counterproposal.

■ Your Children and Your Family ■

The first thing to recognize about a divorce is that it is actually a death: the death of an ideal. This has nothing to do with money and everything to do with your family, especially your children. The best advice I ever heard about going through a divorce was to try not to say negative things about the soon-to-be-ex-spouse in front of your children. It only makes their pain worse (and any child who tells you he is happy that you are getting divorced is probably lying). Studies show that children would prefer their parents stay together even if they are unhappy. One useful piece of advice I got was to buy a notebook and, at the end of every day, write down every angry and sad feeling you have. This way your misery is directed at pen and paper instead of your children.

■ Taking Stock of Your Assets ■

The next thing to do is to take stock of your marital assets. You can use a modified version of the "What You Own and What You Owe" chart that you filled out in Chapter 1, which includes all of the assets that need to be taken into account in a divorce. Among these are each spouse's salary, inheritances received by one person before the marriage, securities, insurance policies, real estate, and any other quantifiable assets such as cars and collectibles.

How your assets are treated depends upon the state you live in—most states are considered "common-law" states, but a few are "community-property" states, for which there are special rules. In a common-law state, all jointly owned assets acquired during the marriage are split 50–50. In contrast, however, any gifts you gave each other—such as jewelry or golf clubs—belong to the recipient.

Community-property states are: Arizona, California, Idaho, Nevada,

Divorce Worksheet: Who Owns What?

| | Who Owns It? | | |
Assets	Partner #1	Partner #2	Joint
1993 Honda Accord	X		
1995 Buick Century		X	
House			X

New Mexico, Texas, and Washington. (Although it is not technically a community-property state, Wisconsin's marriage and divorce laws are consistent with those of the community-property states.) In these states, any income earned by *either* spouse during the marriage, and any property purchased with that income, should be split 50–50 in a divorce.

☞ **Wake-up Call:** Regardless of what your divorce decree says, if your ex-spouse's name is still listed on your employee retirement plan, he or she will receive benefits if you die. When you get a divorce, remember to change the beneficiary on your plan.

Most divorces these days are no-fault (uncontested), so you do not need to prove things such as adultery, substance abuse, or physical abuse. Even so, the divorce process is never fun. The law entitles both parties to "full disclosure," which usually involves written documents signed and notarized as well as by face-to-face questioning and verification under oath when you go to court. Until both sides have indicated that they are satisfied with the disclosure process, the divorce case cannot receive a trial date (or a hearing date for an uncontested divorce). You do not need to have a trial if you are able to reach a settlement before your trial date, but you still must go through full disclosure before the settlement can be approved by the court.

If you have a good relationship with your soon-to-be-ex-spouse, then you might decide to work through a mediator, rather than through a pair of adversarial lawyers. A mediator is a specially trained individual who takes all of the information you have given him (mostly numbers) and works to try to achieve a settlement so that the couple never has to go to court. Mediation can also produce very quick results, in contrast to a divorce trial, which can drag on for months. It's also less expensive, even if you hire a lawyer who also acts as a mediator, which is what I recommend. This works well because he can then draft the documents for the divorce decree.

Before you enter into negotiations, there are some steps you can take to make sure you get what you need. Make a list of the your absolute "must haves," your "wants," and your "willing to negotiate" items. Consult with your attorney and even a CPA to figure out how any settlement would play out five years from now. Then as you go through the mediation or trial process, you will have a checklist to help you think clearly about what you are giving up and what you are getting in return.

In a contested divorce or a particularly bitter one, let your lawyers do the talking. If there are last-minute points to hammer out, don't agree to anything hastily. Instead, postpone the trial, which is generally easy to do, so you have the time you need to think through each issue.

When you get the proposal for the final agreement, sleep on it. You don't have to agree to it right away. Make sure you understand and are comfortable with every single phrase, and there are absolutely no ambiguities. I have seen too many instances in which an unclear sentence has resulted in thousands of dollars of additional legal fees when it comes to payment of college costs, increase in alimony or child support, and other matters.

☞ **Wake-up Call:** Whether you go through a trial or mediation process, take detailed notes of everything that is said. That way you can have records and proof of what the other party verbally agreed to, even if the mediator or attorneys failed to keep a record.

■ Custody and Child Support ■

These go hand in hand because the person who has custody of the children is the one who is paying the day-to-day expenses and needs child support to cover those costs. The laws vary by state, but there is a general formula for how much child support the noncustodial parent is expected to pay based on his or her income. Keep in mind that bankruptcy has nothing to do with an obligation to pay child support. One spendaholic client I had tried to get out of her child support payments when she declared bankruptcy after her divorce (her ex-husband had custody of her daughter). But child support and alimony are considered sacred and you can't discharge your obligation to your own family by using this legal technique.

☞ **Wake-up Call:** Child support has no tax consequences—the person who pays it cannot deduct it, and the person who receives it does not declare it as income.

Most states require a standardized form on which you list your child's or children's expenses, and that gets filed with the court along with your individual income and asset statements. But many people forget to fill in the extras that are not listed on the form. For example, summer sleep-away camp alone can often cost several thousand dollars a year, and there may be school or religious tuition and sports fees. I know from personal experience that a middle-school child who wants to play soccer year-round can be asked to spend over $1,000 in equipment, tournament fees, team fees, and travel to out-of-state tournaments.

The best way to remember all your expenses is to think about each season, write each child name under the season, and then list every activity. With kids as over-scheduled as they are today, all of those extras can be just as expensive as day-to-day expenses. And don't forget summer day care if you have children who will require that while you work.

✔ Common Expense Checklist for Custodial Parents

__ Child's share of household expenses (rent or mortgage, utilities)
__ Food, including school lunches
__ Clothing
__ Transportation

__ Child care
__ Athletic expenses/Lessons
__ Health care
__ Orthodontics
__ Miscellaneous: Tutoring, haircuts, cable TV, travel, etc.
__ College

The "Divorce Hotline" website *(www.divorcenet.com)* and the "Budgeting for Child Support" website *(www.divorcehelp.com/WR/W40 Budget.html)* contain detailed information and worksheets that will help you itemize your family's expenses, assets, and debts. These worksheets will also help ensure that you don't miss any major expenses when calculating the amount of child support you'll need.

■ College Costs ■

Clearly, college is a big issue, and the general rule of thumb is that if each parent is making about the same amount of money, each will contribute equally to saving for college. Otherwise, the expected contribution is based upon income at the time of the divorce. If, at the time your child goes to college, there have been substantial changes in either parent's income level, you can go back to court, but this policy is difficult to change. There should also be a reduction in your child support received during the years your child is at college, if you are the custodial parent—you are still providing a home, but you child is incurring living expenses away from home. One common practice is to reduce child support by 50 percent and then have each parent send the college student a monthly allowance.

Receiving an allowance from each parent can actually go a long way in healing the wounds of divorce that children feel. College may be the first time in their lives since the divorce that they feel their parents are trying to work together on their behalf, as one recent college grad explained to me. She said that just the fact that her parents were cooperating to help her financially meant as much as the money she received.

The best way to make sure your ex-spouse pays college expenses is to have funds set aside in a college trust with an impartial third-party trustee, such as a bank, and ask for some proof of regular investments. Make sure to include this stipulation in your divorce agreement.

■ Who Gets the Deduction? ■

Another issue to settle is who gets to claim each child as a dependent; this should also be spelled out clearly in your divorce agreement. Technically, if your child does not live with you, you can only claim him or her as a dependent if you provide more than half of his or her financial support. If your child lives with you, you can claim him or her as a dependent, even if you provide less than half of his or her financial support. This deduction was worth $2,650 in 1997. Sometimes the custodial parent claims all dependents, while other times, dependents are split between the parents.

■ Alimony ■

More and more fathers are staying home to raise their children, so it is not just women who are looking for alimony during a divorce negotiation. These days, both parents often have flourishing careers and one may decide to stop working altogether or to work part-time in order to be with the children. If you are the parent who stayed home, you should get financial credit in a divorce for the earning power you gave up, if your career has suffered. This is where a good lawyer or tax advisor can help you calculate your lost earnings, and how much you'll continue to lose by reentering the workforce at a lower salary. Most states, however, have guidelines for appropriate alimony amounts based on your ex-spouse's salary, so it can be difficult to negotiate for more.

☞ **Wake-up Call:** If you and your spouse were married for ten or more years, you are entitled to a portion of your ex-spouse's Social Security benefits when you retire or if you become disabled. The amount that you are eligible to receive is based on your ex-spouse's income. You also may be entitled to a portion of his or her veterans' pension.

One important tax consideration to keep in mind is that alimony is tax-deductible to the payer and taxable income to the recipient. So if you are negotiating to receive alimony, figure out what the after-tax value is going to be for you. For example, my friend Maria received $2,000 per month, but after taxes it was more like $1,400. She did not realize this until she filed her first tax return on her own.

Some attorneys and financial advisors recommend that the alimony amount in a divorce decree be fixed in stone. But I recommend against this. What if your ex-spouse suddenly has stock options that makes him a millionaire, or her income doubles? You were part of the "team" that made it possible for his or her success, and you should be able to share in it. See if you can negotiate to get copies of your ex-spouse's tax return every year (the downside is that you will have to provide the same). It will help you get your fair share in the event that all of your sacrifices—whether they enabled your ex-spouse to spend eighteen hours a day for ten years at his or her job, or put your partner through school—pay off in the years after you divorce.

■ Life Insurance ■

Life insurance is a critical piece of divorce planning, especially if you are relying on your ex-spouse to pay a fair amount of your children's future expenses—perhaps alimony, child support, college, and medical expenses. In my case, I purchased a term life insurance policy on my ex-husband's life that would provide that money if he were to die before his financial obligations to his children were fulfilled. I purchased it myself because that way I could make sure that all the premiums were being paid so the policy would not lapse. If you decide to do that, you will be responsible for the premiums, so take that cost into account when you figure out how much to ask for child support. The advantage of owning a policy yourself is that you know it is in force.

I will never forget a situation about twenty years ago when the ex-spouse of an acquaintance was killed in a car accident. The situation was obviously traumatic enough for everyone, but she felt assured of her financial stability because he had taken out a large insurance policy just in case something like this happened. Unfortunately, the ex-spouse had been traveling overseas on business and had neglected to pay his annual premium—it was four months overdue. He was a kind man and I am sure that he did not intend for this to happen, but the results were disastrous. Because it was a term insurance policy, there was no cash value, and she had absolutely nothing for child support or college. Two months after he died, she had to go back to work full-time with three children under the age of twelve.

To ensure that you have enough to meet your expenses in the event that your ex-spouse predeceases you, you should ask for a life insurance policy that would cover spousal and child support and college funds. You can use the life insurance capital needs analysis from Chapter 4 (page 244) to help figure out how much you need. If you own the policy yourself, you can opt to cancel it once the kid are grown.

If for some reason you don't own the policy, make sure your divorce decree stipulates that you receive a canceled check within twenty days of the date the premium is due. That way if he doesn't make a payment, you'll have ten days before the policy is subject to cancellation (which usually occurs after a thirty-day grace period) to try to straighten out the situation.

■ Medical Insurance ■

Health insurance is another issue. If you do not have good coverage for yourself and your children through your own job, you need to stipulate in your divorce decree that you and your children continue to be covered under your spouse's policy. Again, make sure the decree requires regular notification that the insurance is still in force. This way, if your ex-spouse is angry with you and tempted to get back at you by dropping you from his or her policy, the threat of court action can serve as a very powerful deterrent.

☞ **Wake-up Call:** In most states, a divorce decree automatically cuts you out of your ex-spouse's will. And even if it doesn't, few states have laws preventing divorced men and women from disinheriting their ex-spouses and children. Never rely on your spouse's will to provide you or your children with any of his or her assets.

■ Your House ■

The simplest way to divide the value of your house is to sell it and divide up the proceeds after the mortgage(s) is paid off. This can be a simple arrangement if you have no children. Or, you can negotiate to give up some other assets (such as a luxury car or a share of your spouse's retirement plan) in return for your spouse's share of the remaining home equity if you want to stay in the home.

If you have children, however, it is a different matter altogether. Kids do better when they have as few disruptions in their lives as possible, especially in the first year or so of a divorce. If you are a custodial parent, it may make sense to negotiate for residency until your children move out or graduate from college. At that point, the house can be sold and the proceeds split.

Paul and Kellie agreed that the child support he was paying would cover housing, so they decided to forego any complicated formulas about mortgage payments, utilities, and other related costs. Once the kids had graduated from college, they equally shared the increase in the value of the house when it was sold. If you can make such an arrangement with your ex-spouse, it will make life much easier when the time comes to sell.

There also should be a provision that when you are ready to sell, the occupant has the right to pay the other parent cash for his or her share of the home equity, instead of having to sell the house. If the occupant does not want to stay, the other parents should have the same option.

But there is a problem, and it is a big one. Many divorcing couples have most of their money tied up in home equity. That means that if the noncustodial parent wants to get on with his life, he may need his share of the home equity to do so, especially if he wants to buy a new home. I have often seen this issue become the biggest impediment to an amicable divorce. But before you dig in your heels (if you are the custodial parent), make sure you can afford to stay in the house. It certainly will provide continuity for your children. But you don't want to overvalue continuity when a more affordable living arrangement will provide you with a higher cash flow and less tension—which will also help you be a better parent. You may be able to find an apartment or a smaller home in your area so that your children do not have to change schools.

Kate found herself in that position a couple of years ago—she and her husband owned one of the largest houses in their town. When she and Sam divorced, they sold the house, and she moved to a small condominium with her two teenage children. She thought it was going to be a terrible trauma and the kids would be mortified, but they love being closer to the town center and their high school, because all their friends can drop by whenever they want. And Kate says she does not miss having to deal with the cleaning and maintenance of twenty-two rooms. The main thing is to weigh all these competing interests before you make a final decision.

If you and your ex-spouse agree to sell the house, my recommendation is to have your lawyers make the arrangements once you settle on a realtor. Get two professional appraisals, and ask at least two realtors to look at the house and estimate its fair market value. The court will rely on the professional appraisals, but they often vary from what you can actually get when you sell the house. The real estate market is so volatile that if you list your house when there are only a few other houses in the same price category, you may get much more than if you do so when there is a lot of competition.

Unless you bought a brand-new house, you both have done work on it, ranging from planting the flower beds to stripping three floors of paneling from the stairwell of your old Victorian. It is hard to place a value on "sweat equity," but if you have done most of the work around the house and put your own money (gifts from parents, for example) into it, you should get that back, as well as some additional compensation for your hard work.

As far as tax issues are concerned, now that there is a $500,000 capital gains exemption, you probably won't have to argue about who is going to pay that tax. If you make more than $500,000 in profit on the house (the net amount after deducting what you paid for the house and the capital improvements you made), splitting up payment of the tax will have to be a negotiating point.

☞ **Wake-up Call:** Some mortgage documents call for you to pay off the mortgage when a divorce decree is issued, even if the deed has been transferred to one spouse's name. If that's the case and you don't have the means to pay it off or you don't want to sell, see if you can negotiate a refinancing package with your lender.

■ The Deed Is Done ■

Whether your divorce took six months or six years, it probably has consumed your life. Just as when any other major event ends, there is a huge emotional letdown. Now, all of a sudden, everything is settled and it is time to look ahead. My rule of thumb for anyone who has just gotten divorced is to avoid making any major financial decisions for a year.

But this does not mean that you should ignore your finances altogether. Now is the time to take a look at your postdivorce budget and use all the techniques I have given you in this book to stick to it. I have worked with many divorced women and men, and there is a huge tendency to overspend in the first year to assuage the pain of your life change.

You also need to have new wills and other legal documents such as a living will and a durable power of attorney drawn up. If you were fortunate enough to end up with a sizable investment portfolio, you also should start interviewing financial managers as soon as possible. Ask your attorney and accountant for their recommendations as well as any wealthy friends you have. You may have never had to balance a checkbook before, and now you have to pick the person who is going to manage your money. A financial planner can help educate you so that you are standing on your own two feet very shortly. I remember one former client who indeed had never balanced her checkbook and did not know the difference between a stock and a bond. Within six months she had studied personal finance, met with me numerous times to ask questions and make sure she was on track, and then she picked her own investment manager. If she can do it, so can you.

■ Innocent Spouse Provision ■

In 1998 Congress finally passed a bill that protects "innocent spouses" who had no way of knowing that their ex-spouses were not being absolutely honest on their joint tax returns. (This is especially prevalent among individuals who own their own businesses or salespeople working on commission.) Until this bill was passed, if your ex-spouse's tax problems occurred during your marriage, they could haunt you long after the divorce decree had been signed.

Typically the IRS holds both husbands and wives who sign joint tax returns liable for taxes owed during the year, even if they later divorce. That's because if it turns out after your divorce that your ex-spouse deliberately or accidentally filed false information on your tax return, the IRS assumes that you reviewed it and agreed that the information was correct. But many spouses sign tax returns without even looking at them. I once watched a couple sign tax returns—one signed, then deliberately placed an elbow over the numbers while the other one signed without ever looking at it. (We were in a lawyer's office, and they were his clients, so I didn't feel comfortable interfering.) Don't do that!

If you feel that your spouse deceived you about the amount of taxes owed, you can apply for "innocent spouse" relief. Call the IRS and ask for Form #8857, "Request for Innocent Spouse Relief."

TILL DEATH DO US PART

A divorce is almost always preceded by marital problems, so in a way, you have time to prepare for the separation. The death of a spouse you loved, cherished, and planned a life with is doubly hard. I have had clients whose spouses died unexpectedly and those who nursed their spouses through months or years of illness with loving care. Even in the second case, when you know your spouse is going to die, it is a shock when it happens. Often, adequate plans have not been made in advance so that financial problems occur just when you are most vulnerable.

Maria was a stockbroker married to a lawyer who suddenly died of a brain aneurysm. When he died, they were just trying to have their first baby. Scott was only thirty-eight years old, and the thought of either of them dying had seemed absurd. The funeral was packed, the eulogies were moving and funny, and friends and family gathered at Maria's home for dinner. And then, she said, "It was all over. I was left alone, in my house, to deal with the fact that Scott would never be walking in the door again."

Maria found that her friends were supportive at first, but did not seem to know how to behave around her—whether to mention his name, allow her to grieve, reminisce about old times, or talk about the future. Some of them drifted away, not because they didn't care, but because they didn't know what to do. They felt she should get on with her life, and she felt stuck in the past. Fortunately, she went to a therapist who suggested a support group for widows and widowers. That helped on the emotional side, but she had to deal with the financial implication of her new status as well.

Any assets that Scott owned himself passed through the probate process. The same was true of assets for which he named his estate as the beneficiary. Even though Scott was an attorney, he did not have a will. He was in a partnership with another lawyer, but there was no buy-sell agreement backed by an insurance policy that would pay Maria for the equity that Scott had built up in the firm.

It takes up to nine months to settle an estate, and in the meantime money is tied up and unavailable to beneficiaries. Fortunately, Maria had a good job and Scott had a fairly large insurance policy with her as beneficiary, so she was able to get her money from the insurance company within about 30 days. Scott's insurance agent delivered the check, and suggested she use it to buy a variable annuity (which carried a large commission). Maria was financially sophisticated, but she was still so emotionally distraught that she followed his advice without consulting anyone else. It was a terrible investment decision based on her circumstances, because she needed money immediately, and there was a very large "sales charge" (back-end load) of 8 percent if she cashed it in. The moral of the story is, no matter how financially sophisticated you are, when you are faced with a devastating emotional loss you need objective advice from an attorney, accountant, and/or financial planner before you make major financial decisions.

☞ **Wake-up Call:** Every asset that passes through the probate process becomes part of the public record, and if you are fortunate enough to have inherited substantial funds, you may find yourself the target of salespeople trying to sell you inappropriate investments (or, as in one case I know, one widower got a call from someone asking to borrow money).

My rule of thumb is the same in this situation as in a divorce: Do not make a major decision for a year. In my old neighborhood in Atlanta twenty years ago, a lovely widow in her seventies was persuaded to sell the home she had lived in for forty years with her husband, just six months after he died. The rationale of the real estate broker was that she should buy a smaller house. She moved two streets away, and realized the moment that she moved in that she had made one of the greatest mistakes of her life. All her memories of her husband were in that other house, and that was where she wanted to be. I used to watch her on her daily walk, always passing slowly by the house, reminiscing about the place where she had raised five children and enjoyed a wonderful marriage.

One other point to keep in mind is medical insurance. You should be able to keep medical insurance from your deceased spouse's plan—check with the plan administrator. And if you have been named the beneficiary of any retirement plans, you need professional advice about how to handle those plans—whether to roll them over to a spousal IRA or to start taking distributions. This is a complex issue, so make sure you are dealing with an expert who understands all of the financial and tax implications.

The only good news about becoming a widow or widower is that the pain does decrease over time. As one friend told me, "It is something you never really get over, but it moves farther and farther toward the back of your mind. That's when you know that you are moving forward through the grieving process, and you are ready to move on with your life."

REMARRIAGE

First marriages that ended badly are never fun, but they do teach you certain lessons about how to make a second marriage last. A second marriage is certainly a fresh start, but this time the bride and groom tend to be a little less romantic and a little more pragmatic about the problems they may face. They know that money can be the great divider, and they are probably not surprised to learn that stepchildren can try to sabotage even the happiest marriages from the start. If the second marriage fails, then the truly brave move on to a third marriage. In fact, some of the happiest marriages I know are third marriages in which the common theme seems to be: "This time we got it right because we took the right steps from the beginning." But why wait until a third marriage to get it right? Every second, third, and fourth marriage is just as vulnerable to splitting up over money issues as a first marriage.

I know a couple who is blissfully happy today, the man on his second marriage and the woman on her third. But it almost didn't happen because of a problem that cropped up about four days before the wedding. Because Genevieve would be wealthy from an upcoming inheritance and had an attorney of her own, Alex was happy to go with her to talk to him about a prenuptial agreement. Genevieve's attorney drew it up and suggested that Alex sign it in the office. But Genevieve and Alex had already talked to me about this issue (though they weren't clients), and I recommended that each have his and her own attorney to consult about this sort of agreement. That way, the soon-to-be-weds could stay out of the emotional fray.

When Alex's attorney saw the proposed agreement, he went ballistic. They were going to be living in Alex's house and on his income until Genevieve received her large inheritance in ten years. In the meantime, Genevieve would not be working outside the home. Yet the prenuptial agreement was worded so that Alex would get absolutely nothing in return for his financial contributions if they split up.

The problem was solved by buying a ten-year term insurance policy on Genevieve's life with Alex as beneficiary. In addition, she put a provision in her will, leaving him a portion of her inheritance if they were still married when she received it. This near-fiasco could have been avoided if they had gotten financial counseling before consulting Genevieve's attorney, who never asked about Alex's assets. Your first step, as always, should be to get some financial counseling, even before you consult an attorney. That way your lawyer will have the numbers he needs to advise you about wills, trust, and prenuptial agreements.

A financial planner can also serve as a kind of mediator if you find that you are having trouble blending your saving and spending habits, which probably are different. Frequently the most critical issue is whether you are going to keep your money separate or combine it. Usually I recommend three checking accounts, just as I do with a first marriage. Deposit all paychecks into one joint account, from which all regular bills should be paid. Then each spouse can write a check for a weekly or monthly allowance and deposit it into his or her separate account. You and your partner can do whatever you want with that money—no questions asked. If either one of you elects to save or invest that money, it's still yours alone.

Setting a budget for your joint account helps you handle special situations. The budget should include all regular bills, each partner's allowance, as well as any miscellaneous items, such as dining out. So, if you've already spent your entertainment money for the month, but a new movie just opened with your favorite star, you can take your spouse and cover it with money from your personal account.

■ Life Insurance ■

A new marriage necessitates reviewing the beneficiaries of your various retirement plans and life insurance policies. (For tax reasons it's usually best to name your spouse as beneficiary of the retirement plans. This way, income tax does not have to be paid the year of death and can be postponed by the surviving spouse until he or she starts to take the money out.) To determine whom to name on life insurance policies, ask your financial planner for a capital needs analysis, with various scenarios. Your life insurance goes to the beneficiaries you name; if your will says something else, (if you forgot to change it, for instance) that is irrelevant. Naming your children as beneficiaries is one way to ensure that, in the event of your death, they receive the money you want them to have instead of it going the stepchildren of your second or third marriage.

There are several reasons you may want to increase your life insurance:

- If you are financially responsible for your new spouse and/or his or her children.
- If you plan to own or buy a home jointly with your spouse. You should buy enough insurance to pay for your share of the mortgage. Otherwise, your partner may be stuck with a mortgage that is higher than he can afford to pay.
- If you have children and you plan to own or buy a home jointly, your spouse should get enough insurance on your life to buy your share of the house in the event of your death, so that your children are assured to get their share of the house's value.

☞ **Wake-up Call:** Picture returning from your honeymoon and finding out that the trip you thought your new groom paid for was actually put on an already maxed-out credit card. Believe me, this isn't uncommon. The best way to protect yourself from credit surprises is to ask your financial planner to obtain credit reports on each of you and review them with both of you. If your report has a few surprises—or you suspect that your fiancé's does—it helps to have a third party interpret the results and help you understand what really matters. It may not be a very romantic thing to do, but in today's world it is a necessity.

■ The Value of Prenuptial Agreements ■

Prenuptial agreements can protect assets that you bring into the marriage, and can also regulate assets acquired during the marriage. But they can be the source of mutual distrust. To make the process as painless and fair as possible, each one of you should hire your own attorney. They can do the negotiating for you. Remember Genevieve and Alex? Your attorneys can consult with you, so that you never have to have a discussion directly with your fiancé about a prenuptial agreement. You can even sign them in separate meetings, if that seems helpful to your relationship.

Prenuptial agreements can cover what happens in the event of divorce or death. Generally they won't hold up in court if:

- you didn't have legal representation and your partner did
- your partner coerced you into signing
- your partner withheld important financial information

■ Dealing with Different Spending Styles ■

Joanie and Phil seemed perfectly compatible all through the dating phase of their relationship, and they did not have one disagreement about planning and paying for the wedding (which they did themselves). Even the honeymoon seemed to portend little or no stress when it came to money. They had split everything down the middle, down to the last dollar. Then, they came home, the first month's bills of their married life came in the mail, and they realized that they each had very different ideas about how they would manage their money once they had tied the knot.

Joanie grew up without a lot of money and was accustomed to watching her pennies. Joanie assumed that both of their paychecks would go into one account, bills and living expenses would be paid from it, and they would save whatever was left over in both their names. Phil also grew up without much money, but now that he earned a nice income, he enjoyed occasional indulgences and spending sprees (as on his brand new Boston whaler fishing boat!) Phil assumed that they would contribute equally to their living expenses, and would each get to keep what was left over from their own salaries. They are the classic example of the couple who never talks about money before marriage, and then once they are married, it seems as if it is all they do talk about. Things got so bad between Phil and Joanie that a friend suggested they consult me, because she was seriously worried about the rift that their different financial styles were causing in their marriage. It took a while for each of them to concede that they did not have the "right" way of doing things, but they cared enough about each other and their marriage to try the "No-Argument Plan" (see Chapter 3, "Settling Down," page 134).

If you discover that you and your spouse have incompatible spending styles (I am still amazed at how much people overlook about each other when they are dating), I recommend consulting with a psychologist, social worker, or some other professional therapist to discuss the differences and figure out how to come to terms with each other's priorities. Not doing so could cost you another marriage.

■ Stepchildren and Money ■

Finally, once you hammer out these issues as best you can, clarify the financial arrangements with your children and stepchildren. A great deal of tension can arise in blended families around the issue of money. Young children might worry that their stepmother will try to cut their allowance, for example, and older children may be concerned about their inheritance. Reassure them that you have taken steps to secure each family's assets and be as candid as you feel is appropriate.

BOOMERANG KIDS

Picture this: You just redecorated your son's room as a guest room and suddenly his dirty socks are all over the floor, just as when he was a teenager.

How about a fresh start in the parenting department? A second chance to cook and clean and pick up after your kids long after you thought they'd moved out of the house for good? More and more adult children are moving back home after living on their own because of job loss, tuition expenses, or simply wanting to lower their expenses and boost their savings.

You may have thought your children would move on after college—while at the same time they were planning to move back in! The average college-aged student nowadays expects to live with his parents until age twenty-four. Some of them move back in after living alone and seeing just how expensive that is!

While you may be flattered that they want to return home, there can be some emotional tolls and financial strain on both of you as a result. You may be spending more on food, cleaning, gas, laundry, and utilities, while at the same time you have lost part of your house and some of your own privacy. It is easy to get resentful very quickly.

It's best to remember, and to remind your children, that they are now paying guests in your house, and they need to follow your house rules. It's hard to consider your child a guest, but this is probably a time when you must save for your own retirement. Set a time to discuss the new arrangement and ask your child to think about the areas you want to cover: rent, food, use of the car, house rules (concerning loud music, friends coming over), chores, and a set move-out date. For rent, you must ask for some amount, even if it is a modest $25 a week, to reinforce the point. I know some parents who charge $150 a week. Take every penny and throw it in a retirement plan. If you don't want to do that, put it in a savings account and give it to your child as a parting gift when he moves out.

If your child is eating most meals with you and raiding your refrigerator, he should be expected to pay a share of the food bills. Again, I've seen some clients charge $20 a week and others $100, depending on the situation.

Your child should do some chores around the house. If paying for rent or food is a problem, then ask her to do additional chores in exchange for those things.

House rules are critical because this is your space now. If you don't want your son to have his girlfriend sleep over, you have every right to say it is against house rules. You don't even have to say why. Set rules about everything that may make you feel uncomfortable, such as quiet hours, friends visiting, using the living room, or sharing the home computer. Don't forget to mention your financial liability, because you are responsible and can be sued for whatever happens in your house.

■ And Here Come the Grandchildren ■

Some parents get even more than they bargained for when their children move back in with grandchildren in tow. This is another situation when a family meeting is a necessity. Even if you are delighted to have your grandchildren around, they bring with them extra work and expense.

Be sure to come to some agreement about money issues, such as paying your grandchildren for chores and their allowances. And make it clear that you do not intend to sabotage your child's attempt to teach your grandchildren financial responsibility—if their parents say no, grandma and grandpa promise not to contradict.

Make it clear up front that you are not the last-minute babysitter of convenience. I had one client who was so tired of being used that way that she started charging $4 an hour when her daughter decided to go out to clubs at the "last minute." The club-hopping stopped and so did her daughter's tendency to see her mother as a doormat. It was a win-win financial and emotional solution.

INHERITANCES AND OTHER WINDFALLS

You've been booted out the door of your old company with a severance package of $150,000 in hand. Your favorite uncle remembered you in his will—$250,000. Your doctor slipped up in the operating room and after two years of disclosure, he agrees to a settlement of $500,000. Your brilliant brother sold his software business and your share (thanks to kicking in $10,000 at the start) is now worth $2.5 million. You won the Powerball jackpot—$250 million!

After you've popped the champagne cork, and gotten over the shock that you no longer have to worry about how to pay your bills—but before all your relatives and friends and rogue investment advisors knock on your door with their ideas for how to spend your money—you need to hire the best attorney, CPA, or financial planner you can find and put a message on your answering machine saying that all inquiries should go through him or her. This includes family and friends, because you have to keep a cool head. If your windfall was public knowledge, you may even want to get an unlisted number, as a former client did when his company went public and he was on the front page of the business section of the newspaper with an accompanying article stating exactly how much he made.

If you find yourself in this fortunate position, start thinking about what to do with your money. But before you decide to give it away, you *must* read the next chapter, "Happy Endings," and the section in Chapter 4 about how much you will need for retirement.

A windfall is a big financial challenge. It is a challenge most of us would like to face, but nonetheless requires strategic decision making. Pay off your credit cards, for sure. But don't pay off your mortgage without running the numbers with an expert. There are so many tempting options. Invest in that fancy car you've always dreamed of? Book that vacation you've wanted to take for years? Buy a new home in a fancier neighborhood? Pour it into the stock market? Or put it in the bank?

Give yourself a real treat so you can experience your windfall, and then hold onto as much of the rest as you can. My three words of advice are: Invest, invest, invest! When you read the next chapter and see how having enough money at retirement can make it the happiest time of your life (even though it can be the most expensive time of your life), you will understand exactly why preserving capital and investing it is the smartest way to go.

BANKRUPTCY

In the real estate boom of the 1980s, too many people invested too much money in real estate, usually by taking money out of their other investments and then taking on large mortgages to make up the difference. At the time, it made sense, because the early and mid-1980s saw an unprecedented increase in the value of real estate. But where there is a boom, there is always a bust, and it hit big-time in the late 1980s. The problem was twofold. First, if you wanted to sell your home, there were no buyers. Second, even if you were lucky enough to find a buyer, the market value of your home had likely depreciated to the point that it was less than the mortgage you were carrying. So if you wanted to sell your house, you had to come up with cash to make up the difference between the sales price and your mortgage. It can be hard to find that extra $10,000, $20,000, or $50,000 that your lender wants in cash just so you can get your house off your back.

If this did not happen to you, you are probably thinking, "Anyone who got in this position must have been an idiot." But that certainly was not the case. I had one very sophisticated former client with an MBA from a top business school who knew exactly what he was doing when he poured a ton of money into his new million-dollar house. He disregarded our advice not to take money out of his investment portfolio so he could make a large down payment. His large mortgage payments and the house upkeep (including landscaping of about $20,000 a year) consumed a large part of his income. After all, as he explained to us, he owned a thriving office furniture business that was exceeding revenue expectations by about 30 percent a year, which meant that he was pulling down a huge salary. "Alison and I figured that with my income alone (Alison will stay home with the kids), we can replenish my investment portfolio within two years. Then we are back where we stared and we have the mansion we have had our eye on for years."

You probably can guess the rest of the story, but I will fill you in. A major recession hit in the late 1980s. One of the first things that companies did was stop buying office furniture, so Dave's sales plummeted. He had to lay off half his workforce, some of whom had been with him for twenty years. His outstanding invoices were not being paid because companies were in trouble, but his longtime bank—facing pressures of its own—still wanted regular payments on the building mortgage and his business line of credit and was unwilling to negotiate a new payment schedule. Dave then laid off half of his remaining sales force, because there was no net income. With no income to pay the bank, he had no money to pay himself. Almost eighteen months to the day after they bought their dream house, Dave and Alison declared bankruptcy.

If you have declared bankruptcy or are facing it yourself, you are not alone. In 1997, a record 1.3 million individuals filed for bankruptcy, up from roughly 350,000 in 1985. Part of the reason has been the change of laws; nearly 70 percent filed under provisions of Chapter 7, which makes it easier for borrowers to escape many of their obligations by declaring. There are several different kinds of bankruptcy, and people commonly choose to file Chapter 7, because it usually allows you to keep an interest in certain assets such as retirement plans, your house, cars, and personal items. Currently, legislators are trying to make it more difficult to declare Chapter 7 bankruptcy, but no bills have been passed to this effect.

Keep in mind that even if you file for bankruptcy, you will still owe alimony and child support as well as taxes and, usually, student loans. Some other debts will still need to be paid regardless of which option you choose. This just underscores the importance of hiring an attorney *before* you declare bankruptcy, especially because it stays on your credit report for between seven and ten years. Office supply stores sell fill-in-the-blank-forms, or you can represent yourself in court, but I certainly do not recommend it. When you declare bankruptcy, you are taking a huge financial step and putting a big black mark next to your name, so make sure you know what you are doing before it is too late.

The good news is that you *can* make a fresh start after bankruptcy. Dave and Alison moved to an apartment and she got a job that she enjoys, even though their household income has increased to the point where she no longer needs to work. Dave went to work for an office furniture maker, and they say that the experience actually strengthened their marriage and taught their children a valuable lesson. They used a terrible situation to make a fresh start out of life. If they can do it, so can you.

✔ Fresh Start Checklist

Signs that you are financially alert. Check off all those that apply to you:

__ My "fresh start" has been a painful experience, but I try to view it as an opportunity for personal and financial growth.

__ I've chosen a new job or career and I've picked a field with projected growth.

__ I've started a new business and I have enough savings to sustain me through at least the first year.

__ I've started a new business and I have written up a business plan.

__ I'm dealing with a divorce and I am trying to waste as little money as possible on lawyers to fight purely emotional battles.

__ After my divorce, I waited about a year before making any big financial decisions.

__ After the death of my spouse, I waited about a year before making any big financial decisions.

__ I was unclear about how to handle my new financial situation, so I consulted a financial planner.

__ When I decided to remarry, I sat down with my spouse to discuss our spending styles and how we plan to manage our finances.

__ I've updated my will and life insurance policies to reflect my changed status.

__ When my son (daughter) moved back home, I asked him (her) to pay a reasonable monthly rent, help with food costs, and set a moving-out date.

— When I got my windfall, I bought_____, which I've always wanted, then paid off my credit card bills, and invested the rest.

6

Happy Endings

In the beginning of this book, I talked about my parents' courting and planning their future together while gazing up at the moon. They grew up in Maryland, where they were love-struck teenagers, and settled in Atlanta. But they return every summer to Maryland, where they still, at ages seventy-eight and seventy-nine, look up at the moon from the porch of Golden Hill, a clapboard farmhouse on the Chesapeake Bay that has been in our family for generations.

Granted, my parents recognize that their future has a little less longevity than it did sixty-two years ago, when they first met and retirement was a hazy event that was going to happen fifty years in the future. And even though no one who knows my parents would ever call them old—they have more energy than many twenty-five-year-olds—they now make plans on a more short-term basis, focusing on things such as whom they will visit over the holidays and where they would like to travel.

Graced with good health, they stay so busy we have to track them down by E-mail. They walk several miles a day, and still clean and repair Golden Hill twice a year themselves—a week of twelve-hour work days each time. Of course they worry about their health failing, but because they have been frugal and have bought the right Medicare and

Medigap insurance, they are confident they can handle any medical crises. If not, they know they have four children who will step in, because that's how they raised us.

I am not saying it was easy for them to accumulate enough money to have a pleasurable retirement. As children, we were sometimes embarrassed because we did not have as many fancy clothes as did our friends. I know my parents went without things as well—I remember, as a very small child, having a car in which you could view the road through a hole in the floorboard. But as adult children, when we get postcards from Turkey or China (always on a trip that they managed to get a "great deal" on), we know their reluctance to spend money has paid off. They are still very frugal—but they "woke up and smelled the money" during their childhoods, when they lived through the Great Depression, and it has affected the way they have dealt with money ever since. My parents have earned every moment of happiness they have.

☞ **Wake-up Call**: If you are not yet contemplating retirement, or have not yet retired yourself, you may be inclined to skip this chapter. Don't. Whatever age you are when you "wake up," you need to know what lies ahead so you can plan. Or, you may have parents who are facing retirement soon—or for whom it's already a reality.

Not everyone is as fortunate as my parents have been in enjoying good health and accumulating money for retirement. Being forced to take early retirement from your job ten years before you planned to, paying for more college expenses than you anticipated, living through a medical or financial crisis, becoming widowed or divorced, having a business fail, having to take on financial responsibilities for your parents, or having bad luck with investments can all leave you with a nest egg that is much smaller than you had hoped for.

But even if you find yourself in a somewhat less fortunate situation, there are ways to have Happy Endings. I vividly remember two former clients who had spent too much and saved too little during their working lives. Neil was "offered" an early retirement package, but in truth he was being downsized. The only good news was that the package was quite generous in relation to what he would have gotten had he worked a few more years for the company. (During the last ten years, about one third of companies with over two hundred employees have offered early retirement packages.)

As I do with all clients, I prepared a year-by-year long-term cash-flow analysis showing, hypothetically, their income and assets for the rest of their lives (I usually assume living to about age eighty-five or ninety if it is a couple, because odds are that one of them will live that long). Neil and Anne were ages fifty-nine and fifty-six at the time. Using conservative assumptions and taking full Social Security benefits into account, my projections showed that they would run out of money at about age seventy. Of course, no one can predict the future, but a long-term cash-flow projection, year by year, is a great way to get clients to "wake up."

I was very worried about their reaction when I had to give them this bad news. For some reason they felt they were set for life and had even been "gifting" (the financial term for giving up to $10,000 a year, which does not need to be declared for tax purposes) money to their children. In addition to my projections, I also showed them how long they were expected to live. On the one hand, they were thrilled; on the other hand, they suddenly became alarmed about their finances. After the initial shock, Neil said to me, while Anne nodded, "We had better take this plan home, get out our red pens, and start cutting expenses. Then we'll bring it back to you so you can run the numbers again and we will figure out what to do next."

"What to do next" turned out to be stopping the annual gifts to their children, selling their house and moving to a smaller one, and becoming conscious of every penny. If only all of us behaved this way when we were faced with bleak financial news! Neil and Anne "woke up" in time to change their lives and truly enjoy the final season of their lives. They even said that after they had made these radical changes, they were happier because they felt in control of their money. "It feels so good to be frugal," said Anne, "that we wish we had done this twenty years ago."

In this chapter, we will tell you how to feel good about your money during these years of relaxation. Of course much of the advice about managing our expenses in earlier chapters continues to be applicable throughout retirement as well. Most financial advice is good for any season—especially that you remain awake and aware of your financial situation.

If you are like most people, you have worked hard all your life—either in the office or at home—and you want to have financial security now, when you may not have a regular paycheck coming in every month. You probably have Social Security and maybe even some kind of pension plan in addition to an individual retirement plan (or plans) and savings of your own.

But first of all, regardless of your financial status, congratulate yourself on reaching this landmark season of your life! I hope you realize that this is probably the best time in U.S. history to have done so. Why?

Because with each succeeding generation, this has become a longer and healthier season. We live twenty years longer than we did in 1920, and the average life expectancy for men is seventy-two years and seventy-nine years for women (that's an average of seventy-six years).

The financial world had adjusted accordingly. For years, when you reached age 100, if you owned a permanent (cash value) life insurance policy you were considered "actuarially dead" and received the full death benefit (which would mean—you guessed it—you'd have to pay taxes on part of it). These days, there are special riders to make sure that even if you live well past 100 this will not happen.

The ideal time to plan for retirement is before you enter this season of your life. But this chapter is designed to serve as a guide whether you are thinking ahead or are already retired. In either case, you will benefit if you do what my parents still do—spend some time contemplating the future.

PLANNING FOR THE TWO STAGES OF RETIREMENT

In the past, when you daydreamed about retirement you may have fantasized about days spent on the golf course, evenings on the dance floor, walks on the beach, and so on. But you probably did not imagine days when you could no longer drive, or dances where you were on the sidelines, confined to a walker. I have spent a fair amount of time in a wheelchair and on crutches myself, and had to depend on others for such basics as eating meals and getting dressed, so I know how frustrating and debilitating it can be. It's certainly not something we like to think about. But the likelihood is that you will reach that point sometime in your life.

Many people don't realize that for most of us, retirement has two distinct phases. Ideally, during the first phase, you and your spouse will be healthy and able to live independent lives. If you need extra income, one or both of you may even work part-time. The second phase consists of less active years. If your health is not as good and you need daily assistance, this may be the time when you will be paying someone else to take care of you. Thanks to the high cost of health care, Phase Two can be much more expensive than Phase One.

The smart thing to do is to plan for both stages of retirement. How much money do you need to support you in each stage? How much income will you have?

■ Phase One: Taking Off ■

For many people, the first stage of retirement turns out to be the ultimate "fresh start" in life, rather than a period of winding down, as others might imagine. Traveling to far-off places, visiting your children or grandchildren, and taking up a new hobby may be on your agenda. All of this takes money, and there will also be plenty of new expenses you couldn't have foreseen. People planning for retirement twenty years ago never would have thought of budgeting for a new computer, for example, along with monthly online service fees. That's why a budget continues to be a necessity, even at this stage of your life. Can you afford to keep paying $1,000 a year in swim club fees or symphony subscriptions? You can't know for sure unless you look closely at all your expenses.

To help you envision the first stage of retirement (if you are not already in the midst of it), consider the following questions and the financial impact of each. If you are married, answer these questions together.

- At what age do you want to retire?
- Would you like to continue working part time?
- Would you like to stay in your current home, purchase a smaller one, move to a different locale, or purchase a vacation home?
- What do you want to do with your free time and which of these activities will cost the most money?
- Are you facing any medical risks?
- Can you support yourself financially if your spouse dies?

■ Phase Two: Slowing Down ■

In Phase Two, whether your health declines or you just slow down, you will probably need help in daily living. This phase is a lot less pleasant to imagine, but it's critical that you do so now, when you still can plan for it.

The standard rule of thumb is that during retirement you can live on roughly 70 percent of the income you had when you were working. But with some assisted care facilities and nursing homes currently costing $2,000 a month or more, it's clear that for many of us, 70 percent just won't be enough, especially in the later retirement years. I suggest budgeting at least 80 percent. Here are some questions to ask yourself, designed to help you envision what your life might be like:

- Do you want to stay in your home? Can you afford home health care? Are you planning to move in with your children? If so, do they know this?
- Can you afford a lengthy hospital stay? What about round-the-clock nurses at home?
- Would you be interested in moving to a continuing care facility?
- Do you have a will, living will, health-care proxy, durable power of attorney? Inadequate retirement planning could mean that you're kept alive against your wishes.
- Do you want an elaborate funeral or a simple service, cremation or a burial plot? Does your family know what you'd like?

Chapter 4, "Building Up," contains more detailed information about how much money you'll need to have in the bank at retirement (see the chart on page 196). The following table shows which of your living expenses are likely to increase in retirement, and which are likely to decrease.

■ Friendship Counts ■

The issue of building a support network during your retirement transition years may seem out of place in a financial book, but, believe it or not, retirement is a season when friends can make more of a difference than money. Retirement is stressful for everyone because it is a major life transition. When you retire, you are facing a huge change in your lifestyle, and perhaps that of your spouse as well. If your identity has been tied up in your work, all of a sudden you are just one more retiree heading out to the early bird special at the local restaurant. You no longer have a job title, an office, daily deadlines, and responsibilities. If you were a manager, no one is reporting to you.

This can be especially trying and stressful on a marriage if you have been a stay-at-home spouse. When the breadwinner retires, it is difficult to get used to him or her hanging around the house all the time. The entire relationship has changed, because the daily rules have shifted and at least one party (whoever was earning a paycheck) is probably feeling a loss of power. The old stereotype of the husband following his wife around and being underfoot in the kitchen all day actually holds true in many marriages. Sometimes when I am easing couples into retirement, I feel more like a therapist or mediator than a financial planner.

If these are feelings you are facing, the sooner you deal with them the

Retirement Expenses

	From Pre-retirement to Phase One	From Phase One to Phase Two
Business extras	↓	—
Business gifts	↓	—
Child care	↓	—
Clothing	↓	—
Commuting	↓	—
Dues	↓	↓
Gifts and entertainment	↑	↓
Home	↑	↓
Insurance (homeowners', auto, and life)	↓	↑
Leisure and hobby	↑	↓
Lifestyle	↑	↓
Long-term care	—	↑
Medicare, Medigap, and long-term care premiums	↑	↑
Medical care	↑	↑
Retirement savings	↓	↓
Social Security and Medicare contributions	—*	—
Travel	↑	↓
Volunteering	↑	↓
Weekday lunches	↓	↓

*Unless working part-time.

better. There is a tendency to make up for loss of power at work by either asserting it at home (giving orders all day) or giving up responsibility altogether and spending your time doing nothing. Either approach puts a strain on your marriage and can lead you into a spiral of depression. When clients can't seem to adjust to their new situations after six months, I often recommend that they see a therapist. Any time you have to adjust to a major change, talking to a professional about it can only help, and you should not be ashamed of doing so. It is well worth the money and time, and is an investment in your future.

Social support can be more important than financial security during those first years of retirement, according to a recent University of Michigan study. Researchers found that during the first four years after retirement, the size of a person's social network was a stronger influence than financial or physical health on whether their life satisfaction changed for better or worse.

There are support groups for recent retirees, and if you have hobbies (and if you don't, get some!) you can develop a network of fellow hobbyists. My favorite example is of a Fortune 500 executive. He had always loved motorcycles and dreamed of criss-crossing the county on a Harley Davidson, but had never felt he could follow that dream because of his position in the business world. Soon after retirement, however, he and his spouse bought Harleys, joined the Harley club, and have been revving their engines ever since! One minister I know who had to retire early because of illness took up watercolor painting, one of his youthful passions. He has started several new friendships while attending artist's workshops and has even won prizes for his work.

Another friend who ran an auto parts business took a two-year, full-time course in furniture building when he retired and now crafts exquisite pieces of furniture that often take six months to make. He sells them for a tidy profit, but the money is not the issue—he is following his dreams. I often go to a local diner early in the morning to have breakfast and write, and the same group of retired men eat there on a certain day each week. Their topic of discussion (and often argument)? The stock market! It is obvious from overhearing their conversations that each spends a fair amount of time during the week following the market so that he can be as knowledgeable as possible for that weekly breakfast. But of course, social contact is a big part of the reason for their weekly get-together. So whatever your fantasies have been, now is the time to fulfill them!

PART-TIME FOREVER

Some people love to work so much, they never give it up completely. Others simply need the money. Once you complete the income and expense worksheets in this chapter and in Chapter 4, "Building Up," you will be able to estimate whether you can meet your financial obligations with your current income and savings. Remember that you will need an estimated 70 to 100 percent of you preretirement income to maintain the same standard of living as when you were working. It all depends on your retirement expenses, which you can estimate by looking at the Retirement Expense List (see page 300). We will talk about Social Security in a minute, but you can generally assume that it will pay you about 40 percent of your annual preretirement earnings if you retire at age sixty-five—but the more you earned yearly, the lower that percentage will be. For example, if you had steadily increasing earnings during your life and you made $20,000 last year, your Social Security retirement benefits might be $8,000 a year. But if you ended up earning $100,000 a year, Social Security is obviously not going to pay you 40 percent of that ($40,000). If you look at the Social Security retirement benefits chart, you will see that the more your income increases, the slower the amount of your Social Security benefits increase.

The good news is that only about 10 percent of people over the age of sixty-five are considered below the poverty line, down from 30 percent in 1970. The bad news is that the median income of retirees today is just under $12,000, and over half of that is from Social Security. If we project a 3 percent inflation rate, in ten years, today's purchasing power of $10,000 will be reduced to about $7,300, and in twenty years, to just under $5,500. If you retire at sixty-five, you are expected to live to age eighty-two if you are male, and to age eighty-five if female—so living on a fixed income could be a real problem for you.

If you are a woman, the statistics are even less heartening. Of the elderly poor we talked about, 75 percent are women. A quarter of all women over age sixty-five live in poverty. Social Security makes up 90 percent of income for over half of elderly women.

I once had to deliver the bad news to a new widow in my church that after her husband's estate had been settled and debts were paid, her total annual income was going to be about $6,500. Her income was cut dramatically because the Social Security and pension benefits she was receiving were cut back almost 50 percent after her husband's death. They had been barely making ends meet before he died. We talked about the possibility of her taking a full-time job. She called later to say that, after talking with her children, she decided instead to sell her modest home and move to another state to live with her daughter.

If you find yourself in a position where you need part-time work for income, go back and read the sections on starting your own business and on developing an existing career or changing careers in Chapter 5, "Fresh Starts." Part-time employment after retirement is such a burgeoning industry that there are career counselors and résumé services that are specially trained for those who have recently retired or who have been retired for a while and want to reenter the workforce. And many employers are waking up to the benefits of having mature, experienced workers on the job who will tend to stay with the company for the long term.

Now that age discrimination is illegal, it should be easier to get jobs than ever before. But, of course, that doesn't mean that doors always open easily. The harsh reality is that often it is hard to get your foot in the door to see the human resources manager when you are old enough to be his or her mother! I had a client who retired after a long and distinguished executive career at a medium-sized company. Mary wanted to work part-time in a challenging position and had a wealth of experience to bring to the table. The problem was, the last time she looked for a job was twenty years beforehand, and what worked then does not work now. Also, many of the jobs these days are in small start-up companies where the corporate culture is very different from a Fortune 500 or even an established medium-sized company (and, as she said, the average age of the employees seems to be about twenty-five). At my recommendation, she took a refresher course in how to search for a job, prepare a résumé, and improve her interviewing skills so that she appeared as young and energetic as possible, and even change her wardrobe. The trick was to repackage all of her skills to show how valuable her knowledge of the evolution of how companies work is in today's market, and to prove that she has the ability to keep up with a culture and employees who are so much younger.

Not all retirees continue to work because they have to. Many of today's retirees find playing bridge or golf boring. They want more of a mental challenge and work provides it for them. If you are lucky, perhaps you can arrange a part-time consulting job with your old firm. Or, as we talked about in Fresh Starts (Chapter 5), you can start a small business on the side in preparation for retirement and keep working at it once you quit your main job. Even at my father's age, he still has a small mechanical engineering business that brings in extra income and gives him tremendous mental benefits because he still feels active in the workplace. Wherever he is, he faithfully calls in every day for messages, and returns them promptly. He is frequently working on mechanical drawings when I visit. His business also provides him with important personal and social contacts, as well as contact with former business associates, many of whom are also "semi-retired."

GETTING YOUR BENEFITS

Now let's take a closer look at your income and assets to see exactly what your financial situation in retirement is or will be. If you have not checked on what your Social Security benefits will be at retirement, chances are you are going to be disappointed. When clients find out their estimated benefits from the Social Security Administration (SSA), they are always shocked at how low they are. I guess we expect to get more because we have put so much in. Unfortunately, the rate of return—the percentage of your Social Security contributions that you get back—has dropped as follows, according to *Fortune* magazine: 135 percent if you retired in 1940; 24 percent in 1950; 15 percent in 1960; 10 percent in 1970; 8 percent in 1980; 6 percent in 1990; and 4 percent in 1998. That 4 percent if you retired last year looks pretty pitiful, but keep in mind that during your working life you also had another benefit provided by Social Security: insurance in case you became disabled or died with a family to support.

Social Security is a topic that always raises lots of questions. What can you expect? How do you get it? And who is right about its future viability? Should you count on cost of living increases? If they don't happen, what will this do to your cash flow?

Today, Social Security is a program in trouble. A guaranteed source of income for Americans over sixty-five since it was established in 1935, it has seriously eroded over the years. Current Social Security benefits are a far cry from those of its heyday in 1972, when benefits were linked to the nation's inflation rate, guaranteeing recipients that their monthly payments would rise with each year's cost of living.

Now the burden on working Americans grows each year. Payroll taxes siphon off 6.2 percent of the first $65,400 a person earns—an all-time high. Congress and the White House continue to debate how to keep the program solvent into the next millennium.

Social security is a double-edged sword. It does provide a basic level of retirement income. But the flip side is that it engenders a false sense of security, lulling many people into thinking they don't need to sacrifice very much to save for retirement because those government checks will just keep rolling in. Of course, if you've read the earlier chapters of this book, you know I've tried to dispel that myth during every stage and season of your life.

Times have changed since 1935, when there were sixteen workers paying into the system for every retiree receiving benefits. Now, because people are living longer, and consequently collecting their benefits for so much longer, only three workers pay per retiree, and by the year 2020, the ratio will be two to one. Unless massive changes are made, deficits are projected to begin in 2012 and the system will run out of money in 2029.

What does all this mean to you? First of all, the closer you are to retirement, the better the chance that you will actually receive benefits that are projected by the SSA. Your retirement benefits depend on the number of quarters (three-month periods) you have worked, your annual income in each of the last 35 years of your working life, and your age at retirement.

The higher your earned income, the more your monthly benefits will be, although these increases are not proportional. For example, if you received $30,000 during your last year of work, your monthly benefits would start at $1,059. If your income was double that, the benefits would only be 15 percent higher, or $1,217. The average monthly payment in August of 1998 for retirees was $768 (the amount differs for widows/widowers collecting their spouse's benefits and for people who are receiving disability benefits). Women average lower payments than men—because of periods when they left the work force to raise children and their lower rate of pay in general.

Regardless of your level of benefits, Social Security is an important part of your retirement planning. The best way to start is to find out your estimated benefits by contacting the Social Security Administration. See the Appendix for more information. The chart on the next page may help you come up with an estimate, but it's best to get the numbers directly from the system.

The report you get will show your estimated annual benefits at age sixty-two, at your "normal" retirement age (sixty-five to sixty-seven, depending on your year of birth), and at age seventy. These are estimates of future benefits with an actual dollar amount at that time. The closer you are to retirement, the better idea you'll have of how far that amount will actually go.

Social Security Retirement Benefits

Your Age	Your Family	Your Earnings in 1995				
		$20,000	$30,000	$40,000	$50,000	$59,000 or more
45	You	$825	$1,108	$1,248	$1,380	$1,485
	You and your spouse*	$1,236	$1,661	$1,872	$2,072	$2,228
55	You	$825	$1,107	$1,227	$1,320	$1,381
	You and your spouse*	$1,236	$1,659	$1,841	$1,979	$2,072
65	You	$798	$1,059	$1,142	$1,196	$1,217
	You and your spouse*	$1,197	$1,589	$1,714	$1,793	$1,824

*Your spouse is assumed to be the same age as you. Your spouse may qualify for a higher retirement benefit based on his or her own work record.

Note: These figures are calculated in today's dollars. They assume your earnings are steady and that you'll work until full retirement age. To find the correct amount, select the age nearest yours and move right until you reach the column for the salary nearest yours. If you are younger than 45, use the numbers for age 45 to provide a conservative estimate of benefits that will be available to you.

Source: Social Security and author's estimates, based on previous years.

If you are unhappy with the SSA's decision about your benefit levels, you can file a "reconsideration." You also can ask to have any deadlines waived until your situation is resolved.

☞ **Wake-up Call**: It's hard to remember how much you made thirty years ago. That's why I recommend you get an updated statement from the Social Security Administration (see the Appendix for information) every couple of years during your working life. Make sure that the SSA has properly recorded your income for each year.

Also, take a look at how your benefits will vary according to your retirement age. If you retire at sixty-two, generally you will only get 80 percent of what your benefits would be at "normal" retirement age. Conversely, you will get an extra 8 percent for each year you work past normal retirement age (see chart on page 309). If you're married, your nonworking spouse will get 37.5 percent of your benefits if you retire early, and 50 percent at your normal retirement age. And beginning with workers retiring in 2000, the definition of "normal" retirement age will rise to sixty-seven.

The younger you are, the more likely your benefits will be less than projected now. As a safety measure, you might assume that your actual benefit will be 75 percent of current estimates.

It is hard to know whether you should take early Social Security distributions, wait until your normal retirement age, or defer as long as possible. The chart on page 306 will give you the answers, based on different investment returns and your longevity. Once you decide when you want to start getting benefits, get in touch with Social Security at least six months before that date. That way, if there are any discrepancies about how much you earned, you can get them resolved before benefits start. This also gives you time to set up a direct deposit plan.

One of the biggest problems in matching Social Security records occurs when women change their names after marriage or divorce. So check for records under every name that you've had. And make sure that you use your exact name, as listed on your Social Security card and on forms at work such as W-4s. I found this out the hard way when I filled out a W-4 form as Ginger Applegarth instead of Virginia Applegarth (my legal name)—getting it straightened out was a major challenge.

One last thing. When you get in touch with the Social Security Administration, do it in writing or go to an SSA office. Use the telephone only as a last resort because, in my experience, this is the most time-consuming way to get the information you need. Whether you make contact in person or by phone, take copious notes, including the name and ID number of the employee who helps you.

■ Benefits from Work ■

Whether you wok for a large or small company, the benefits information you get is no doubt confusing. And even your personalized benefit statement, which you should receive every year, may look like Greek to you.

Sasha is my best example. She called me in a panic because I had advised her to sit down with her employee benefits manager and go over her projected benefits, since she was planning to retire in a few months. Poor Sasha—she had been completely confused about her 401(k). Her company retirement benefit statement showed her the lump sum she would receive if she decided to take the entire amount at retirement. It also showed what her annual income would be if she'd decided instead to take monthly payments for the rest of her life by converting it to an annuity. Until she went over the statement with her benefits manager, Sasha had thought she was entitled to both, and she was dead wrong.

Fortunately, her company also had a pension plan and she would be receiving an annual income from that. Sasha's husband had a pension plan as well, so they would have enough to support themselves—even if not in the manner they had planned. Unfortunately, not everyone is as lucky as she is.

As a financial planner I look at the projected retirement benefit statements from a lot of different companies and even I sometimes get confused. That is why it is so important to sit down with your employee benefits manager at least a year before you plan to retire and start collecting your retirement information so you can evaluate your options. For your pension, you may have to choose between a *single life only plan* (when you die, payments stop, and there is no more money left for your beneficiaries); or a *joint and survivor plan* (your monthly check will be less, but your surviving spouse will likely get one-half or two-thirds of your benefits after your death, until he or she dies). You can also choose a *ten-year certain plan* (you get payments for life, but if you die before you receive ten years of benefits, your beneficiaries get payments for the rest of the ten-year period).

As morbid as it sounds, the biggest factor here is the state of your health. If you are married, and both of you are in good health, you probably want to choose the joint and survivor annuity because you're

Social Security: Retirement Age Affecting Benefits

Full benefits are equal to the primary insurance amount, or PIA. Normal retirement age is the age at which full benefits are payable. Benefits can be significantly lower or higher than the PIA, depending on age at retirement.

Year of Birth	Normal Retirement Age (NRA)	Credit for Each Year of Delayed Retirement After NRA	Benefit, as a Percentage of PIA, Beginning at Age				
			62	65	66	67	70
1941	65 and 8 months	$7\frac{1}{2}$%	$76\frac{2}{3}$	$95\frac{5}{9}$	$102\frac{1}{2}$	110	$132\frac{1}{2}$
1942	65 and 10 months	$7\frac{1}{2}$%	$75\frac{5}{6}$	$94\frac{4}{9}$	$101\frac{1}{4}$	$108\frac{3}{4}$	$131\frac{1}{4}$
1943–1954	66	8%	75	$93\frac{1}{3}$	100	108	132
1955	66 and 2 months	8%	$74\frac{1}{6}$	$92\frac{2}{9}$	$98\frac{8}{9}$	$106\frac{2}{3}$	$130\frac{2}{3}$
1956	66 and 4 months	8%	$73\frac{1}{3}$	$91\frac{1}{9}$	$97\frac{7}{9}$	$105\frac{1}{3}$	$129\frac{1}{3}$
1957	66 and 6 months	8%	$72\frac{1}{2}$	90	$96\frac{2}{3}$	104	128
1958	66 and 8 months	8%	$71\frac{2}{3}$	$88\frac{8}{9}$	$95\frac{5}{9}$	$102\frac{2}{3}$	$126\frac{2}{3}$
1959	66 and 10 months	8%	$70\frac{5}{6}$	$87\frac{7}{9}$	$94\frac{4}{9}$	$101\frac{1}{3}$	$125\frac{1}{3}$
1960 and later	67	8%	70	$86\frac{2}{3}$	$93\frac{1}{3}$	100	124

Source: Social Security Administration, Office of the Chief Actuary

For example: Joe was born in 1963. His normal retirement age, as recognized by the Social Security Administration, is sixty-seven years old. If Joe actually does retire at sixty-seven, he receives the full 100 percent of his benefit (presently the average benefit is $768 a month for retired workers, so we will assume that Joe, retiring at age sixty-seven, will receive $768 a month). If Joe were to retire at sixty-two, he would receive only 70 percent of his benefit, or $538 a month. If Joe were to wait until age seventy to retire, he would receive 124 percent of his benefit, or $952 a month. For each year that Joe waits to retire, he will get an extra 8 percent of his full benefit.

likely to get the most money back with that option. If you are single and your health is not good, then a ten-year certain plan makes sense. That's because even if you die five years after retirement, your designated beneficiary will receive payments for another five years.

I never recommend the single life only plan because its payments stop when you die. You could have $200,000 in your 401(k) plan that you've converted to an annuity, and die after receiving only $15,000 in benefits—and your heirs won't get a penny of what is left.

Other options include taking your money out in a lump sum and paying taxes on it, or rolling it into an IRA and betting on you own investment skills or that of a professional investment advisor, and then withdrawing funds from it over time. With all these options, you can see why I recommend a financial planner who will prepare a long-term cash flow based on each one of these scenarios (all of which have different tax consequences) so you know which one to pick. The choices you make about how you handle the money in your company plans are irrevocable.

You may also be eligible for veterans', state and/or federal employee benefits. See the Appendix for contact information of various offices.

ASSETS

■ Mastering Your Assets ■

At the beginning of this book, you had the opportunity to fill out a net worth chart that gave you an idea of where you stand today. When you get to retirement, this gets especially confusing because of the differing ages at which you can withdraw your money from your retirement accounts.

Two of the most frequent questions I'm asked by retirees and soon-to-be retirees are, "Which assets do I use up first—the ones in my retirement plans or the ones I have on my own?" and "When can I take the money out without penalty?"

The first answer is easy: Use up your nonretirement assets first. That's because when you sell them, you will pay a lower tax rate on any profits you have made from the sale. The reason: You paid for your nonretirement assets—such as mutual funds or a vacation home—with after-tax dollars, and you may have paid taxes on dividends and capital gains along the way. In contrast, most—and for most people, all—of the money you put in retirement plans was pretax, which means you got to deduct that amount from your income in the year you made the contribution to a retirement plan. Also, all of the dividends and capital gains were sheltered from taxes each year as your retirement accounts grew. What does that mean? In most cases, every dollar you take out of a retirement plan will be taxed as earned income. Ouch!

Let's look at tax-deferred plans by category, in terms of when you can take distributions and what the tax consequences are. You can start taking withdrawals without penalty from all company retirement plans at age 55, provided you are no longer an employee of the company (that is, if you quit or were fired). Starting at age 59½, there are no penalties on any withdrawals from any of your other retirement accounts. When I say penalty, I mean a 10 percent penalty on any money you withdraw in any year. So if you take out $50,000, your penalty is $5,000—and you must pay income taxes on the money as well.

There is a blanket rule for all retirement plans except the Roth IRA— you have to start taking minimum distributions from them by age 70½. "Minimum distributions" are based on your age and the beneficiaries of your plans.

Once you reach age 70½, you can no longer contribute to a regular IRA. But you can put up to $2,000 in a Roth IRA, and you never have to take the money out. If you are looking for a "safe harbor" for money you plan to leave to your heirs, this is a great way to build up an estate because your contributions stay tax-sheltered and can remain untouched for as long as you live.

SELLING YOUR HOUSE

Whenever I talk about retirement with my clients, I make sure that the issue of selling their houses comes up. Some couples are in denial and don't want to think about it; others can't wait to sell and move to condominiums where someone else is responsible for the yard work. In fact, it is not unusual for each spouse to have a different viewpoint.

Caroline and Peter debated this issue for months before they walked through my door; in fact, it was the marital tension about this issue that brought them to me. They were smart because they were fifty-six and fifty-five and planning ahead, before they might find themselves in a situation where their only remaining asset was home equity.

Selling your house is a huge emotional and financial decision, and you need to think it through before you decide to go ahead. Ask yourself the following questions:

1. Do I have enough assets and income for the rest of my life without having to tap into my home equity?
2. Do I want to stay in my home, and if so for how long—a few years, as long as I can be independent, forever?
3. Would a smaller house make more sense from a maintenance and financial standpoint?
4. If my plan is to sell and move to be nearer to my children (and probably grandchildren), can I develop an independent social network there so that my days are fulfilling and I do not become an emotional burden to my family?
5. Does a retirement community sound appealing?
6. Does owning a mobile home with the ability to travel wherever I like make sense for my retirement dreams?
7. What will happen to the house if I need to go to a nursing home?

The first thing to do is to complete the worksheets in this chapter to see if you will indeed have enough income and assets to support you through retirement. Once you assess your financial situation, you will be better able to decide whether to sell. If you are contemplating selling, don't do so until you have figured out where you are going to move. A retirement community? A smaller home or apartment? A mobile home?

If you do plan to sell your home, go back to Chapter 3, "Settling Down," and read the advice included there on selling a house. But be wary! Many real estate agents target retirees, especially new widows and widowers. Make sure that *you* want to sell your home, and that you are not being pressured by a real estate agent or your children to do so.

☞ **Wake-up Call**: Let your homeowners' insurance company know when you retire; some companies give discounts to retirees or long-term policyholders.

REVERSE MORTGAGES

If you completed the income and expense worksheets and realized that much of your money is tied up in home equity but you don't want to sell, you are in luck. There is a relatively new type of program that can allow you to remain in your home and have a monthly income as well. It is called a *reverse mortgage*.

The big problem with home equity is that it doesn't pay the bills. But if you consider yourself house poor, strapped for cash because the bulk of your money is tied up in your home, a reverse mortgage might be right for you.

A *reverse mortgage* (also called a "home equity conversion plan") is almost the mirror image of a mortgage. With a regular mortgage, the homeowner starts out with the debt and makes monthly payments of both interest and principal until the mortgage is paid off. In this case, the homeowner ends up with all the equity in the form of the house.

With a reverse mortgage, the opposite is true. The homeowner is paid a monthly income (or can draw from a home equity line of credit), but each payment reduces the homeowner's equity until the house is actually owned by the lender. The good news is that even if you use up all the equity, you can continue to live there and own the home until you die. Your only obligation is to pay real estate taxes, insurance premiums, and regular maintenance.

If the owner(s) dies before the lender becomes the outright owner, the house is sold at the owner's death to repay the loan. It also could be sold prior to that if the owner moves into a relative's house or a nursing home.

If you have enough income to qualify for a home equity loan, you might consider that instead of a reverse mortgage. The advantage is that you can pay that back over time and therefore will not lose your house. But the beauty of a reverse mortgage is that you don't have to have substantial income to qualify, and if you live in the house long enough, you can get monthly payments long after the equity in your house has been used up. Even better, the lenders cannot go after your estate for their shortfall to cover their losses. In essence, a reverse mortgage is an annuity because it guarantees you a certain income for the rest of your life.

■ The Pros and Cons ■

Just like traditional mortgages, reverse mortgages have up-front costs. They tend to run about the same as those of a traditional mortgage, and include things like origination fees and insurance premiums. A reverse mortgage is probably not worth the up-front costs if you plan to move within the next few years. Similarly, if you want to keep your house in the family to pass down to your children, this is not a good option for you.

Reverse mortgages may be the solution for someone who wants to remain in familiar surroundings with memories of loved ones, or even for caregivers who want to care for their elderly relatives at home instead of moving the retiree into a nursing home. You may lose your home eventually, but for the time you are alive, you can hold onto what may be your most prized possession—your home.

■ Signing Up ■

The amount of money that you can obtain through a reverse mortgage depends upon the program you use—Federal Housing Administration-insured or Federal National Mortgage Association (Fannie Mae) reverse mortgages. The Federal Housing Administration's program, the Home Equity Conversion Mortgage (HECM), and Fannie Mae's program, Home Keeper, are the two largest and most widely used reverse mortgage programs.

The amount of monthly income will depend on the age of the home owner, the value of the home and the prevailing interest rate at the time the loan is closed. If you are sixty-eight years old, single, and live in a $250,000 house, you could receive a monthly payment of between $300 and $800, depending on your interest rate. A couple will get a lower monthly income than a single home owner because one is likely to outlive the other by several years. Both the FHA and Fannie Mae require borrowers to attend informational sessions explaining the program before the deal is completed.

Some states have publicly funded programs for low-income residents, but most reverse mortgages are private. If you go through a private reverse mortgage program, check into the financial stability of the institution involved by calling your state banking department and asking about its financial strength rating.

LIFE ON THE ROAD

When Gloria and Bill told me they planned to sell their $200,000 house and buy a recreational vehicle (RV) when Bill retired in six months, I thought they were nuts. Somehow my outdated prejudices about RVs got in the way of the reality of just how smart their decision was. I used to think owning an RV was, well, tacky! Then I did a little research and realized that they were making a terrific decision.

Purchasing an RV is a way to see America in the comfort of your own home. In fact 25 percent of full-time RV owners travel more than

15,000 miles a year. They can be as expensive or cheap as you like—25 percent cost more than $50,000 and 21 percent cost less than $20,000. There really is an option for everyone. If you want to downsize your lifestyle, have sold your house and need to find another place to live, want the freedom to travel and see family, like the idea of experiencing multiple communities (or just traveling on your own), a recreational vehicle may be for you. It is also one of the least expensive housing options you have, so if your income and assets come up short, an RV may be just the answer.

But before you drive off into the sunset, make sure you really like to drive, that you enjoy waking up in a different place every few days or weeks, and that you can survive in such a cramped setting. Other aspects to consider: Not only will you be away from your normal social network, but you will also be unable to see your regular physician(s) for treatment.

CHOOSING A RETIREMENT COMMUNITY

Before I tell you the true story of our three-month-long search for a retirement community for a client, let me warn you in advance that you should give yourself six months to a year to look around before you make a final decision. Unfortunately in my client's case, we did not have that luxury.

Ruth was a high-powered executive who lived in the Far East and was finally coming home to retire. She asked us to investigate retirement communities for her, and although we had never done so before, we thought it would be an easy, fast process. We could not have been more wrong. The problem is that the term "retirement community" can mean anything from apartment buildings that are rented exclusively to retirees to life-care communities to nursing homes.

The term "community" was very important in Ruth's decision because she is extremely well-educated and has traveled the world for years for business. This meant that she wanted to be around people like her who are eager to attend the symphony and plays, go on educational trips, and provide stimulating conversation. A pleasant climate was also very important to her, as was being near the water.

The one drawback was that Ruth did not have enough money to gain automatic entrance into any retirement community she chose. That limited her options a bit, but we were determined to find the right place for her. Together we considered twenty possibilities all over the U.S. in a two-month period. Ironically, her final choice was a retirement community recommended by friends who lived in a nearby community in California. She is now moved in, firmly ensconced in the community, and extremely happy.

☞ **Wake-up Call**: The best retirement communities often have a waiting list of two years or more, so it's smart to shop around and get your name on a list well in advance of your projected move-in date.

Remember when you went to camp? The best retirement communities can be just as fun—offering you a wide variety of interesting activities with people of similar ages in a safe environment.

But first impressions can be deceiving. Beautiful landscaping and a finely appointed dining room are not worth a three-week wait to have your leaky shower repaired. And these centers can be very expensive. Lifetime care communities can charge you more than $100,000 just to guarantee your lifetime residence there, plus another $20,000 in annual fees.

So if you're shopping around for a retirement community, you need to know:

- the types of communities available;
- the services you want and may need, both now and in the future;
- how to find the community that is the best fit for you; and
- how to look behind the public face of a retirement community to judge its quality and value.

■ Life-Care Communities: Care for the Rest of Your Life ■

If you're looking for a place to settle down for the rest of your life and you're concerned about paying hefty medical expenses, a life-care retirement community may be for you. This program guarantees that regardless of your future financial situation, you will be allowed to remain a resident. It also guarantees health-care coverage for life.

These communities fund the care by adding a surcharge to your fees and by establishing a benevolent fund to pay for residents who can no longer make their monthly payments. Keep in mind, however, that life-care retirement communities also look very carefully at the health and the financial status of the applicants before accepting them.

■ Continuing Care ■

Continuing-care retirement communities provide a combination of residential living and health services that are either on-site or off-site as part of a contract. These are not just apartment complexes requiring their tenants to be a certain age, or nursing homes (although each of these may be components of the community). They are neighborhood-like communities with an emphasis on group and individual activities (which is why most retirement communities require that at least one daily meal be eaten in the common dining room). You start in your own apartment and then, if you need more care, you move to the nursing facility. Applicants are screened for physical and mental health, financial stability, and ability to fit in with other residents. In a way, it's like applying for college, but your stay will probably be a lot longer (some residents are as young as sixty-five).

■ Fees ■

The cost of continuing-care facilities can be considerable. Usually there is an entry fee, paid up-front, and a monthly fee that might not include all of your health care. The amount of the entry fee may depend on the size and type of dwelling you choose, your age, and your health. Entry fees can be hefty, ranging from $30,000 to as much as $500,000 or more, depending on geographic location, the size of the living quarters, quality of services, and the extent of medical services included. An average amount is about $75,000.

Monthly fees also vary widely from facility to facility. Find out if the fee changes (and by how much) over the course of your stay or if you need increased care. Medical care isn't always included in the fee structures and some communities require you to purchase long-term care insurance. The good news is that about 15 percent of your entry fee and 25 to 35 percent of your monthly fees are tax deductible as medical expenses.

■ Finding the Right Fit ■

Selecting the retirement community is a daunting task because each one offers different services and accommodations for different fees, and the contracts are full of legalese.

When you visit:

- stay overnight (most communities require an overnight visit, anyway)
- spend time on your own checking out the facilities and chatting with residents you meet—not just your official hosts, dinner companions, and panel of interviewers
- wander through the skilled-nursing facility and see how the residents there are treated and whether you would want to spend the last part of your life there. Make sure the nursing facility residents are fully integrated into the life of the community

In addition, you should carefully examine the contract agreement, specifically looking for the following issues:

- descriptions of the living quarters—size and type, maintenance and housekeeping responsibilities, and furnishings—and whether utilities are included
- the type of medical care provided, whether it offers on-site doctor and hospital services, nursing care, and various therapies
- recreational and educational activities
- menus and the accommodation of special diets. How many meals are served each day? Are the meals part of the monthly fee, or will you be charged separately?
- is personal assistance, such as help bathing and dressing, provided if necessary?

■ Accreditation ■

If possible, you should select a continuing-care retirement community that has been accredited by the Continuing Care Accreditation Commission of the American Association of Homes for the Aging. You might also check out *New Choices*, a magazine designed for older people that ranks various types of retirement communities on a regular basis. Although it is hard to find at newsstands, you can generally find copies at your local library, or see the Appendix for contact information.

No matter which continuing-care retirement community you choose, you are committing a huge investment of your money and time. There is no substitute for good research and the Continuing Care Accreditation seal of approval.

This is perhaps the most important decision you will make for the rest of your life. So take your time, research it thoroughly, and don't be swayed by any sales pressure. (The best communities don't have to sell themselves, anyway; they will probably have waiting lists of at least several months). Then you can enjoy the fruits of your labors because you will know you've chosen the best place for you.

CHOOSING A NURSING HOME

In all of my years as a financial planner no one has ever walked in my door and said, "I would really like to spend the last years of my life in a nursing home." Actually, the opposite is true. When I start talking with clients about financial seasons, and specifically retirement, just the term "nursing home" can engender incredible fear and denial. One client of mine, Harriet, feared she would end up in a nursing home because she was single and had no one to take care of her. Having experienced her mother's care in a poorly run home, the thought of winding up there herself so terrified her that she refused to discuss the possibility at all.

No one wants to spend the last season of his life in a nursing home, but it may be a necessity. According to the U.S. Department of Health and Human Services, 43 percent of Americans currently age sixty-five or older will enter a nursing home—and if you are a woman, your chances are 50 percent greater than if you are a man. Twenty-five percent will stay more than a year, and 10 percent will stay more than five years. If you (or your parents) end up needing a nursing home, you want to be sure you find one that meets your particular requirements. So how do you choose?

Let's hope the old days of nursing home abuse and neglect are on the way out. The federal government has taken an active role in monitoring nursing homes and sanctioning those that do not treat their patients well. Still, it is important to shop around long before you think you might actually need one, because, just like retirement homes, nursing homes often have a waiting list of two or more years.

Several organizations can help you navigate the maze of choosing a nursing home. Medicare, for one, offers a twenty-five point checklist with a ranking of one to ten that covers basic information, quality of life, quality of care, safety, and other concerns. It also gives you an accompanying guide that tells you how to visit a home and evaluate each of the categories.

The American Association of Homes and Services for the Aging, a nonprofit organization, publishes a guide to finding the right nursing home on its website (*www.aahsa.org*). I have included it here because it gives you a more general overview of how to prepare for a nursing home visit.

■ What Does Every Good Nursing Home Have? ■

[American Association of Homes and Services for the Aging]
Look for the following when choosing a nursing home:

1. A current operating license from the state.
2. An administrator who has an up-to-date state license.
3. Certification of Medicare and Medicaid if these programs are important to you now or in the future.
4. A location that suits the resident and makes regular visits by family and friends possible.
5. Handrails in the hallways, grab bars in bathrooms, and other features aimed at accident prevention.
6. Clearly marked exits and unobstructed paths to these exits. All nursing homes must comply with state and/or federal fire safety codes.
7. Bedrooms that open onto a corridor and have windows, as required by law.
8. A physician who is available for emergencies.
9. No heavy odors, whether pleasant or offensive. A good home will not use highly scented sprays to mask odors.
10. Hallways wide enough to permit two wheelchairs to pass with ease and wheelchair ramps for easy access into and out of the home.
11. Kitchens that separate food preparation, garbage, and dishwashing areas and keep perishable foods refrigerated.
12. Toilet facilities designed to accommodate wheelchair residents.
13. An attractive resident dining room with tables convenient for wheelchairs and food that looks appetizing. Notice, too, whether residents who need help are receiving it.
14. Residents who look clean and are dressed appropriately for a full day of activity and social interaction. A policy that encourages residents to go outside.

15. Commitment to a philosophy of care in which physical and chemical restraints are used minimally or not at all.
16. An activity room or designated space for residents who are able to be involved in reading, crafts, and social activities.
17. A friendly and available staff who appear pleasant, caring, and accommodating to residents and visitors.
18. A volunteer program.
19. An active resident council or some type of resident participating program that enables residents to recommend changes within the home.
20. A residents' bill of rights or a stated policy that identifies and respects residents' individual rights.

■ Where Can You Get Additional Information? ■

Contact the American Association of Homes and Services for the Aging (AAHSA) to find out if your state has an AAHSA affiliate. AAHSA affiliated state associations operate in thirty-nine states across the country.

Order a copy of AAHSA's *Directory of Members*. This book gives you instant access to a nationwide network of some 5,000 not-for-profit nursing homes, continuing-care retirement communities, assisted-living, and senior housing facilities. You'll find a complete contact information and a list of each facility's services. See the Appendix for AAHSA's contact information.

■ Medicaid ■

Medicaid is designed for people who receive federally assisted income payments. For a couple of years, ending in 1998, it was a felony to "spend down" (give away) your assets so that you could qualify for Medicaid and have your long-term care needs paid for that way. Today, laws have changed to legalize this, but there is still a multiyear waiting period between the time you get rid of your assets ("go broke") and the time at which you can qualify for Medicaid. In addition, many financial advisors and individuals have ethical concerns about employing this strategy, so make sure you're comfortable with this technique before you decide that it's worth it.

HEALTH INSURANCE

■ Medicare and Medigap ■

Every once in a while I get a call from a panicked friend whose parent is having trouble getting health insurance. Usually, the problem is that he or she neglected to sign up for the medical insurance programs for seniors during the open enrollment period, when you can sign up regardless of health. Before you panic, read the information below and you will figure out how you can get yourself (or your parent) in both programs even if you missed the open enrollment period, which is usually within six months after you turn sixty-five, or one particular month a year thereafter.

Be assured that if you are confused, you are not alone. Even experienced financial planners often refer their clients to experts who specialize in elder-care law, such as attorneys, accountants, social workers, and other financial planners. It is a specialty unto itself.

Senior health insurance is changing at warp speed. The reason is clear: Medicare, Medicaid, and Social Security now account for 40 percent of all federal spending.

Before Medicare was established with the Social Security Act of 1966, seniors had few options for medical insurance unless their employers continued coverage as part of their retirement benefits. Now, one of the great things about turning sixty-five is that you are eligible for government-sponsored medical insurance. But don't harbor the misconception that Medicare will cover all of your medical expenses. Nothing can be further from the truth.

Medicare is designed to cover relatively short-term catastrophic medical care. It does not provide coverage for long-term custodial care, such as basic nursing-home care, so it is not a substitute for long-term care insurance.

Medicare offers four options, each with its own deductible, coinsurance, time limits, and premiums. *To be properly covered, you'll need Medicare A and B and either C or Medigap, which is designed to plug the holes in Medicare coverage—and you'll still need long-term insurance.* The annual costs of long-term care can amount to several thousand dollars, depending on age, health, benefit amount, benefits paid, etc. But that's better than having all of your retirement savings eaten up by costly medical bills.

Here is a summary of each program:

Medicare Part A (Hospital Insurance)

This program covers inpatient hospital care, skilled-nursing facilities, home-health care, and hospice care (under certain circumstances). You are automatically entitled to coverage if you are sixty-five or older and are entitled to Social Security or disability benefits.

There is no premium; it is free. The catch is that there is a deductible of $764 for each "benefit period" (which I'll explain in a minute), plus you have to pay co-insurance charges of $191 a day for the second and third month in the hospital. After that your coverage runs out and you must pay all costs yourself. A benefit period starts after you have been out of the hospital for sixty days. It is not uncommon for doctors and family members to play hospital roulette by taking patients out of the hospital and caring for them at home for sixty days so that they can qualify for a new benefit period.

If you must stay in a skilled-nursing facility, you must pay $95.50 a day for the 21st through the 100th day of care. After that, coverage runs out entirely.

Medicare Part B (Supplemental Medical Insurance)

This program offers optional insurance that covers doctors' fees and services in and out of the hospital and other medical expenses. In 1998, the cost was $43.80 a month with a $100 annual deductible.

Unfortunately, Medicare Part B does not plug the holes in Medicare Part A. It does not cover long-term nursing care or other expenses, which is why everyone needs additional medical and long-term care insurance.

Special managed-care programs have been created that allow you to pay a small extra premium and co-payment per visit if you buy Medicare Part B. If you go to doctors or hospitals outside these programs, however, which are typically offered by health maintenance organizations (HMOs) and preferred provider organizations (PPOs), your bills will be much higher.

Medicare Part C (Medicare + Choice)

This new program was created by the Balanced Budget Act of 1997. It requires you to use specific doctors, hospitals, and services in order to have your expenses covered. The good news is that it generally pays the deductibles and co-insurance charges that Medicare Parts A and B fail to cover and is designed to be used as a less expensive alternative to Medigap.

The cost is usually an additional premium that varies by age and state. To be eligible, you must have both Medicare Parts A and B.

Medigap

This private program offered by insurance companies or managed-care organizations was designed to plug the holes in Medicare coverage. Typically it covers Medicare deductibles and co-insurance payments, in addition to a variety of other benefits. With Medigap, patients can choose their own health-care providers. One exception: Medicare Select (less expensive than Medigap) restricts you to your health organization's services if you want full coverage.

When these policies were first sold, the offering organizations often took advantage of their subscribers. Some seniors were sold more than one policy (now prohibited by law), and it was virtually impossible to judge which policies covered what medical costs. Now both state and federal rules regulate Medigap policies. There are ten basic types of Medigap plans (see chart below), which are standard in all states.

Standardization means that it's easy to compare Medigap plans, and make a purchase based on price and the quality of the insurance company. Be sure to buy from a company that has been selling Medigap insurance for at least five years. If you purchase your plan from a managed-care program, make sure that it has an excellent reputation in the community.

Almost no one can afford to get by with just Medicare Parts A and B because the co-insurance and deductibles for a long-term hospital or nursing home stay are so expensive. Do your research on the Medicare + Choice options available in your community, and get prices on the Medigap insurance policies that are sold in your state. You can't make an informed decision without doing that research. Once you purchase additional coverage, you will at least experience the relief of knowing that the emotional stress of a long-term illness will not be compounded by financial worries.

☞ **Wake-up Call**: Make sure to buy the additional insurance within six months of signing up for Medicare Part B. After that, any medical conditions you may have might preclude you from being able to get a policy.

Ten Standard Medigap Plans

Benefit	A	B	C	D	E	F	G	H
Part A hospital coinsurance (days 61–90)	X	X	X	X	X	X	X	X
Part A hospital lifetime reserve (days 91–150)	X	X	X	X	X	X	X	X
100% for 365 lifetime hospitalization days	X	X	X	X	X	X	X	X
Parts A and B Blood	X	X	X	X	X	X	X	X
Part B 20% co-insurance	X	X	X	X	X	X	X	X
Part A inpatient hospital deductible		X	X	X	X	X	X	X
Part A skilled nursing facility care co-insurance (days 21–100)			X	X	X	X	X	X
Foreign travel emergency			X	X	X	X	X	X
At-home recovery				X			X	
Part B deductible			X			X		
Part B excess charges						100%	80%	
Preventive medical care					X			
Prescription drugs								Basic

■ Long-term Care Insurance ■

In addition to all this, you'll still need long-term care insurance to cover nursing-home or in-home care that lasts longer than several months. The premiums for that may seem high, but when you look at the deductibles and co-insurance they cover, it is certainly worth the price.

Back when long-term care insurance was first being developed and marketed in the 1980s, I had a client who insisted on buying a policy, even though he and his wife's combined net worth was over $5 million. It turns out that both his and his wife's parents had experienced long-term illnesses in their later years, and all of the money they hoped to leave to their children was eaten up in medical expenses. Daniel and Anne-Monique had worked very hard to build up their net worth and had an extremely sophisticated estate plan designed to avoid taxes so their children would get the largest possible inheritance. They did not want to see their money spent on nursing homes or home-health aides. Unlike many people, they were well aware that Medicare did not cover 365 days of nursing home care a year, and they certainly would not qualify for Medicaid.

I found the best policy we could for them—but when I think about it now, it was a fairly primitive one. Long-term care insurance has come a long way in the last dozen years since I worked with Daniel and Anne-Monique. Back then, the policy owner had to be hospitalized before any nursing-home care benefits would kick in. Home-health care was not covered at all. Mental disorders were usually not covered unless there was organic evidence (impossible for patients with Alzheimer's disease, which at that time could not be definitively diagnosed without an autopsy of the brain after the patient had died).

Now all of the above and more is usually covered, which certainly is a good thing as America's population ages. Forty-two percent of Americans sixty-five and older will enter a nursing home during their lifetime, and the current average annual cost of a one-year nursing-home stay is $46,000. Even home-health care, the least expensive alternative for someone who needs regular medical attention, costs an average of over $1,000 a month.

The best time to get long-term insurance is when you are in your forties—the earlier the better. When you are younger, the premiums are less, and after a certain period of time, you may be able to keep the policy in force without paying premiums.

☞ **Wake-up Call**: In 1996, the Health Insurance and Portability Act gave long-term care tax-favored status by making the premiums tax-deductible and the benefits tax-free as long as a policy met certain conditions. That is good news indeed, but by singling out long-term care insurance for such beneficial treatment the federal government is sending us a message that Americans had better take care of their own long-term care needs, because the federal government won't.

The premiums for this type of insurance are not cheap, but unless you have investable assets of $2 million or more you probably need it, especially if you want to preserve some assets for your children. In fact, in many families both the parents and the children contribute toward long-term health care premiums. After all, long-term care insurance will relieve your children of a substantial financial burden in the future, so you should not be shy about asking for their help with paying the premiums now—as long as it won't cut into their ability to save for their own retirement. If you are shopping for long-term care insurance for your parents, make sure they understand that you are not pressuring them to buy the coverage just so you can stick them in a nursing home.

There are several ways to keep premiums down. One is to enroll in group insurance, which is almost always cheaper than private coverage. Many employers are now offering long-term care insurance as an optional employee benefit: In a recent survey, 8 percent of employers offered group long-term care insurance, which was up 2 percent from 1990. Usually the employee, the employee's spouse, and the employee's parents are eligible to purchase coverage. Other ways to trim premiums include choosing a longer waiting period, lower benefits, or coverage that ends after perhaps five years instead of offering lifetime protection. As with life insurance, however, the amount of the premiums is not the most important consideration when purchasing long-term care insurance—in fact, it is one of the *least* important considerations.

What matters most are the policy benefit amounts and the specific terms of the contract. These policies are complicated, but asking the following fifteen questions will help you select the one that is right for your circumstances:

1. Is this policy "qualified" under the Health Insurance and Portability Act of 1996?
Purchase a policy that is "qualified" because only those policies allow you to take a tax deduction for the premiums and pay out tax-free benefits.

2. Is this policy guaranteed for life—it is "noncancelable"?
Make sure that the insurance company cannot cancel your policy if it finds out that you are in poor health. Note that virtually no companies issue policies with guaranteed premiums because no one can predict future health care costs.

3. What is the waiting period, and does it only have to be met once?
The waiting period should be no longer than six months, and you should only have to meet that requirement once during your lifetime. That means that if you use the benefits, then get well again, then need long-term care again, you don't have to wait another six months for additional benefits.

4. Does it cover home-health care, as well as skilled-, intermediate-, and custodial nursing-home care?
These provisions give you an option to stay at home and receive care, as well as to receive all kinds of care in a nursing home. That way, you can use your benefits even if your condition changes.

5. Do I have to be hospitalized before benefits begin?
Purchase a policy in which hospitalization is not required. You may simply start needing home-health care, and your private insurance plan or Medicare will not pay for an unnecessary hospital stay, so you would have to pay these costs out of pocket.

6. What are the conditions that "trigger" benefit payments—what do I need before benefits begin?
The conditions should consist of cognitive impairment of any kind; should explicitly include a diagnosis of Alzheimer's disease; and should include the inability to perform two out of five or six activities of daily living—usually eating, bathing, dressing, using the toilet, "transferring" (moving unassisted from a bed to a chair for example), and continence.

7. What are daily reimbursements for home-health care and nursing-home care?
Know the cost of these services in your area so that you choose a policy that adequately covers those costs. Your insurance agent or a state elder-care agency should be able to give you this information.

8. Is there an inflation clause, so that my daily benefits increase over time?
The cost of home-health and nursing-home care has skyrocketed in the last few years, so make sure that your policy benefits keep up with those costs. Again, your agent or state elder-care agency can help. You may not be able to afford the highest annual increase available, but take the most you can afford.

9. How long will benefits be paid?
If possible, you should purchase a policy with the longest benefit payment. Usually this is about six years for home-health care and lifetime for nursing-home care. When you consider that 10 percent of Americans are expected to spend five years or more in a nursing home, having lifetime coverage makes sense.

10. How long is the preexisting clause in effect?
This clause excludes preexisting conditions (medical conditions or ailments you already have prior to purchasing the policy, which are usually listed on your application). Your policy should have no more then a six-month preexisting-conditions clause; after that, all medical ailments should be covered.

11. Is there specific guaranteed protection against policy lapse and reinstatement?
This protects you if you are having physical or mental difficulties and forget to pay the premium; you can have the policy reinstated even if your premium is late.

What specific expenses are covered under the policy?
It is very important that you know which medical and ancillary expenses will be covered, because you'll want to choose a policy that reimburses you for expenses rather than one that pays you a flat daily rate (also known as an indemnity policy). The following expenses should be explicitly listed in your policy contract as covered: respite care (temporary nursing home stays or extra home-health care to give your primary caretaker a "break"), home modification, hospice care, caregiver training, professional health-care services, therapeutic devices, personal-care adviser, and bed registration fees if you are moving to a nursing home.

13. How long has the company been selling long-term care insurance?
Choose a company that has a good track record in the sales and administration of long-term care insurance. This means that the company has a history of dealing with these kinds of claims and has a good idea of its expected payments over time on the policy you buy. Make sure you purchase insurance from a company that has been selling long-term care insurance for at least five years.

14. What are the company's financial strength ratings from the major insurance ratings services (A. M. Best, Standard & Poor's, Moody's, and Duff & Phelps)?
You want to choose a company with solid financial strength so that if expenses are substantially greater than expected, the company can handle them with ease. Not all companies have ratings from all of the services, but you should choose from a company that has at least two financial strength ratings. We talk about insurance company financial ratings in "Building Up" (Chapter 4), and it is important to be well-informed.

15. May I have a sample copy of the exact contract of the policy I would be purchasing from your company?
Here is where you will probably get the answers to most of the questions listed above. Do not depend on what an insurance agent tells you verbally; it's what's in the contract that counts. These policies are very complicated and your agent may not know all the answers to your questions, or may give you incorrect ones out of lack of knowledge about the specific policy you are considering. It is worth spending the money to have an attorney, financial planner, or fee-only life insurance adviser review the contract for you (make sure they have a strong understanding of long-term care policies).

Even if you are uninsurable for life insurance, you may very well be able to purchase long-term care insurance. Don't let life insurance uninsurability keep you from checking out long-term care insurance. Only deal with an agent who has several years of experience with long-term care contracts, because these policies are constantly evolving at a very rapid rate.

If you are considering purchasing a long-term care contract through work, your employee benefits manager should be able to help you or refer you to the company that is selling the group insurance. Just as with other insurance policies (or any financial products), *never* buy a long-term care policy over the telephone or through direct mail. These policies usually are very expensive and have very poor coverage. If you have adult children, they can help you review the various contracts and sales proposals you receive. If your parents are the ones purchasing the insurance, be sure to offer (actually insist, but gently) that you be involved in the decision-making process. There are even elder-care consultants now who can review policies, help you get the home-health care you need, and help you choose the appropriate nursing home.

PASSING IT ON: ESTATE PLANNING

■ Good Planning Can Be Your Financial Legacy ■

Recently I met individually with a number of employees at a television station in the Boston area. It was not surprising to find out that out of about twenty-five employees, ranging in age from twenty-four to early sixties, only two had wills. Many had children and many had built up substantial assets by investing well in the company retirement plan. But when I asked about wills, I got the same answer I usually get from clients: "I have been meaning to do that, but I just have not gotten around to it." Over half of Americans do not have wills, so if you fall in that category, you are hardly alone.

If your estate planning is not up-to-date, you may find it comforting and amusing to know that even some of the best investment experts in the business haven't done their estate-planning homework either. A couple of years ago, I was speaking at a large investment conference, along with a number of Wall Street gurus and very successful mutual fund managers. Of course the main topic of conversation among us was the stock market and how well everyone had done, but as the only financial planner in the group, I asked how many of these speakers had updated their wills and trusts and felt comfortable with their current estate plans. A few volunteered that they had very sophisticated plans, but more than half gave me sheepish looks that revealed the truth—they are just like the rest of us. We love focusing on investing, because it means winning, but no one wants to think about dying.

For many of us, the words "estate planning" have about as much appeal as a root canal. The problem with putting off a root canal is that it leads to additional pain and suffering. With estate planning, avoidance leads to pain and suffering felt by your loved ones. The grief of having lost you is mixed with the anger of untangling a mountain of legal and administrative red tape that has been dumped in their laps. Don't give your family a root canal.

You may think you don't have enough money to worry about estate planning. You're wrong. Proper planning begins the moment you become an adult with your first bank accounts and student loans. The need grows as your assets grow and your family relationships become more complex.

Here's a quick quiz to see if you *shouldn't* worry about estate planning:

1. You don't care who gets your money or how much each person gets.
2. You don't care who gets disinherited, even if it is a spouse, child, or needy parent.
3. You don't care how much of your money gets eaten up in estate taxes (state and federal), administrative costs, court fees, and legal bills.

There are very few people who pass this test.

If you have assets to pass on, the best thing to do is make the process as easy as possible for your loved ones when you die. This is especially true if you have a desire about how a particular asset is to be handled. Otherwise, you run the risk of creating animosity between relatives that can last for the rest of their lives. My thoughts turn to an elderly New England woman whose house on the coast of Maine had been owned by her family for generations. Ever since her grandchildren were small and came to spend part of their summers with her, she had told them that she never wanted them to sell the house—that it needed to stay in the family.

As they grew older, she asked each grandchild individually to promise not to sell if she left the house to them in equal shares, instead of to their parents (her children, who were financially comfortable). When the grandmother died, and the market value of the house was determined to be almost twice what had been thought, two of the five grandchildren immediately wanted to sell their shares to the other three for cash. They were not willing to accept payments over time because they were both strapped for money.

The other three grandchildren, in order to keep the house in the family, bought the shares of the two who wanted to sell, and in order to so do had to use up assets they had earmarked for their own children's education or take second mortgages on their own homes. As you can imagine, the accusations of broken promises "made over a lifetime to our grandmother" and the counter-argument of, "but we never thought the house was worth so much" flew between the two groups. The result was—as it usually is when money disputes are involved—certain beneficiaries (in this case, three of the grandchildren) are no longer speaking to the other two.

Ironically, the grandmother had enough money to leave the house and the rest of her assets in a real estate trust that could have had very specific terms for keeping ownership in the family, along with enough resources to pay for its upkeep. Her mistake was relying on the verbal promises of her grandchildren, which is a natural thing to do. But you can't count on verbal promises when money is involved.

What is estate planning after all? It's an overall strategy that coordinates the disposition of everything you own—house, bank accounts, investment portfolios, life insurance, and retirement plans. You probably have the genesis of an estate plan and don't even know it. If you have a life insurance policy or a retirement account like a 401(k) or an Individual Retirement Account, you probably named your beneficiaries in those documents. The problem is that in doing only a part of the process, you may have disinherited someone who is depending on you— usually one of your children.

When you think of estate planning, you probably think just of a will. You're right to an extent. A proper will is the cornerstone of a good plan. But estate planning is much more than a will. It lays out a road map for coordinating your trusts, joint property, insurance policies, and retirement plans. That's because these assets are outside the jurisdiction of most wills, and these assets can take on lives of their own during "probate," depending on what each document says. Probate is the court process in which a deceased person's estate is administered, whether the person died with a will or not. The process includes the appointing of a representative, notifying creditors, inventorying the estate, and distributing the estate according to the deceased person's will.

Maybe your will specifically said that you "leave everything to my dear daughter Amy," but the beneficiary of your life insurance is still your ex-husband, while your house is jointly owned by your mother, and the retirement plan names a trust to control those monies. Your dear daughter Amy gets nothing. Just think of how Amy will remember you and resent her family members who received the money she should have had. I have rarely seen a situation where a family member who knew he should not have gotten an inheritance "did the right thing" and gave it to its rightful owner—or even shared much of it.

Proper estate planning involves consulting with an estate-planning attorney and includes signing some other key documents, such as a durable power of attorney and a "living will," that coordinate these aspects of your life with all of your other financial holdings. It's easy to see how important proper estate planning is if you want as much of your money as possible to go to the people or organizations you wish to benefit.

■ Why You Need Estate Planning, ■
Even if You Already Have a Plan in Place

Chances are, you may already have drawn up a will or taken some or all of the other steps outlined here. Even so, there are a number of important "life events" that should send you running, not walking, to a competent estate attorney.

If you marry, you will probably want to change your beneficiary on various assets to your new spouse. If you then get divorced, you'll probably want to change the will again, because the original will probably become automatically invalid, and you'll want to name new beneficiaries. You may unintentionally disinherit a child by not including language in your will providing for any "living or future children" or by listing children by name either in your will or in your list of insurance policy or retirement plan beneficiaries—in that case, a new sibling arriving later, after you first drew up the will, would not be named. If your will provides for "naturally born children," you will have disinherited any current or future adopted ones. I recently heard of a case where parents had named each of their seven children by name in their wills. But then they had a "late in life" baby and forgot to change their documents. Both parents died in an automobile crash. So the last child got nothing and the first seven inherited their entire estate.

Some states do not recognize wills drafted and signed in other states. If, for instance, you move from a community property state to a noncommunity-property state, your entire estate planning needs to be rethought. In terms of marriage, "community property" means that one-half of the earnings of each spouse is deemed the property of the other spouse. States that recognize community property are Arizona, California, Idaho, Louisiana, New Mexico, Nevada, Texas, and Washington. In other states, the income is considered the distinct property of each spouse.

If you are fortunate enough to inherit or otherwise receive a sizable sum of money, your current plan (or nonexistent estate plan) may leave your assets prey to every possible dollar of estate and inheritance taxes imaginable. Finally, your parents may have finally broken down and admitted to you that they are going to need your help at retirement. You will no doubt want to make some provision for them, especially if you can't count on your siblings or spouse to provide for them in your absence.

The rule of thumb I give my clients about estate planning is: Make your plan as airtight as possible. Review it yearly and after every major life event.

Before you meet with your attorney to draft documents and discuss your estate plans, imagine every possible scenario. If you are married, imagine each spouse dying first, and regardless of marital status imagine your situations now, five, and ten years from now. If you are not married but have a partner, it is more complicated because your partner does not have the rights that a spouse would have under state law. If you have children, what are their ages? Might you have more either naturally or through adoption? As morbid as it sounds, the key is to "brainstorm" about how your family circumstances would be affected by your death.

■ Minimizing Estate Taxes ■

Do your heirs another favor: Plan your estate for taxes. You may not think you are wealthy enough to owe estate taxes, especially if you heard about the "great new law of 1997" that made estates under $1 million tax free, but think again. Jessica and Thomas came to me for financial planning never imagining that they needed estate tax planning as well. But each had a $500,000 life insurance policy purchased individually through work, and when they totaled up their assets they were astounded to discover their estate values at death would be $1.8 million. They never thought of themselves as wealthy, because of course their life insurance death benefits were only available if one of them died. But the IRS would certainly consider them wealthy.

There was another provision in the 1997 law that had small-business owners jumping up and down for joy. Starting in 1998, small-business owners had an estate tax exemption of $1.3 million. I remember receiving a call soon after the law passed from a jubilant contractor

Estate and Gift Tax Exemption

Year	Exclusion
1998	$625,000
1999	$650,000
2000–2001	$675,000
2002–2003	$700,000
2004	$850,000
2005	$950,000
2006	$1,000,000

saying that his estate tax problems were over. Unfortunately, I had to deliver the bad new that, in addition to other restrictions, his beneficiaries had to operate his business for ten years after his death in order to qualify for the tax exemption. Since none of his children had the least interest in inheriting his business—one was a lawyer, another a social worker, another a banker—this exciting new provision in the law was meaningless for him.

Every U.S. citizen has a credit that prevents federal tax on a portion of his or her estate's assets. The amount used to be $600,000, but a law was passed in 1997 that slowly increases that amount to $1 million over ten years.

That sounds like a lot of money, but if you think of the increase in real estate prices and the stock market, as well as retirement plans at work, there are plenty of people whose estates would get stuck with taxes simply due to inflation. Estate planning is most assuredly not just for the rich anymore. And some states have state taxes as well that start at much lower amounts.

The first step is to figure out how much you are worth at death. If you're like most people, you're probably worth more dead than alive. That is because, in addition to all the assets you own now, your estate value at death includes the death benefit of life insurance policies that you own, death benefits from your retirement plans, and mortgage insurance that pays off the balance of your loan upon death.

If you own property with anyone else, you need to figure out what happens to your share of that property when you die. For example, your will may state that $400,000 is to be given to your children, and the rest to your wife. But if your entire estate is valued at $600,000 and most of it is made up of your $400,000 house that you own jointly with your wife (with right of survivorship), your children will only get $200,000.

If you think your estate reaches a value of around $600,000, you have reached the danger zone when it comes to paying estate taxes. The IRS may value your assets much higher than you do, bringing its value to over $1 million, so it is smart to play it safe. Your estate is federal tax-free as long as its value does not exceed the amounts listed on the "Estate and Gift Tax Exemption" chart, which increase each year and level off at $1 million in 2006. You can give that amount away during your lifetime or at death. After that, the federal tax bite starts at 18 percent and caps off at 55 percent for the very wealthiest estates.

It is a mistake to think that if you are married you don't have to worry until your taxable estate reaches $1.3 million in 1999, for example. Each person's estate is treated separately. The "unlimited marital deduction" allows you to leave everything to your surviving spouse with no federal estate tax due at that time. But if you leave it all to your spouse, then you, in effect, lose your $655,000 exemption in 1999 (or a greater exemption if you die in a later year). Example: Let's say you are married, and your assets are worth $800,000 and your spouse's assets amount to $400,000. You die and leave everything to your spouse, who now has $1.2 million in her name. If she dies a year later, in 2000, her taxable estate will be worth $1.2 million. After her $675,000 exemption, the other $525,000 will be hit with a federal estate tax whammy of $165,050. This means that money that could have gone to your beneficiaries will instead be paid to Uncle Sam.

This marital deduction mistake is avoidable, as long as you leave your assets to someone other than your spouse. To return to the example, if you had left $600,000 in a trust for your children or other beneficiaries, it would have not been taxed—a savings of $155,800. The remaining $200,000 would go to your spouse. Furthermore, the trustees of your trust can give your spouse all the income and as much principal as they deem necessary, because as long as the trust is not in your spouse's name, it will not get taxed as part of her estate. When she dies, her estate will only be worth $500,000, so no taxes will be due.

☞ **Wake-up Call**: You can't escape death, but how about taxes? Every dollar that is paid in taxes is one that could have gone to your heirs. Don't take any chances by waiting to contact a lawyer to put an estate plan in place.

Even if your estate is small, there will be expenses at your death. There are administrative costs, court costs, legal fees, probate expenses, and sometimes state inheritance or estate taxes, even if your estate is worth only $50,000. All these vary, depending on your state of residence.

☞ **Wake-up Call**: Give copies of your life insurance policies to your beneficiaries, or at least tell them where they can find a copy. Don't store them in your safe deposit box; that will cause a delay in filing for death benefits.

All these costs mean that your estate will have to come up with the cash to pay them, and for many nonmillionaires, the bulk of their estates is their homes. If your executor does not have enough cash in your estate to pay taxes, he or she is going to be forced to sell your house, business, or other nonliquid assets in order to raise the money. It doesn't matter if your relatives live there, the real estate market has tanked, or that it would normally take a year or two to find a buyer for your business. All that matters is that those costs are usually due and payable within nine months of your death.

One other thing to consider is gifts that you may have given to anyone, especially your children. Any financial gifts you have given over the years are counted against the bottom line. So if you've given away $100,000 in assets, it counts against your remaining exemption. If you die in 1999 after making the gift, your remaining exemption is $655,000 minus $100,000, or $555,000. It gets especially murky when you have loaned or given money to your children to help them, say, make a down payment on a house. This needs to be documented; otherwise your child may have to pay the state back the entire amount immediately, or your estate may get socked with "unreported gift" taxes. The documentation should say how the child is expected to pay back the money; the usual way this is handled is that whatever he has borrowed is taken out of his share of the estate proceeds that would come to him.

Tips to minimize your estate taxes:

1. If you are married and you have everything in joint tenancy with right of survivorship and your spouse's name as the beneficiary on all of your retirement plans, depending on the value of your estate you may have just lost your chance to save big bucks. Put anything over $600,000 in a trust in another person's name so it won't be subject to taxes at your spouse's death.
2. Annual gifting: In 1998, you can give up to $10,000 to anyone

Your Net Worth at Death?

What You Own

A. Bank Accounts			
Checking	+		
Savings	+		
Money Market Funds	+		
Total Bank Accounts		+	(A)
B. Investments			
Mutual Funds	+		
Stocks	+		
Bonds	+		
Life Insurance (death benefits)	+		
Annuities (death benefits)	+		
Investment Real Estate	+		
Total Investments		+	(B)
C. Retirement Plans (Death Benefits)			
401k or 403b	+		
Company Plan	+		
IRA	+		
Keogh	+		
Total Retirement Plans		+	(C)
D. House (Market Value)	+		
Total House		+	(D)
E. Cars			
Car #1	+		
Car #2	+		
Total Cars		+	(E)
F. Personal Property	+		
Total Personal Property		+	(F)
G. Other Assets			
Loans Receivable	+		
Collectibles	+		
Business Interest	+		
Other	+		
Total Other Assets		+	(G)
H. Total of What You Own (add totals of A–G)		+	(H)

continued on next page

Your Net Worth at Death? (cont.)

What You Owe

I. Mortgage			
First Mortgage	+		
Home Equity Loan	+		
Total Mortgage		+	(I)
J. Credit Cards			
VISA	+		
MasterCard	+		
Other	+		
Other	+		
Total Credit Cards		+	(J)
K. Car Loans			
Car Loan #1	+		
Car Loan #2	+		
Total Car Loans		+	(K)
L. Other Debts			
Education	+		
Life Insurance (cash value)	+		
Other	+		
Other	+		
Other	+		
Total Other Debts		+	(L)
M. Total of What You Owe (add totals I–L)		**+**	**(M)**

Your Net Worth at Death

Total of what you own (H) minus Total of what you owe (M)	–
Your net worth at death	

you'd like without paying taxes on it and it doesn't count toward using up your unified credit amount. This is a great technique for slowly passing on your holding to heirs. This is also useful if you have a rapidly appreciating asset such as land about to be developed since all the appreciation will occur outside of your estate in the hands of your recipient. After 1998, the $10,000 will be indexed with inflation. Caution: If you name yourself as custodian for a minor in the account, it's included in your estate—a real concern if you are a grandparent giving money to a grandchild.

3. For the wealthy, those of you who have already ensured the finances of your children, you can create a generation-skipping trust. This trust bypasses your children and goes directly to your grandchildren. In 1998, the tax-free amount you can use is $1 million (in the years to follow that amount will increase with inflation).

4. For the charitably minded: Set up a durable trust. You put assets in it, naming your favorite charity as the ultimate beneficiary. You can take the tax deduction now while continuing to receive income from it for as long as you're alive. At your death, the charity gets the assets.

But before you give away any of your assets, make sure that a competent financial adviser prepares cash-flow scenarios for you showing how your finances will be affected without that money. The assumptions should be very conservative: Assume that you will live five years past the year in which you are actuarially expected to die, and assume that you'll have significant medical problems requiring nursing or home care for the last few years of your life. With increases in health-care costs as well as in longevity, you need to protect yourself first.

Never give away assets based on the promise of the recipient (usually one of your children) to "take care of you, no matter what." Too many trusting parents have died with empty wallets and broken hearts because their well-meaning children did not come through for them as promised.

Finally, remember that the worst estate planning is no planning at all. You've been given an opportunity for tax relief. So use it.

LIVING TRUSTS

A trust is a legally recognized arrangement where one or more persons (trustees) take title to property to hold it for the benefit of another person (beneficiary). Living trusts, also called loving trusts and revocable trusts, are specifically designed to avoid the probate process. By doing so, you will save estate administration fees, maintain your privacy, and speed up the distribution of your assets. Living trusts are too complicated to handle without a professional's advice.

Living trusts certainly have lots of advantages, but they're unnecessary for a great many people. At its most basic, a living trust is a trust you set up during your lifetime. But in popular estate-planning jargon, the term "living trust" specifically refers to a *revocable* living trust. This is one that you set up during your lifetime and that allows you to terminate it, change trustees, change beneficiaries, and move assets in and out of it whenever you want without an attorney. An irrevocable trust doesn't give you such freedom.

To figure out whether a revocable trust makes sense for you, you need to look at what a trust does—while you're alive and after you've died.

■ While You're Living ■

I have very mixed feelings about living trusts. On the one hand, they can have financial and personal benefits. On the other hand, I find that there has been much hype surrounding them which has created unrealistic expectations, misinformation, and misuse. Let me give you an example. A new client, Helen, told me that she had created a living trust, which was particularly important to her because she was single and getting older and wanting things "taken care of." It sounded good so far. Then I found out that the only knowledge Helen had about living trusts was gained by going to a seminar that had been advertised in the newspaper, jointly given by an attorney and an insurance agent. (This is a common marketing technique and there is nothing wrong if done appropriately; the attorney drafts the document and if insurance is needed, the agent sells it.)

But here was the problem. Helen's Yankee thriftiness kept her from having an attorney look at her situation, prepare the living trust, and make sure her assets were transferred into it. A friend had told her that office supply stores sell blank living trust documents and you can just fill in the blanks. So that is what she did and that was *all* she did. But she never transferred any assets into her trust, so it sat completely empty, and the language of her store-bought contract was inappropriate for the laws of her state of residence.

To transfer assets, you must contact all the companies where you have registered ownership of your assets, such as mutual fund companies, your local Registry of Deeds (for your house), banks, etc. Request the forms that allow you to change the legal ownership of the assets from the companies to the trust, then fill them out and send them back to the bank, Registry of Deeds, etc.

Whether it was said at the seminar or Helen misunderstood, she believed that she had escaped all estate taxes by creating a living trust. It would be great if that were true, but it just ain't so. Helen needed real documents, created by an estate planning attorney who could also help her with other estate issues.

There are, however, important benefits of living trusts that everyone should consider. While you're alive, a living trust allows you to transfer control of your assets to a trustee or successor if you become disabled or incapable of managing your affairs. But you can do that with a durable power of attorney; you don't have to create a trust to do it.

With a trust, you have to transfer ownership of your assets into the name of the trust. This painstaking process is called "retitling." The advantage a living trust offers over a durable power of attorney is that if something happens to you, all of your assets are already placed neatly in a single legally binding basket: the trust. In contrast, with a durable power of attorney, you are authorizing someone else to make financial decisions on your behalf if you become incapable of doing so.

A living trust also allows you to name successor trustees. With a durable power of attorney, you can usually name only one person to take over if you become incompetent.

■ Advantages After Death ■

The real advantages of a revocable trust kick in when you die. First, all property in the trust avoids the probate process. This means that if you have a large estate, you can save substantially in attorney and executor fees. Find out the laws in your state, as most states have laws setting standard attorney and executor fees as a percentage of the probate estate.

By avoiding probate, you may save upwards of 2 percent of your assets, or you may be able to use an adult family member or close friend as executor who will charge very little or nothing. On the other hand, if you set up a living trust to avoid probate costs, you should check out the going rates for area law firms and professional executors. Consider possible expenses carefully: The cost of setting up the trust may be more than the probate costs that you would avoid.

If you own property in states other than the one in which you legally reside, putting that real estate in the living trust will prevent your heirs from having to go through probate in every state in which you own property. That in itself is a hassle that can make a living trust well worth the effort.

Another major advantage of a living trust is that most of us prefer to keep our personal finances private. Wills and probates are public record and anyone who wants to pay a nominal fee can go to the local courthouse and get copies. If you are worried about any of your heirs being taken advantage of by unscrupulous salespeople, that's one reason a trust may make sense for you.

Here's an example: Marion was 50 and had set up a living trust for a very specific reason. She was sharp as a tack, but she could tell that over time her husband Warren, fifteen years her senior, was going to have a harder and harder time managing his affairs if she were not around. Unfortunately, there are people out there who make it their business (and make their living by) looking at assets that pass through probate, targeting elderly and wealthy individuals. Marion wanted to protect Warren from a barrage of phone calls and letters, as well as to protect him from making bad financial decisions.

I know it is sickening to think that people make their living by capitalizing on death, but they do. Women are particular targets. Soon after my friend Martha's husband died and his probate assets were made part of public record, she started getting letters and phone calls. Martha was wise enough to hire a financial adviser to help her through this difficult time, and also to throw all the letters in the trash and say, "Thank you, I'm not interested, do not call me again," and hang up whenever she got a sales call. This is good advice for everyone.

Trusts and their assets are not public. This is especially useful if, among other estate-planning situations:

- You have a large estate.
- You have experienced an unfriendly divorce.
- You are remarried but are not on good terms with your children or stepchildren.

- Your children will be inheriting unequal amounts of your assets.
- You want to leave money anonymously to a charity.

Some insurance agents and investment managers "prospect" for new clients by getting public information about large estate settlements through probate court records. If you're concerned about the ability of your beneficiaries to manage money, or you're concerned about their gullibility, the privacy of a revocable trust could be helpful. You can also have terms in the trust that will protect them as well.

The major disadvantage of a living trust is that it does not escape estate taxes upon your death—though unscrupulous legal advisors, investment managers, and insurance agents may advise you otherwise. It's to their benefit for you to set up a living trust so they can receive legal fees, investment fees, and insurance commissions. And even if you have a living trust, you still need a will, because you will inevitably have assets that you did not put into your trust, or that you didn't realize you owned. Your will should name an executor and guardians and should state that all of your probate assets will "pour over" into your revocable trust.

Living trusts may be overkill if you have a simple estate-planning situation and don't have privacy or unusual distribution concerns. If you do need one, see a competent estate-planning attorney rather than simply filling out a preprinted "revocable trust form." It's worth a few extra hundred dollars to make sure you have an airtight estate plan with coordinated wills and trusts.

✔ Happy Endings Checklist

Signs that you are financially alert:
__ I check with Social Security once a year to make sure they record my income correctly.
__ I have thought about how I would like to spend the two stages of retirement.
__ I have filled out a retirement expense calculator for each stage.
__ I have estimated my retirement income.
__ I have worked out a budget for retirement.
__ I'm spending down my nonretirement plan assets first.
__ I have consulted with an estate-planning attorney.
__ If my estate will be worth over $600,000 at my death, I have set up a trust to avoid estate taxes.

Did I Wake You?

Congratulations! You should consider yourself now truly "awake" when it comes to your money—and it will affect the rest of your life. That's because when you really start thinking about money and your future, you will never be the same again.

Put this advice into action and you will begin to "smell the money"—the financial possibilities that will present themselves during every stage of your life. It doesn't matter what your money status is now or what season you are in. You now know how to get money to start with (getting out of debt, spending less, and saving more), how to make the most of what you have (using tax-sheltered retirement plans and investing for maximum returns), and how to plan for your future. If you can take a small step every day, you will wake up tomorrow that much closer to your goals and your dreams.

☞ **One Last Wake-up Call:** When you wake up every morning, don't forget to think of each new day as an opportunity to wake up about your money. Make it an automatic response and you will be able to smell the financial possibilities in every season of your life. Your financial future starts today, and being awake and aware means you will be successful.

Wake Up and Smell the Money is designed to be a guidebook for every season of your life, one you can refer to again and again as your seasons—and those of your loved ones—change. I hope that you'll write to let me know how *Wake Up and Smell the Money* affects your life. The letters I got from readers of *The Money Diet*, my first book, were truly inspiring. They also included some terrific advice that I have passed along in this book. Tell me what has worked for you, so I can pass it on to readers—after all, that's what we are on this earth for, to help each other. If some piece of my advice did not work for you, I want to know about that too; what I am looking for is feedback and a personal connection with you. I answered every letter I received from readers of *The Money Diet*, and I will do my best to honor that commitment for this book, too. I want to hear from you!

You can reach me at the following address:

Applegarth Advisory Group, Inc.
10 Mount Vernon Street, Suite 225
Winchester, MA 01890

Appendix

AGING/RETIREMENT

- American Association of Homes and Services for the Aging (AAHSA)
  901 E Street, N.W., Suite 500
  Washington, DC 20004-2037
  Publications: 800-508-9442
  www.aahsa.org

- American Association of Retired Persons (AARP)
  601 E Street, N.W.
  Washington, DC 20049
  800-424-3410
  www.aarp.org

- AARP Home Equity Information Center
  601 E Street, N.W.
  Washington, DC 20049
  www.aarp.org/hecc

- Department of Veterans Affairs
  800-827-1000

- **Federal Employees Retirement System**
  Office of Personnel Management
  P.O. Box 686
  Washington, DC 20044
  206-606-0500

- **National Center for Home Equity Conversion**
  7373 147th Street West, Room 115
  Apple Valley, MN 55124
  612-953-4474
  www.reverse.org

- **National Council on the Aging, Inc.**
  409 3rd Street, S.W., Suite 200
  Washington, DC 20024
  202-479-1200
  www.ncoa.org
  info@ncoa.org

- **National Eldercare Locator**
  800-677-1116
  http://web.ddp.state.me.us/beas/locator.htm

- *New Choices* **magazine**
  28 West 23rd Street
  New York, NY 10010
  212-366-8800
  newchoices@readersdigest.com
  www.seniornews.com/new-choices

- **Social Security Administration**
  800-772-1213
  www.ssa.gov

CHILDREN

- *Baby Bargains*
  by Denise and Alan Fields
  Windsor Peak Press, 1997

DIVORCE

- **Budgeting for Child Support**
  www.divorcehelp.com/wr/w40budget.html

- **Divorce Information**
  www.divorcenet.com

FINANCIAL ADVICE

- **American Institute of Certified Public Accountants (AICPA)**
  1211 Avenue of the Americas
  New York, NY 10036-8775
  212-596-6200
  www.aicpa.org

- **Certified Financial Planner Board of Standards**
  1700 Broadway, Suite 2100
  Denver, CO 80290-2101
  303-830-7500
  www.cfp-board.org

- **Institute of Certified Financial Planners (ICFP)**
  3801 E. Florida Avenue, Suite 708
  Denver, CO 80210-2544
  800-282-PLAN
  www.icfp.org

- **International Association for Financial Planning (IAFP)**
  5775 Glenridge Drive, N.E., Suite B-300
  Atlanta, GA 30328-5364
  404-845-0011
  www.iafp.org
  info@iafp.org

- **National Association of Personal Financial Advisors (NAPFA)**
  355 West Dundee Road, Suite 200
  Buffalo Grove, IL 60089
  888-FEE-ONLY
  www.napfa.org
  info@napfa.org

- **Society of Financial Service Professionals**
  (formerly the American Society of CLU & ChFC)
  270 South Bryn Mawr Avenue
  Bryn Mawr, PA 19010-2195
  610-526-2500
  www.financialpro.org
  custserv@financialpro.org

HOUSEHOLD FINANCE

- **Checks in the Mail**
  800-733-7387
  www.checksinthemail.com
  info@checksinthemail.com

- **Consumer Credit Counseling Service (CCCS)**
  check local phone book for phone number
  www.cccsedu.org
  cccsinfo@unicom.net

- **Consumer Federation of America (CFA)**
  1424 16th Street, N.W., Suite 604
  Washington, DC 20036
  202-387-6121

- **Current Checks**
  800-426-0822
  800-204-2244
  www.currentchecks.com

- **Designer Checks**
  800-239-9222
  www.designerchecks.com
  info@designerchecks.com

- **Equifax**
  P.O. Box 105873
  Atlanta, GA 30348
  800-685-1111
  www.equifax.com

- **Experian (formerly TRW)**
  P.O. Box 949
  Allen, TX 75013-0949
  800-682-7654 or 888-397-3742
  www.experian.com

- *The Money Diet: Reaping the Rewards of Financial Fitness*
  by Ginger Applegarth
  Viking, 1995
  Penguin, 1996

- **TransUnion Corporation**
  P.O. Box 390
  Springfield, PA 19064-0390
  800-888-4213
  312-408-1400
  www.transunion.com

INSURANCE

- **A.M. Best**
  Ambest Road
  Oldwick, NJ 08858
  800-424-2378
  www.ambest.com
  customerservice@ambest.com

- **Duff & Phelps Credit Rating Company**
  17 State Street, 12th Floor
  New York, NY 10002
  Hotline: 212-908-0200
  www.dcrco.com
  hotline@dcrco.com

- **Moody's Investors Service**
  99 Church Street
  New York, NY 10007
  212-553-0300
  www.moodys.com

- **Standard & Poor's**
  25 Broadway
  New York, NY 10004
  212-208-1002
  www.ratings.com
  ratings@mcgraw-hill.com

- **Veterinary Pet Insurance**
  4175 East LaPalma Avenue, Suite 100
  Anaheim, CA 92807
  800-USA-PETS
  www.petinsurance.com
  usapets@primenet.com

- **Weiss Ratings**
  4176 Burns Road
  Palm Beach Gardens, FL 33410
  800-289-9222
  www.weissratings.com
  wr@weissinc.com

INVESTING

- *A Commonsense Guide to Your 401(k)*
  by Mary Rowland
  Bloomberg Press, 1998

- *The New Commonsense Guide to Mutual Funds*
  by Mary Rowland
  Bloomberg Press, 1998

- **Money Central**
  www.moneycentral.com

- **Morningstar**
  225 West Wacker Drive
  Chicago, IL 60606
  312-696-6000
  www.morningstar.com
  www.morningstar.net

MAJOR PURCHASES

- **American Automobile Association**
  1000 AAA Drive
  Heathrow, FL 32746
  800-JOIN-AAA
  www.aaa.com

- **Bank Rate Monitor**
  www.bankrate.com

- **Consumer Reports New and Used Car Price Service**
  New: 800-888-8275
  Used: 800-258-1169
  www.consumerreports.com

- **Fannie Mae**
  3900 Wisconsin Avenue, N.W.
  Washington, DC 20016-2892
  202-752-7000
  www.fanniemae.com

- **Federal Housing Administration**
  Homes hotline: 800-218-0250
  www.hud.gov

SELF-EMPLOYMENT/SMALL BUSINESS

- **American Marketing Association**
  250 South Wacker Drive, Suite 200
  Chicago, IL 60606
  800-AMA-1150
  www.ama.org
  info@ama.org

- **Independent Business Alliance**
  111 John Street
  New York, NY 10038
  800-559-2580
  www.ibaonline.com

- *Working Solo*
  by Terri Lonier
  John Wiley & Sons, Inc., 1998
  www.workingsolo.com

- **Small Business Administration**
  409 3rd Street, S.W.
  Washington, DC 20416
  800-U-ASK-SBA
  www.sba.gov

- *The Small Business Money Guide*
  by Terri Lonier and Lisa Aldisert
  John Wiley & Sons, Inc., 1999

TAXES

- **Internal Revenue Service (IRS)**
  Help line: 800-TAX-1040
  Publications: 800-829-3676
  www.irs.ustreas.gov

Index